Somebody Should Have Told Me!

The Life of a Driven Woman

Paula Mann

Somebody Should Have Told ME!

First published in the United States of America in 2011

This book was also reprinted in the United States of America.

Copyright © 2013 by Paula Mann Publishing.

Library of Congress Control Number: 2011907790

ISBN: Soft cover 978-0-989-20070-7
ISBN: eBook 978-0-989-2007-1-4

All rights reserved. Without limiting the rights under copyright reserved above, no part of this book may be reproduced or transmitted in any form or by any means, electronic or mechanical, including photocopying, recording, or otherwise by any information storage and retrieval system, without the prior written permission of both the copyright owner, Paula Mann and Paula Mann publishing.

Paula Mann Publishing
P.O. Box 1071
Seabrook, Texas 77586
Phone-832-633-8050
www.paulamannpublishing.com

From The Author

I first give praises to The Almighty God for bringing me through my life experiences thus far, scarred but not broken. His grace and love enable me to share some of my own experiences as well as those of others in this book.

I thank my husband of eighteen years, "Donald", for being patient as I spent many hours on my computer. A special thanks to my friend, Eric Nelson from Nichburg, Alabama. To my children, grandchildren, stepchildren, and godchildren, I love you all! May God continue strengthening us as we bind these families together in love and harmony through prayer!

Paula was born June 12, in southern Arkansas, the sixth child of seven children, made up of five girls and two boys. She, her older siblings and baby brother all benefited from a loving mother and father. She enjoys dancing, singing, writing, participating in Church Activities, and spending as much time as possible with her family.

She has two children, three step children and three beautiful grandchildren who she lovingly describes as "her second heartbeat!" Having seen just a little too much growing up, she developed her idea of how to make her life better than that of the older women of her time. Paula was anxious to grow up and start living her life as a wife and mother. Her mother was the insistent, contributing factor in her getting an education, at the University of Arkansas, Pine Bluff, in Arkansas. Despite her mother's hopes and dreams, Paula became pregnant by her high school sweetheart, and got married during her sophomore year. Juggling a baby, a marriage and college became quite challenging and threatened her ability to cope.

After college, she landed a job and began teaching, near her home town. Thinking that life was finally about ready to begin, there were set backs at her every turn! She began writing a book, that had no name, but the trials and tribulations of life, cause her to abandon her writing for several years. She spent a number of years having fun, trying things that she never had dreamed of.

Paula moved to Houston Texas in January 1982 were she continued to teach in public schools. She became the mother of a daughter fifteen years after her first child's birth. She remarried in 1995 and has been married now for over seventeen years. Two years ago while cleaning a closet in one of her Guest rooms, she ran across the manuscript that she had begun so long ago, and decided that it was time to finish it.

In loving memory of my parents
Mr. Ivy Daniels Sr. and Mrs. Savanah Thomas-Daniels (RIP)

Dedicated to my grandson: Bryan Shedrick Boyette Jr.

Nana loves you so much!

"When life deals us lemons, we make lemonade!"
Evil is always lurking, but it must never steal the beauty within you!
Let us remember one another in prayer
When we pray silently, Satan can't hear it!

They should have told me to remain a child, a dependent, until I learned to manage on my own.

They should have told me that I needed to remain single until I completed my education.

Did they tell me, and I did not listen?

They should have told me that as a woman, I was fragile.

They should have told me that I was vulnerable and totally unequipped to manage life with a man before I knew how to manage life without one.

They should have told me that life in the real world was totally different from that of the imaginary.

They should have told me about the devastation that disappointment brings.

They should have told me that it was impossible to have a relationship with a man without first having one with God.

They should have told me to use birth control to ensure that I did not have a child prior to completing my education and marriage.

They should have told me . . .

Somebody Should Have Told ME!

Preface

Marriages and relationships end for many different reasons and can have devastating effects especially on young people. It can be a difficult, frustrating, heartbreaking, and an overall traumatic experience for both the young and old, male and female.

In the case of infidelity or just plain loss of Interest, we often lose our self-confidence and become overwhelmed when a partner decides they no longer want the relationship. We ask ourselves, "What is wrong with me?", "Is there someone else?", "What does she/he have that I don't?" or "Where did I go wrong?"

Rejection in most cases can almost stop your breath! These types of situations are common but no less painful when it happens to us. Not everyone respond to these situations in the same way, but for the most part, everyone goes through pain when adjusting to the changes. Quite often, the individual who walks away may feel pain, although his/her pain may come from just knowing that their action is hurting another, and it's seldom enough to change anything.

They, more often than not, still walk away! In many cases, the devastation of the loss of a partner or lover is much like the death of that person. The mental attitude of the individuals involved determines the success of the transition from lover to friend or, in many cases, from lover to enemy. It is truly, in my opinion, a thin line between love and hate. Some older men/women of today have been down that old "Breakup" road a few times and have learned to deal with situations in their own way.

Dealing with emotions of a breakup without help can sometimes have overwhelming results! Some of which will be addressed within this book. Couples can be counseled, and sometimes relationships are saved; however, both individuals must be willing to participate and give it their all. Thirty-five percent of couples who are counseled remain together after an extramarital affair.
In most recent years: psychologist, psychiatrist, and counselors have been instrumental in helping individuals cope with the loss of a partner.

Many are effective and well equipped to help you work through the many emotions and the drama that goes along with separation.

These occurrences magnify even more when it happens to very young individuals who have less experience with love and relationships. The entire situation becomes complicated further when children are involved.

Sometimes we find it hard to go to a perfect stranger and lay our heart on a table to be dissected. As a result, we suffer through pain, confusion, loneliness, bewilderment, uncertainty, and embarrassment, existing day by day until we grow accustomed to the absence and/or until another lover gradually takes his/her place. The latter is quite dangerous and can have lifelong effects on the individuals' actions, reactions, relationships, and their children for the rest of their lives.

I have found that most young people sympathize with one another and gain fulfillment in knowing that they are not alone in their situation. They gravitate toward friends and others who are in or who they know have been in similar predicaments. They have a tendency to cling together, comforting one another, sharing the latest news about the fathers and mothers of their children, and the latest development in their declining relationships.

Although this avenue is far better than dealing with situations alone, this too can have negative and very adverse effects in the long run. Getting caught up in the "girl or man if I were you I would" advisories can be misleading if the advice is taken and acted upon.

When I went through my first separation and divorce, I was so focused on myself that I neglected to focus on the real and true needs of a child who was adjusting to the loss of a father. When this happens, our children suffer from the loss of both parents. These mistakes are common, but through my own personal experiences, as well as through the raising of my own children, the light bulb in my mind just popped on one day! It was late, but just in time for me to apply some of what you will read here, to my own life.

Hopefully, reading this story will help you in your relationships and the raising of your children, if there are any involved. Countless numbers of young people are still suffering and allowing their children to suffer because they don't know what to do or where to turn. Writing this book has allowed the resurfacing of some of the pain I had suffered over the past years. It caused me to abandon my writing for days at a time, before being able to tackle the task again.

Although years have passed and I believe I am healed as much as I can be, to revisit the closed doors of my past has been both painful and therapeutic.

Growing up, I witnessed so much that was inappropriate; seeing husbands and wives fighting, cheating, arguing, and so much abuse, that I vowed not to live that way when I was grown up and married.

Much like everyone else, my childhood experiences has affected my whole life! Most of us have a story to tell, but not everyone choose to write about it. It has been as though I was equipped with antennas that helped me sense when to roll and when to fold. I have rolled many times and have fold just as many, minus one. Confused now aren't you?

Read my story to understand what minus one means. There is life after we crash and burn! I have been hurt and I have caused hurt! As far as my hurt and those who caused me pain, I forgive them without their asking. For those of whom I have hurt, I have humbly asked forgiveness, for "I am truly sorry!" Life has a way of balancing things and time heals most wounds. Although time helps in the healing process, quite often, a scar remains.

Many of my friends have asked me "Where did you get the idea of writing a book like this?" I will tell you as I told them, "Honey, I have been on this earth for quite some time now, I've had lots of experiences, made a lot of mistakes and truly have learned from them all.

I have plenty to tell!"

Somebody Should Have Told ME!

My Inspiration

Like Frank Sinatra's most beloved song "My Way", I truly did do it my way! I had grown up in a loving family with both parents actively striving to see that we all would grow up to be productive members of society. Although they accomplished that goal with all seven of us, in my personal life "I" messed up so many times, making bad decisions without conferring with God.

To be able to mess up and emerge scarred but unbroken is a testimony in itself—a testimony that I share with you in this book and will one day share with my grandchildren.

My elder child "Bryan," was on the roller-coaster ride with me, as I messed up over and over again, in pursuit of my place in this world. I searched for my one true love, and my purpose for living. Just when I had given up all hope of ever knowing the full reason for my existence, I found it all and a bag of chips. The lyric for "My Way" tells the story of a man who is dying. He looks back over his life and takes full responsibility for the ups and downs, the twists and turns of his life.

He realizes how content he is with the choices he made and through it all, as he approaches deaths door, he maintains a very high degree of his honor. Paul Anka was vacationing in France in 1967, when he heard a French pop song, "Comme d'habitude," (as usual) performed by Claude Francois.

He acquired publishing rights free of charge before returning to the United States and asked Frank Sinatra to sing it. Sinatra turned him down, but Paul Anka was persistent, and rewrote the song with Sinatra in mind. Anka approached him again when he was performing at Caesars Palace in Las Vegas, Nevada. Although Paul Anka was himself a professional singer, he insisted that only Frank Sinatra could do the song the justice it so deserved.
Frank Sinatra recorded Paul Anka's version of "My Way," December 30, 1968. It reached number 27 in the United States, while its record is still unmatched in the United Kingdom, becoming the recording with the most weeks inside the Top 40. When I heard the song for the very first time, even though I was quite young, I loved it!

Through the years, I have kept the original record. I had it on eight track, then cassette, and now on CD. Little did I know how relative to my own life, this song would become? Perhaps Paul Anka was drawn to the song because it described his journey in some way; however, as you progress through these pages, you will come to know why the song has such meaning to me and my life. Although I did it my way, it was not without consequences.

Chapter One

My immediate family consisted of five girls and two boys, our mother who we all called Mama and our father, who we all called Daddy. My parents, Betty and William Casey, were respectable members of the community who raised us in the admonition of God. They were somewhat strict but not uncomfortably so. Being the sixth child of seven, I can imagine that Mama and Daddy were getting a little worn out with raising kids, and softened a bit, by the time that my baby brother and I became teenagers. I am especially proud to have been born and raised in the country, because we were spared the exposure to city living and all that goes along with it.

The fast life and drugs had not filtered down into the small towns when I was a kid. I thank God for that! Today they are everywhere, and the most a parent can do is educate their children to the fact. There is no doubt that had it been around, we like so many others today would have been at risk. As far back as I can remember, our family had very close ties, but the very core of our family was traumatized when my baby brother, "George" and I were hit by a speeding car. I was in the first grade, but like most children I was as curious as could be. While waiting for the school bus one morning, my cousin, "Lillie" told me that they had some delegate's at their house. "What are delegates," I asked? She laughed and told me that I had to come see for myself. All day at school, I thought about the delegates. I asked my first grade teacher what they were. When she replied, well, "I really don't know what Lillie could be talking about! We call people who come from other churches to visit within our community, delegates, but that usually takes place during the summer months, and this is September. You let me know what they are when you find out, Ok!"

I could not wait to get home so that I could see those delegates. After school I asked my mother if I could go down to Lillie's house to see the delegates. She immediately said no, but I was so curious. I could be over to Lillie's and back before she missed me, if I hurried, I thought! If Mama found out I disobeyed her, I would surely get a spanking that I would never forget. I debated for an hour or so, before my curiosity got the best of me.

I decided to take George with me, because, I would be less likely to get a spanking if he went along also. Being only three years old, he seldom got spanked. I knew my mother well enough to know that if I were caught, she would go much easier on me, if George was with me. When I saw Mama busy, I grabbed George by the hand and away we went. I told him about the delegates and that we had to hurry before mama missed us. We ran as fast as we could.

Once we arrived at Lillie's, her mother told us that she was across the road at her brother's house. I unlatched the gate and turned around to latch it back again, when I heard George say, "I bet you can't catch me!" I called to him, but he kept running. I called again, but he continued to run. He headed for the road as fast as he could. I knew I had to catch him before he got to the road, because mama would kill me if I let him get hurt. I started to run as fast as I could, still calling to him. As we approached the highway, I could hear a car coming. Running as fast as I could, I called out. "Don't go onto the road, a car is coming".

He stopped right in the middle of the road, turned around saying, "I told you, you could not catch me," jumping up and down with excitement. I knew that a car could not see us until it topped the hill and that could be too late. I had to get to him before the car did! I ran into the road to deliver him to safety, but the car hit us both at the same time. I vaguely remember being in my cousins house with everyone around me. My first grade teacher who lived in our community was working on me, doing I don't know what. It all seemed so much like a dream. We went to the hospital by ambulance, but it was several days before we regained consciousness.

At the hospital, I remember waking up for short periods of time. As I looked around the room, George was in the same room as me, with tubes filed with blood in his nose. He seemed to have been sleeping, but Mama sat in a chair between us, crying and praying. I am told that we were in the hospital for almost a month; George with a broken collar bone and internal injuries, and I had internal injuries and both legs were fractured badly. My dress was caught underneath the car causing it to drag my body until it came to a stop. I took a direct hit but George was hit indirectly because I pushed him out of the way as much as I could. At home I received my homework every day from my first grade teacher.

She would spend at least two hours each day after work, helping me to keep up with my class. That was done from the goodness of her heart, because mama and daddy sure could not pay her. I guess it helped that we all were friends and attended the same church. Healing was a slow process because I did not go to school for three months. I had problems walking because of the many fractures I suppose! Later, I learned, when my mother was told to get dressed so that she could go to the hospital to see about us, she arrived with two dresses and house shoes, but no bra or underwear.

One of my sisters went to a nearby store to purchase my mother a bra and some under garments. She was just that upset at the news of our getting hurt so badly. I returned to school the following year, and my friends were as glad to see me as I was to see them. Our teacher had kept them informed of my condition, but upon returning, I spent many recesses retelling the story, as they listened intensely. Many of the children said that they were first told that both George and I had died, but the teacher told them better the next morning. I had left them as a first grader, but returned to school as a second grader. Our family finally got back to normal and as I grew up, I always remembered what disobedience had almost cost me.

Mama had taught me from George's birth that it was my responsibility to help take care of him. I tried to step up to the plate, even though I was just three years older than him. Once when she was hanging clothes on the line, in the backyard, she told me to watch the baby who was lying in a bassinet sitting on the porch. He was probably three months old, but she gave me a fan and told me to keep the flies off of the baby by fanning him. I guess I got tired and went to get the fly spray. I sprayed him to keep the flies off, like I had seen mama spray other things. But I did not know that the baby was off limits to fly spray!! As he lay there gasping for air, she got to him just in time I suppose. However, I was never asked to keep the flies off of the baby again!

I spent the weekends and summers of my teen years babysitting my sister's children. My sister's Faye and Ann were both beauticians, and each had five children. On any particular Saturday I had at least five children to watch. Thank God their shops were in different areas, for I am sure I would have babysat all ten of the kids at the same time. Even though I managed to get out of it from time to time, that continued until I graduated from high school. My nieces and nephews were precious to me and as babies, often refused to let anyone care for them other than me, if I was within their sight.

I got a big kick out of that at first, but it soon got old. They didn't seem to understand that I was a teenager and wanted to do big kid stuff some of the time. A teenager of the 1960s in our small town of one thousand and eight, people had a very shallow social life, but just hanging out with others in the same age group was enjoyable.

One of the highlights of each year was that the county fair came to town in September. All of the Boys in the community did whatever they could to earn extra money to spend at the fair. It was usually used to "ride" girls along with themselves and for eating county fair foods. I was awful glad to be a girl, and be able to spend my money just on myself. I enjoyed riding with the boys' money as well, especially when mine ran out. My neighbor, Josh Eden and I had a wonderful time that year as usual, not knowing that it would be the last time we would enjoy the county fair together.

In December of that same year, 1962, our community was shaken again by tragedy. I was thirteen during one of the coldest winters Arkansas had seen in some time. Our neighbors, the Edens three sons went down to the pond to try to ice skate. This was done without the consent of their mother. They skated for a while but then the ice broke and the younger son fell into the freezing water. Josh went over to pull Randle out of the hole, but when he lifted him, the ice broke with him as well! Frightened to no end, the third son, "James" ran home to tell his mother, but by the time they got back to the pond, both boys had been overcome by the freezing water and drowned. It was no time before the news traveled throughout the community and we all arrived at the scene.

The rescue team was dredging the pond for the boys. They were my friends and I was so heartbroken. After about forty five minutes both bodies had been recovered, and their mother was having a screaming fit. "My babies, Lord my babies," she repeated over and over again! Most of the women and children were crying along with her. They would be missed so much. Through the years, I have reflected back on times when we played together and the fun we all had. The funeral was so sad, because the children from the community and their classmates all came to pay their last respects.

I was afraid that I would see them, and their spirits just might come over to play as usual. My daddy told me to put my hand on them, and I would not be afraid anymore. My sister went to the caskets with me, and slowly but hesitantly, I touched the hand of Virgil. It was cold and hard, and that did not set well with me. That night, I was just as afraid as I was the nights prior to the funeral.

By the age of sixteen, I babysat as little as possible. Faye and Ann's older children were growing up and gradually took my place as babysitter.
At my oldest sister, Faye's house, her neighbor, Mr. Evans, would beat his wife. I would run inside to be sure not to look, since my sister had told me to do so. I felt sad for Mrs. Evan, and wondered why she continued to live with him. Faye explained to me that Mrs. Evans did not work and with five children, she needed his money to take care of them.

One evening, I was sitting on Faye's porch, when I heard the neighbors screaming at one another. Mrs. Evans came out onto the yard and was telling him, "If you ever hit me again, I swear, I am going to get you back; I am tired of you beating me." Mr. Evans ran out of the house onto the yard and hit her so hard, it hurt me. She was lying on the ground screaming as he hit her over and over again. Their children were crying, asking him to stop hitting their mother. I could not go inside; I was spellbound as I continued watching. With every lick, I hated Mr. Evans more! He finally let her go, and the children all ran to her, holding onto their mother. I could hear her comforting her children as she continued sniffling. "It's OK babies, Mama's OK!" She sat on the ground with her five babies around her, like little chicks next to the mother hen.

Several hours later, Faye's beauty shop as closed; all of her kids had their baths, and we had sat down to eat when we heard gut-wrenching screams. It sounded at first, like the panther getting ready to strike on the Tarzan show, then like a roaring lion.

When Faye dashed for the door to see what was happening, I was as close as her shadow. Mr. Evans was outside, with the water hose on and was splashing water all over himself, and jumping around as if he was getting stung by bees. It was still light enough to see him in his underwear, and everywhere he touched his body turned pink. Faye told me to stay were I was, and she ran to him.

He screamed and moaned as he splashed water over his body. His face was completely pink on one side. Faye ran back to the house, called the police and asked for an ambulance as she gave the address. She told the police that Mrs. Evans had scalded her husband, and had taken all of the kids away in the car with her. Although I knew it was wrong to hurt people, I thought, "Well, Mr. Wife-beater, I'll bet your favorite pastime has come to a screeching halt."

Although it was terrible, she had been taking beatings for many years. I understood! By the time Faye got back out to the scene, a crowd had gathered. Mr. Evans was in severe pain, saying over and over, "Lord have mercy," softly sometimes, and at other times it became a scream! When the ambulance arrived, and they took him away, the police questioned the crowd.

Since Faye was the first on the scene, they questioned her away from the others. Mr. Evans told Faye to tell the police not to arrest Mrs. Evans, because it was his fault entirely. Early the next morning, Mrs. Evans returned home, and came over to Faye's house. I am sure she was curious to know what happened after she left home. She was a nervous wreck, with tears ever flowing from her eyes. Mrs. Evans neck was blue with bruises and there were scratches on each side. My sister hugged and comforted her, made her a cup of coffee, and sat her down at the dining table.

I sat in the family room as close to the dining room as possible, so that I could hear. I turned the television down to a whisper and told the kids to be extremely quiet, so they could hear TV. I listened as Mrs. Evans informed my sister of so many things she was not aware of. Mr. Evans was not only beating her, he had been touching one of the sixteen-year-old girls in the community, inappropriately. She had confronted him about that for months, and last night she threatened to tell the girl's parents.

After he finished beating her on the front lawn, and they were back inside of their home, he began choking her, to the point that she lost consciousness. She said thoughts ran rapidly through her mind before she lost consciousness. She thought about her children and who would raise them! She wanted to pray before she went to meet her maker!

Why didn't she leave him long ago even if it meant going to the welfare system? When she regained consciousness, and realized that she was still living, he was sitting in his favorite chair staring at the TV. She guessed that he realized she was alive and left her laying there on the floor until she woke up. She was dazed, but got up from the floor when she was able, went to the kitchen where she had four hens boiling in a large pot. She looked out back, and the kids were still playing, unaware that they had almost lost their mother. It was then as if God spoke to her subconscious, she realized that she had to go. She had to leave him, or next time she would die.

Without caring that she had plans to make chicken with dressing for church, she carefully removed the hens from the boiling water. She watched him from the corners of her eyes as she moved around the kitchen. She walked outside where the children were playing and told the elder child, Billy, who was ten years old, to quietly gather all the children and put them in the car. She told him not to let anyone come in the house or get out of the car.

Mrs. Evans told Faye, she went back into the kitchen, poured a half jug of Johnny Fair syrup into the broth, and stirred it. As she stirred, just as God had spoken to her subconscious, it was Satan's turn. She thought of the many years she had taken his abuse, and how close to death she had just come. She remembered how savage he became when she threatened to expose his behavior with the teenager up the street. "He thinks this is his world, and we all just live in it!" she thought. She took the keys to her car, put them in her mouth, unbuckled her belt and placed the straps of her purse through her belt loops, walked over to him as he sat nodding in his chair and turned the whole pot of boiling broth over his head. She told Faye, "I lost it! I lost touch with myself, as if I was someone else." She cried even more.

"He screamed so loud, such a gut-wrenching sound. He hurled himself out of the chair, and that is all I remember,"she said, "I must have run to the car, that's what I had planned to do." Mrs. Evans paused as if she thought of the consequences for the very first time. She placed her hand over her mouth and said, "I know I will have to go to jail Faye." Faye caught her by both hand and told her, "No, no, no, you won't go to jail! Your husband took care of it! He told the police not to arrest you because it was his fault, entirely! John Lee, the head policeman, said no charges would be brought against you, because of the many times the neighbors have called his office asking for a policeman to come get him off of you.

He told me that he wanted to take him down to jail so many times, but you would lie to him claiming you ran into a door, or fell down the steps. I think Mr. John Lee is proud of you! You're OK girl, don't worry. I sent Charlie down to the hospital to check on him early this morning. He is going to have a long recovery period, but he will make a full recovery with scars." Mrs. Evans spent the night in a cheap motel in a little town twelve miles away. Her brother who lived a couple of hundred miles into southern Louisiana was coming to help her move, get a job and even government assistance if necessary until she could do better. Her family had asked her to leave him repeatedly, but now she was ready!

I had heard my sister and her husband, Charlie, talk about Mr. Evans cheating with other women, and I wondered why he would fight her if she was letting him get away with his cheating. Well, maybe he beat her up this time because she was speaking out against his cheating, or maybe she was trying to protect the young girl. Either way, I was really proud of the outcome. Faye hugged her and cried.

When Mrs. Evans's brother drove away with some of the kids in his car, and Mrs. Evans, along with the rest of her children trailed him with her car. "Will Mr. Evans go take the car from her?" I asked. "No, Mr. Evans had better stay away from her, or her brother will tear his head off sister replied. "Why are you crying?" I asked, "you should be happy." Faye looked down at me, and said, "I am happy that she is leaving his old butt, but I am losing a very dear friend." "Can you go and visit her sometime?" I asked. "I can see her from time to time, but it won't be the same. I am used to having her near." She cried.

The women of my youth, seldom left, separated, or divorced their men especially if they had two or more children. Women were less liberated in the 1960s; therefore, many did not work, depending solely upon their husbands to be the bread winner. The women who did work outside of the home usually did what my mother called "days work." They washed, cooked, and cleaned for more affluent families in the morning, only to return home to do the same in their own homes.

Of course, city living was quite different from country living, and the jobs for city women were more plentiful. In our little country town in Arkansas, there was only one company to employ men, and that was the saw mill. Women were not allowed to work there at that time. The men who did not work in the saw mill, did spine-breaking work in the woods, cutting trees and hauling the logs and pulp wood to the saw mill in our town and other towns nearby. Some of the wood was hauled to paper mills in neighboring towns to make paper products.

Georgia Pacific was one such company which employed some of the men from within the area. People, who owned buses and vans, earned extra money hauling the men back and forth to work. Our two grocery stores and the department stores employed only one or two women each. This left the majority of women regardless of race, to be stay-at-home moms, later called housewives, to glorify the occupation. Men were aware of the vulnerability of their wives, causing some to take full advantage of the situation. As a result, many wives were abused and treated with little respect.

By the time I was thirteen, ladies began car-pooling to El Dorado, Arkansas twenty-six miles away to work in the chicken poultry. Suddenly, a few other plants popped up in the same town, and even more women were employed, thus leading to them becoming more liberated. Until then, many women felt that they had no other choice but to stay with their men, no matter the treatment.

My other two sisters Tisah and Nadellie had gotten married before finishing high school and already started having babies. They both finally returned to school and got diplomas to keep Mama off their backs. Tisah had two children, and Nadellie eventually had six. Nadellie was by far the best child of the seven of us. She had five boys and one girl, and adopted another son when she was forty-five years old. This sister was somewhat quiet yet friendly, with the most beautiful smile you have ever seen. I am not saying that the rest of us were bad actors, but we could get a little loud when we all got together to reminisce.

An older brother, Nicholas, had secured a great position at a local chemical plant and was providing well for his family. He had two children within his marriage and two children prior to his marriage. He was the only boy until our baby brother George came along. The three older girls were so proud of their brother, Nick. Mama said the girls loved him so much that they didn't want him to be spanked. Once when Daddy told him to lay across the old trunk to get some licks on his butt, my oldest sister ran and pushed him off of the trunk and onto the floor, laid herself across the trunk, and said, "I'll take his paddling, Daddy." I am told that they did that many times, to keep him from being punished. Quite often, that saved everyone, because daddy did not have the heart to spank after such a display of affection.

Sometimes it worked, and Daddy did not spank him or the volunteer. Sometimes it didn't work, and he had to take his own spanking. Daddy said the girls would stand and cry just as hard as if it were they getting the whipping. Now, George and I were the last two, of seven children left at home; therefore, we heard much about education from both our mother and father. We were a church-going family, and Mama made sure we were there for Sunday school, regular church services, BTU, choir rehearsal, and any auxiliary meetings held.

George had already let mama know that he did not want to go to college, and she finally agreed to his wishes. She always had a way of being a softy for her boys! George would learn a two-year trade. I waited until I thought the time was right to break the news to Mama that I wanted to be an airline stewardess. I had seen pictures in magazines of them dressed in their uniforms, read about the many places they traveled, and I thought, that sounds like the job for me. How else would I ever get to see all the states of the United States, or even other countries? Nobody I knew traveled very far from home, and I had dreams. I was not going to get stuck in this place all of my life.

As an airline stewardess, I would have to be trained, but I could be a stewardess without a college degree. One day while hanging sheets and pillowcases on the line, I told Mama I wanted to be an airline stewardess.

She quickly and very sternly stared me dead in my eyes and said, "No! No, Savannah! Too many of those planes are falling out of the sky. You're my last chance at having one child to graduate from college. I want me a college graduate out of this here family! You are the one, I see it, and I know right here, (pointing to her chest) in my heart." There was no way that I was going to get out of it without greatly disappointing Mama. I was in tenth grade then, and Mama walked, talked, planned, and preached college several times a week until I graduated from high school.

I never knew my paternal grandparents. My paternal grandfather died before I was born, and I was two years old when my paternal grandmother died. Daddy would tell us stories about them and his growing up with them. We have pictures and I have stared at them many times, wondering what it would have been like to actually have gotten to know them or even had a conversation with them. Daddy was born to a family of six boys and one girl. I was raised knowing all of my paternal uncles and the aunt. The boys loved that one sister very much! They protected her, the best they could from any harm or danger.

The boys all had from three to eight children, but the one girl had only one child. She was a sweet woman who later got hooked up with a man who burdened her for most of her life. He moved her far back into the woods and built a log cabin for their home. He was lazy, and made feeding the cows, hogs, horses, chickens, goose, geese, ducks, turkeys, dogs and cats, her responsibility. He was so evil that he refused to get up to get himself a glass of water. He called himself a preacher, but nobody thought much of him, for the way he treated her.

I remember my dad saying many times how he had asked her to leave him, and he and the brothers would all pitch in, in order to get her a place, but she would never leave. She lived and worked like his slave for over thirty years.

She outlived him, but developed Alzheimer's a few years after he died and soon went to her eternal rest. I liked all of my paternal uncles, but one was really mean! He used to fight with his wife, and that made us afraid of him, and as much as we were afraid, we equally disliked him.
She was not our blood, but we did not know the difference. We loved her very much because our mother loved her. She had eight children of her own, but she always found the time to talk, tease, and kid around with us.

Mama would get so aggravated when we would hear her screaming, because our Uncle Slim would have gotten drunk and decided that Auntie needed her monthly whipping. He averaged giving her a good spanking at least once or twice a month. Mama would find Daddy wherever he was and tell him to "come get your crazy brother off of this woman." We would listen and cry because mama would always cry. Mama almost never allowed me to go anywhere with Auntie because of Uncle Slim. One day after much pleading, Mama let me go to our cousin's house with my auntie and her daughter, Lillie. Lillie was a year older than me, but she was my friend and my cousin.

Mama told me, as I begged her to let me go, "I am going to let you go, but I'll bet if your uncle comes and catches Auntie gone, he's gonna run all of you to hell and back. Go on, little lady!" I went along and was having fun with Lillie playing about the yard at Daddy and Uncle Slim's niece Lucy's house. When the phone rang, Lucy answered and quickly turned to Auntie, "Girl, Slim is looking for you!" Auntie jumped up grabbed Lillie and me by the hand, and up to the side of the road we went. We could hear the old truck coming, so Auntie had us to lie down in the bushes on the side of the road, until the truck passed. She held my hand so tight it hurt a little, but I dared not say anything.

As soon as the truck was out of sight, she snatched us up, and we were off running again. When I finally got to where I could see our house, through my tears, I saw mama standing next to the road. I was so glad to see her. I knew Uncle Slim would not kill me if I could just make it to her. I could tell Auntie was scared because of the urgency to her voice, and I could feel her shaking as she held my hand so tightly. "Run to your mama child," Auntie said as we approached Mama. They lived four lots away from us. I continued running; I ran to Mama for dear life! When I got close, she saw my fear. "Um hum, bet I won't have any more trouble out of you wanting to follow Lillie, will I? You know your uncle is crazy," she said, with a chuckle. I never asked to follow them again.

It was a family tradition to meet at our maternal grandmother's house each Sunday after church, along with all of our maternal aunts and uncles and their families. This type of fellow-shipping kept the cousins close throughout the years as well. When grandmother, whose name was Mae Johnson, passed away at age seventy-three, and Papa was alone, the tradition continued. Although I had been close to both my grandmother and my Papa, I became exceptionally close to Papa, whose name was Alvin Merik Johnson, after grandmother died. I would visit him a little more often, to keep him from being so lonely. They had been married for fifty-eight years, and she was his everything. He told me many things that I probably would never have known, had I not spent that valuable time with him. He said he worked for a circus at the age of fifteen, and while traveling with the circus, he met many girls, but at the age of twenty, he met my grandmother. According to Papa, grandmother was the hardest girl to talk to, because she was bashful.

After following her around all night, he finally cornered her when she sat eating a freshly roasted wiener. She told him she could not have a boyfriend because she already had two children, both boys. He was shocked because she was only fourteen years old. After her mother died, my grandmother was raised by an older sister, Sue Lean Payne, who was barren but wanted children very badly. She arranged for her husband to sleep with my grandmother, and as a result, two children were born, both boys. My grandmother cried as she told him the story and said that she was going to take the boys and run away soon. Papa told her not to run away, that he would be back for her and the boys. Two months later, he arrived, but the sister would not allow the boys to go. At their births, old Aunt Sue Lean had her name registered as the mother, via the midwife. As far as the law was concerned, they were her boys. When I heard that story the very first time, I thought, what a crook.

Grandmother hated the idea of leaving the boys, but knowing they would be taken care of, she made the choice to go without them. My grandfather arranged for her to visit the boys every two months until they were teenagers. Grandmother's sister did indeed take excellent care of the boys, and they were affluent enough that the boys shared their own car when they became of sufficient age to drive.

The boys began to visit their mother, and their younger half—brothers and sisters. My mother was the first child of seven born to Grandmother and Papa. They loved their sister so much and would bring her gifts each visit. On her death bed, Aunt Sue Lean asked grandmother for forgiveness and told the boys how badly she had wanted children and what she finally resorted to, to get them. She thanked them for being good sons and asked them to devote the rest of their lives to their mother, my grandmother. They did so lovingly devote the rest of their lives honoring both Grandmother and Papa as their mother and father. They also continued to honor their own father until his death.

Papa was my grandmother's knight in shining armor, and so I now understood why she loved him so much and could never do anything without consulting him. On my last visit with Papa, he told me how much he missed my grandmother, and assured me that he would be going to be with her very soon. I did not want to hear him talk like that, so I asked him to stop. He turned to me with more seriousness in his voice than I had ever heard from him, and said, "Savanah, now listen, death is as natural a thing as can be. Just as sure as you are born, so you shall die. When it happens, I don't want you to waste a lot of time crying over me. I know you'll cry, but let it be because you will miss old Papa, and then move on.

Papa will be right where he wants to be. You know Gal, I am tired! You tell them all what I said to you today, after I am gone you hear!" By then, I was ready to end that conversation, so I just said, "Ok Papa, I will!" It was a Sunday evening; the sun was beginning to set, and a cool breeze blew across the porch. As Papa began to talk even more, "For the first forty years of my life, I did everything under the sun I thought I was big enough to do, but the last forty years, Savannah, I have lived the best I know how, for the Lord." I laughed at the thought of Papa doing something bad.

All I had ever known was my wonderful, loving Papa and his love for the Lord. He prayed for me when I was too shy to pray aloud in Church. "I'll bet what you call bad was actually nothing Papa," I chuckled.
Papa and I both were laughing when he said, "Oh, I was bad Savannah! "Ok then," I replied, "tell me something bad that you did during the first forty years of your life!"

He sat and thought for a few minutes before saying a word, as if he was trying to make up his mind if he wanted to tell me anything at all. He laughed out loud a few times, then, all of a sudden; he began to speak. "Once, old Johnny Sims, Claude Mason, and I were all going with the same woman. She was a bad actor, but we didn't care. This went on and off for several years." Now, Papa had my undivided attention. I listened intensely with my mouth wide open at times, as Papa continued. "We all had wives and children but we thought, if nobody knew, what harm could it do? "Papa!" I said in disbelief that I was hearing him correctly! "Wait Savanah, you ask for this, now listen," Papa exclaimed. I was in the field plowing one day, when old Johnny came running down from across the woods.

He was running so fast, and calling my name, so I stopped the horse, dropped the reins and went to meet him. When I got to him, he was out of breath. He told me that old Elsie had gotten sick and was dying. She had sent for his wife and Claude's wife and had told them everything and asked for their forgiveness.

He was coming to tell me to get home because she had sent for my grandmother also." Papa said he left old Johnny standing in the field and made a mad dash for home. When he arrived, my grandmother was putting on her sweater getting ready to walk out of the front door. Papa asked where she was going and my grandmother told him that Elsie was sick and they say she wasn't going to make it, and she wanted to see her. Papa said he tried to convince her that if Elsie was that sick, it would do nothing but upset her to go visit, so he asked her to stay home. Nothing he said could change her mind and my grandmother told him that if Elsie dies without her knowing what she needed to talk to her about, she would never get over it.

Papa became desperate and told her that if she walked out of that door, to not ever come back. I could not believe my ears were hearing Papa right! He said the look on my grandmother's face broke his heart. He had never talked to her that way before, but she pulled off her shawl and hung it back up, with tears streaming down her face. Old Elsie died that night and Papa said, "I had the nerve to feel relieved". He became quiet as if he had to compose himself, before he could go on. He continued, "The weeks and months that followed are what led to my becoming the Papa you know today Savanah. It worried me so bad, I almost lost my mind.

One day when I was in the woods alone, I fell down on my knees and asked the Lord to help me. I prayed to him that day, with a sincerity I had never had before. I begged for my life because I was dying a slow death. When I finished praying, I knew what I had to do. Six months to the day of Elsie's death, I went to your grandmother and told her everything." My eyes widened a bit when he said that, because I just knew that he would say grandmother came unglued. He laughed and laughed, "Savanah you can't do wrong and get away with it.

The Lord whipped me so bad that I had to tell it on myself! If I had just thought about it, your grandmother was not going to do any more then, than she did when I told her. She cried a little, and when I told her how sorry I was, and I cried too, she put her arms around me and forgave me. Your grandmother was the best woman I have ever known. Try to be good, and live your life so that you won't have to go through what I went through," Papa said. That Sunday my Papa and I became friends and on Tuesday, just two days afterward, in 1978, he died.

Once Papa was gone at age eighty, I told the entire family that Papa said. "We could cry if we must, but after the funeral, he wanted us to go on and live our lives, because he was just where he wanted to be". I never told them about our private conversation, until now. It was a personal and most special moment we shared that I treasure to this very day. Mama continued the tradition of having Sunday dinners at her house. My sisters would all make a dish and Mama would have all the rest of the fixings and our family continued to feast. About once a month all of mama's sisters would bring their families and food to join in with us. This kept the families close.

One of the big highlights of our Sundays was for us to fess up to Mama and Daddy about things that we thought we had gotten away with as children, only to find that Mama and Daddy could tell us more than we realized they knew. It would be until I had children of my own that I understood that parents know each and every one of their children. They know what they are capable of and just about who did what.

I saw my mom and dad disagrees a few times; it was never devastating to me. Mama did not like for daddy to drink, so the majority of their disagreements were as a result of his drinking. Daddy came from a long family line of bootleggers. He loved Mama, and it was apparent whenever he looked at her. Kids can catch on easily to little gestures parents make. I think all dads have their own special chair within family rooms across America. Our dad would come in from work, attend to the garden he and Mama always kept, take a bath, eat supper, and go to his chair to read or watch the news. Mama was always busy doing something, but would often pass through the family room. Us kids would elbow each other and watch Daddy's eyes follow her as long as she was in sight.

He used to tease her sometimes, saying that she had enough back-end (butt), to set a plate full of food on and never waste a crumb. Mama did have her share of butt! Sometimes when she became aware through our sniggles that we were watching Daddy, she would turn around and tell him, "Mind your own business!" She didn't like for Daddy to play with her in that fashion with us watching. The more she fussed, the better he felt, we thought. My mom's sister, Aunt Matilda, and Uncle Bob would physically fight every weekend.

I remember being so frightened every time they would visit because a few of those fights took place in our front yard. It would often be as a result of their both drinking. I had a tendency of feeling threatened when people bigger than me would fight. I thought they would fall on me, and I would in some way end up underneath. My mother never drank, but dad would have a few.
He could still intercede then act as the mediator to calm situations between my aunt and uncle! Mama would tell Aunt Matilda to come visit by herself if they could not visit folk and act decent. A few times, she came to visit her older sister alone, but most of the time Uncle Bob would end up showing up. Mama always said Uncle Bob would come along, only to exercise his rights as Aunt Matilda's husband.

Mama would put her right hand on her hip and preceded to mock Uncle Bob, "Where my wife goes, I go," as he reeled and rocked from being intoxicated! She would then laugh a hardy laugh! I took mental notes of all I saw and heard, and I knew that my life was going to be different. I didn't exactly know how different it was going to be, but I was not going to have a husband who would fight me nor cheat with other women. In the country when someone came to town for any length of time, everyone knew it. It was my twelfth birthday, and Mama had made a beautiful coconut cake with three layers.

It had twelve pink candles, and Mama had written happy birthday on a small card, glued it to two toothpicks, and sat it on the cake. It read, "Happy Birthday Savanah!" She made all of us our favorite cake for our birthday each year. I suppose she had learned most of her cooking skills from Grandmother, because she was an excellent cook. By the time we were twelve, there would be no more birthday parties. Special family dinners and a cake made us just as happy. It was our sign that mama knew we were growing up, and when you are twelve, you can't wait to grow up.

Mama and Daddy talked over dinner about a new boy who had moved into our little settlement, who was deaf and dumb. I remember thinking that the poor kid could not learn. I was feeling bad for him prior to even seeing him. Deaf and dumb were terms used to describe someone who could not hear or talk, I learned later, after Daddy explained it to me. Tomorrow would be Saturday and I was sure that I would get to meet this poor unfortunate kid. Late into the night, I felt ill and ran back and forth to the bathroom throwing up everything that I had consumed at dinner. When I wasn't vomiting, my bowels were loose, out of control. Mama had attended to me all night and had concluded that I had a bug "virus" of some sort. She gave me medicine that slowed the bowels and by morning, the vomiting had subsided. I still felt rotten, but I would take feeling bad over the vomiting and pooping any day.

As I lay in bed wishing I felt well enough to go outside, George ran inside to tell me that the new boy was at the café, and if I wanted to see him, I had better hurry! He had found out that his name was Milton Roy and raved over the fact that the boy could not talk. "But he can most certainly hear," George announced, "because he can dance to the music on the jukebox, Savanah!" Mama had instructed me to stay in bed for the rest of the day, and I would be better and able to go to church with the family on Sunday.

I really wanted to see the boy, so I sneaked out of the house and looked at him through the café window. He looked normal enough, and George was certainly right, he could hear, because he was dancing with Ernestine and wasn't missing a beat. If he could dance with Ernestine, he could certainly dance with me. Ernestine and I were the best dancers in the neighborhood. I rushed back into the house before Mama could realize that I was gone. The following weekend, he returned to the café, and I had my chance to dance with him. As I spoke to him, he understood everything that I was saying, but would write answers to my questions on paper. He told me his name was Milton and I told him my name.

When others would say things and the group laughed, he laughed too. He finally wrote me a note explaining that he could not hear, but he danced to the beat of the music, by feeling the vibrations from the jukebox. He knew what everyone was saying, because he could read their lips. He had gone to a special school that taught him these skills, and he had learned well. Over the next few months, Milton and I became great buddies. He taught me how to communicate using some sign language and through spelling words with hand signals. My dad was really concerned that we were spending too much time together. I guess he thought I would end up marrying this, what older folk called; Deaf-and-dumb boy! Mama held dad at bay.

"Oh Daddy, leave her alone, they are just kids and she has high school and college before she can think about marrying anybody! Savanah is not getting too close to him, because she is learning from him. He is teaching her sign language so that she can better communicate with him. You should see them, she already has learned a whole lot from him," Mama said.

"Let's see if you will say that when we have a little deaf-and-dumb grand baby running around here," Daddy exclaimed jokingly! Older people are usually afraid of things they cannot understand, and my dad was reluctant to my getting too close to Milton. When school was out for the summer, we spent hours talking, and I got to be pretty good with signing. People with more severe disabilities used to be locked away from the general population because of that fear of the unknown and, quite often, because they were ashamed. He was my very first "handicapped" friend, of the many more to come. Of course, Jimmy also thought I was spending too much time with my new friend. I think he was kind of jealous since we secretly claimed each other as girlfriend and boyfriend since fourth grade.

I attended church with Jimmy all of my life. His mother was the youth coordinator, youth choir director, and worked as secretary at one of the local high schools. His father was the piano/organist, head deacon in our church, and an administrator at a junior college, twenty miles from our community. Jimmy was spoiled because his parents were able to give him so much more than the rest of us kids in the church had. He would buy things just for me, and I was flattered to say the least. We were so young that there is really nothing to say about that kind of innocent puppy love.

We attended all church activities together, talked on the phone every day and night when possible. My dad was quite insistent that we did not spend too much time on the phone. He did not like Jimmy too well, because he was spoiled and flaunted his possessions and his superiority over the other kids. That friendship had begun before our ages were in double digits. Jimmy, being two years my senior, went away to college in June directly after graduation, and I was promoted to the eleventh grade. He would come home every other weekend, and we would see each other at church or at my daddy's Café for teens. The most we did was make eyes at each other and smile. We managed a few kisses here and there, when we found ourselves in the position, and that was enough to keep us happy. Just because our lips touched one another's, I thought that was a real kiss and that was as good as it got. Between fourth and seventh grade, we had kissed maybe four times.

By now we knew there was more to kissing than just touching lips, but we did not know how to do it. It would be another year until I was in eighth grade that he would try to teach me how it was supposed to be done. I was to let our lips touch, and then slowly stick my tongue into his mouth. I did just as he asked, but I did not want to get caught, so I did it quick. When he started manipulating his tongue over mine, I thought, that was a bit too much! I would rather touch our lips together and let that be that!

Back then we had party phone lines, an arrangement in which two or more customers were connected directly to the same local loop. Prior to World War II in the United States, party lines was the primary way residential subscribers acquired local phone service. This remained so, especially in the country towns and for rural residents for many years thereafter. Each family had their own ring tone, and after a while, everyone recognized everyone else's ring tone.

There was no way of knowing if someone was using the phone unless you picked up the phone to see if there was a dial tone. It was a rule at our house that if anyone was on the phone when you picked up, you were to immediately hang it up. It was quite a bit of eavesdropping going on mostly by us kids. When I was thirteen years old, I picked up the phone to call Jimmy, knowing I had to make it quick before dad or mama would come through the family room and say something about my being on the phone.

We had just gotten home from evening service at the church, and it was my turn to call to say goodnight. I picked up the phone and heard Mr. Desoto telling the police to come quickly because his neighbors got into a fight, and the husband shot the wife; he said, "I believe she is dead." At that point, I should have put the phone down, but I couldn't. Mr. Desoto went on to give them the address, and the police acknowledged that they were on their way, and would dispatch an ambulance. This was a true emergency! He went on to tell the police, "It happened so fast! We had just gotten home from Church, and she had just walked in her door." The police asked him, "Do you attend the same church?" Mr. Desoto replied, "Yes; she is an usher." I immediately knew that it was Mrs. Williams.

I slammed the phone down. I loved that woman, and she loved me. She was kind, and so very loving to all of the kids at the church. I sat down on the sofa and began to cry.

Mama came into the family room and asked me what was wrong. I told her that I picked up the phone to make a call, and Mr. Desoto was telling the police that Mr. Williams had shot Mrs. Williams and that she was dead. My mom screamed out loud, "Lord no, Lord no!" Daddy came running and asked, "What on earth is wrong?" Now I am crying loud and hard because my Mama is hurting too. She cried when she was sad, but cried when she was happy also. I didn't always understand the reason for her tears, so when I didn't understand, I associated it with pain, and cried right along with her. That night, I fully understood that it was pain that caused her tears, because I was feeling pain as well.

Mama told Daddy what I told her, and Daddy sat her down on the sofa, picked up the phone, and called Mr. Desoto's house. Mr. Desoto had gone back over to the Williams, but his wife confirmed that the tragedy had taken place. Mama was hysterical but wanted to go to help see about the children. Daddy made her sit for a few minutes to get herself together. He explained that she had to get herself together before she could be of any help to the children. Mama soon composed herself, and they left. George went with them, but I refused to go because I just could not stand the idea that I might see her all bloody and dead!

They locked me in and told me not to open the door for anyone. After they had pulled off, and I was all alone, I remembered what Daddy had said when he was talking to Mr. Desoto's wife. He said that Mr. Williams ran away after he shot Mrs. Williams and he was not sure which way he went! I thought, "Where would he go"? He always would come and talk to Daddy about things when he got upset. Would he dare to come here? Now panic began to set in, as I sat on the sofa waiting for Mama and Daddy to return. I heard all kinds of sounds that I had never heard before. The house seems to be popping and cracking, and with each pop and crack, I lost courage. All the doors and windows were locked, but he could look in and see me all alone, with the lights on inside the house.

Mr. Williams could see that Daddy's truck was gone, so would he think about breaking in? I was too scared to move, so I sat there scared to death. Finally, I heard a loud thud on the back porch, more than likely the dog, but fear had taken over. I jumped up, tiptoed to turn the lights out in every room, knowing that he just might be standing in any room that I entered. Making my way back to the sofa, I was relieved that Mr. Williams was not inside with me as of yet! I had not overcome my fear of the dark, so now I was in another fix.

I finally got the courage to crawl to the middle bedroom where mama kept all of her quilts in the closet. In the dead middle of August, I crawled underneath about ten quilts and stayed there until Mama, and Daddy returned. I don't know how long I stayed there, but an hour seemed like three. I came from underneath those quilts, wet with sweat, but relieved to say the least. Mrs. Williams was the only person that I had known in my life to have a total of twenty-six children, and the only person I had known to have been shot and killed in my life.

No, this is not a typo! Mr. and Mrs. Williams did indeed have twenty-six children! As a child, I thought that was probably a world record, only to find years later, that the most prolific woman in the Guinness book of world records was a peasant woman from Russia. She gave birth to sixty-nine children with sixteen sets of twins, seven sets of triplets and four sets of quadruplets.

The Williams had six sets of twins, and all the rest were individual births. He was forty-one years her senior. He had married her when she was only thirteen years old, and he was fifty-four. At the time of the shooting, he was in his late seventies and she was in her late thirties. Mr. Williams was afraid that she had another man. On the night of the shooting, she only asked that he allow the children to change the channel on the television. Because of his age, they did pick him up and take him to jail, but he was released less than a week later and never did any hard time.

Within one year after Mr. Williams killed his wife, he was a basket case. Many times he would come down our little country road in his wagon, pulled by one horse, talking to himself and suddenly pull over, climb down from the wagon and take off through the woods running, the best a man of his age could run.

That behavior continued a few years until his death. For several weeks after Mrs. William's death, I grieved. She had been the kindest woman I had ever known, and I knew beyond a shadow of doubt; she had to be in heaven. She called me her girl! As an usher, she took care of all the girls by not allowing us to slip on the outside when our parents were unable or too busy to watch.

The perfect time to slip out of the church was during offering, and even if we did get past her, she would soon be out there to march us right back inside. It has been many years now, and I still think of her fondly. I remain friends with their surviving children to this very day. We live far apart, and don't visit often, but friends we shall forever be. Jimmy and I maintained our little puppy love relationship throughout my tenth grade year. I was going to the eleventh grade, and he was off to college. Before school ended the previous year, we had been told that our school would merge with the schools in the neighboring town, and those kids were bused to our school.

Chapter Two

Into my class walked the most gorgeous boy I had ever seen in my life. His name was Fred. I knew that because someone called, and he answered as he approached the door. He was about five feet ten inches tall with a slim but muscular build. His skin was as smooth as a baby's butt, with eyes that were so light brown that when he looked at me, it seemed as though he could see right through me. He had a brother there also, who was cute, but Fred was the cat's meow. Most of the girls on campus were talking about him and wanting him to initiate conversation, but he was quiet and reserved. I wanted to know this boy too! After several days, I could see him watching me from the corners of his eye sometimes, but when class was over, he wasted no time gathering his books heading on to the next class.

One day, I arrived in math class a bit early and when he came in, he sat right next to me. I got really nervous and embarrassed, because I knew that, anyone could see me blushing all over. I could feel him glancing my way, but I was frozen in place. I could not control myself in any aspect of the word. I looked at my hands, and they were a little dry, so I hid them underneath the lap tray on the desk. I could not believe that I was so out of control emotionally. When I heard my name being called, I realized that it was the teacher asking me a question. I had no idea what he had asked, so to keep myself from looking even more stupid, I just said, "I don't know the answer!" Then, I thought, "That's just great, now you have made him think you are a dummy!"

I raised my hand, asked to be excused, saying I felt ill. I did not feel sick at all, but I needed to compose myself. When the teacher let me go, I left the room in a rush. I could not return to that class, so I waited until a few minutes before the bell, to go back in. Fred was busy writing notes, and seemed not to realize that I was back. As we gathered our books, Fred said to me, "Oh, here are the notes you missed, and if you need any help understanding them, just let me know. You can copy them and return them tomorrow." "OK," I replied! He was thinking of me when I was out of the room.

That was a great sign! The next day, I told him that I might need a little help with one of the problems from yesterday. He said, "Well let's eat lunch really fast, and I will explain it to you." That was the beginning of our friendship. Over the next few weeks and months, we became even closer. I saw him in every class other than Physical Education and Choir, we ate lunch together every day, and I felt that he thought of me as a special friend. We talked on the phone every night, and on weekends, he would come to the teen café. Even in the eleventh grade, I was not allowed to have boyfriend Company, but the café made it so as we could not tell the difference. I told Jimmy about Fred, and he hit the ceiling. "You're messing around on me Savanah, how dare you," Jimmy said.

We had a few words, but by Christmas, my heart belonged to Fred and Fred alone. In our senior year, Fred and I was a total item, and by senior prom, we were deeply in love. Some would beg to differ, because we were so young; they would probably call it infatuation, but now that I am older and more experienced. I would say that it was true love!

When we graduated from high school, I was still a virgin! I am especially proud of that because today few girls graduate from high school as virgins. Maybe I would not have been a virgin had I grown up in a more recent generation. While most of my friends were actively engaged in sexual intercourse with their boyfriends, I was lying saying I was also sexually active, just to fit in with my crowd. Don't get me wrong, I really wanted too, but the fear of getting pregnant, coupled with my fear of my parents, kept me from participating. I daydreamed of what sex with Fred would be like, and we discussed it on several occasions.

We agreed to wait until after graduation, because we really wanted to get married right after high school. Realizing that one obstacle remained, we prepared our speeches for Mama, who was expecting me to go to college. When we expressed to Mama that we wanted to get married, she shot that idea down before Fred could speak a full sentence. I was going to college and leaving my handsome boyfriend back there for the other girls to drool over. Daddy had become ill and was hospitalized! Mama was making ends meet, but borrowed the money from Uncle Alvin to get me set up for college.

I shared a room in the dormitory with one of my high school friends, "Gail". The next morning, we registered for classes, and the year was off to a great start. Fred and I talked two and three times each week, and he would drive up to the university in Pine Bluff, Arkansas, about once each month. I missed him so much, but I had to stay focused on my classes. Some students don't have to study a lot, and although I didn't study as much as some, I had to study to make good grades. I had left for school in early September, and Fred came up in late September. He arrived around 7p.m, Friday evening, and we began our wonderful weekend together.

There were no curfews, because I signed out, as if I was going home for the weekend. I would never have known to do that, had I not been told by Lisa, one of the upperclassman girls from my hometown.

Yes, I lied! Away from home, I felt free, brave, and grown up! Fred admitted that he had some experience with sex, but I was as dumb as hell. Sex is kind of like riding a bicycle, once you learn, you never forget. I learned really fast! We made love several times that weekend, and I fell deeper in love with each occurrence. Fred was gentle, knowing it was my first experience, but by the time we made love on Sunday evening before returning to campus, I was glad to go. I could feel that I was a bit irritated, and I was not comfortable with that. My parents probably knew that once I tried sex, I would definitely like it. Maybe I was a chip off of the old block.

They had seven kids, and one stillborn, so they must have really liked sex also. I completed my first year of college, worked during the summer in one of the neighboring towns near my hometown, and spent as much time as possible with Fred. Fred worked there part time and talked his supervisor into getting me hired on for the summer. He also maintained a part-time job at the saw mill, with plans to work at the saw mill full time when the opportunity presented itself. The saw mill paid higher wages than the Chicken Poultry. It was a chicken poultry plant that I knew was going to take some getting used to, for me to work there.

The first few nights, I felt really nauseous, but that soon subsided. While at home, I met Jeana, one of my friends from high school for lunch. She was telling me that Fred and Linda were getting a little too close for comfort, so watch things! Linda attended the same school as we did, but was two or three years younger than we were. She always had a gigantic crush on Fred, and it showed every time she looked at him. Although I tried to pretend that it was no big deal, my heart broke. If you can visualize dropping a glass on the floor, you can understand what happened to my heart.

Just the idea made me physically ill. How would I ask him such a question? Should I believe what I just heard? He wouldn't mess around on me! Would he? Days passed, and I watched Fred's every move, as much as possible. On the weekends when we would go out, sometimes we would see her, and I swear that she watched our every move. When we slow danced, I would glance at her trying not to be obvious, and she always looked angry. One night, in particular, he went to the bar to get us drinks, and she made her way to the bar and stood right next to him. While she looked up at him, it seemed that their conversation was a little more than casual. I could see him glancing over his shoulder to see if I was paying any attention too. This would be the night that I decided to push for an answer.

Following the dance as Fred was taking me home, I asked the question. "Why did Linda seem so upset tonight?" "Linda who," he replied? "The only Linda in the room tonight, that's what Linda,"

I said! He explained to me that she just had a little crush on him, and she would come up to him flirting, but it was nothing. He told me so calmly, and so nonchalantly, that instantly, I believed him. Without a doubt, he loved me, so that was that! Marilyn, a woman at work who was at least ten or twelve years older than me, was paying quite a bit of attention to Fred. I thought nothing of it because of her age! Certainly there would not be anything going on. Whenever I came around, I still had his undivided attention.

Marilyn was cute, but surely he didn't want anyone that much older than him himself. While working there, I realized I needed to be in school, so that I could have a career. This was painful labor to me! At eighteen years of age, I could not do this work for the next thirty years, like so many were planning to do. Several of the girls and guys whom we graduated from high school with, worked there, and had no other future plans.

In August, I went back to school, and we began the same routine as the year before. On Fred's first trip to visit me in September, we became engaged. I would go home once each month, and he would come to see me once. Our sex life was irrefutably awesome! The extra money was great, but I was ready to return to school, so that I could finish, marry Fred, find a good job, and start a family. I proudly purchased all of my clothing for school that year, said goodbye to my family and Fred, and began my sophomore year. It would be two weeks before Fred would come to visit, so I consumed myself with my classes.

Good grades were a requirement to land better jobs! He still made his monthly trips to see me, and I continued my monthly visits back home. It was getting harder to deal with Mama and Daddy's same-old curfews. I was grown up now, but to them, I was still their little girl. Gail and I moved off campus for our sophomore year. I had cousins, "Kaye and Patty," who lived off campus, and because I looked up to them, I wanted to be off campus as well. Kaye was my idol. I thought she knew everything, although she was only two years older than me. Her boyfriend was one of the local disc jockeys at the largest radio stations in Arkansas. That opened the door to our being able to do so many things that we never would have been able to do. She eventually married him, and I thought that it was a match made in heaven, although she begged to differ later.

Even though I had a heavy class load and lots of studying to do, I missed Fred dearly. On his first visit to the university that year, like the year before, I had all of my homework completed, so that I could focus on him and him alone. During the month of October, my menstrual period was due on the thirteenth, but it did not come.

My periods were like clockwork, and I became fearful. "Oh please, God," prayed, "I can't be pregnant!" Trying to put it out of my mind, I continued my daily routine. Maybe, just maybe, I was wrong and everything would return to normal. I told nobody, not even Gail. By November 13, I was almost positive that I was pregnant and went to see a doctor for him to confirm what I already knew in my heart.

I was very pregnant, very unmarried, and very scared. Now, what was I to do? I could never tell Mama! She would be so disappointed in me! The speech she gave before I started college ran through my mind as if it was yesterday. I could not eat, or sleep! Gail was in her bed, but heard me crying in the night. She turned the light on, sat on my bed next to me, "You are pregnant, aren't you?" she said ever so gently. "Yes!" I whispered. "I thought so," she said as that familiar little wrinkle appeared between her brows. "For the last couple of weeks,

I have been hearing you crying in my sleep." I cried uncontrollably, but Gail did not want the other girls to hear, so she shushed to quiet me down. "What am I going to tell Mama, how can I ever face her again?" "It will work out! She will be disappointed at first, but she will get over it," Gail insisted. We talked until daylight, she made breakfast and we went to class as usual. I did feel better having told someone else. Now I didn't feel so alone! We decided that I should tell Fred first, and he would help me decide what to do next. When we talked on the phone, I didn't tell him, but he knew something was wrong.

I tried to be cheerful, but he could tell that something was on my mind. He would be to visit the weekend, so I would tell him then, but feared what he would say! Would he be angry with me for ruining his life, because even though we wanted to be married earlier, we always planned to have a baby much later? This was the very first crisis of our relationship, as well as the first real crisis of my life. I could not imagine how he would react, nor predict how it would turn out. Friday came slowly that week, but I anxiously awaited his arrival after class. I was already packed as if the weekend rendezvous was going to be the same as the others before it. He arrived right on time. His usual time of arrival was always between 6:00pm and 7:00pm.

We went to dinner, prior to going to the hotel as usual. He commented, "You are eating like a bird today, you usually eat like a horse," he chuckled. I smiled, but I did not find it particularly amusing. It felt so good to be in his arms again, but the circumstances made it feel different. Thoughts were running through my head like wildfire. Would he hold me the same after I tell him? Will he stick by me or abandon me? I had seen others abandoned when faced with the same situation. As I grow bigger, will he think I am ugly?

We made love early that evening, probably because, I had told him that I did not want to go dancing like we often did. What if he never comes back to visit? I would be the laughing stock of the campus! As we lay in each other's arms, I turned to tell him, but he beat me to the punch by telling me about a tragedy in his family. His favorite aunt was in the hospital dying of cancer. I was sorry for their loss, so I had to let him talk it out. I had to wait! I slept arms as always, but upon waking, I told him that I had something I must talk to him about. "OK," he said, as he repositioned himself to hear. No sooner than I got the words "I am pregnant," out of my mouth, I began to cry! The smile on his face faded in such a way that you would have thought he had lost his mother to death. "I am sorry, I am so sorry," I muttered as I turned away.

I could not bear to look at him! I had given him the worse and most unexpected news of his life. For at least ten minutes, which felt like an hour, we said nothing! I wanted to turn to see his face, but I could not bear what I thought I would see again. He so gently touched my back. I could not move! He stroked my hair, over and over again.

He then caught my shoulder and pulled me toward him and said, "I want a son, and if it is a girl, you are gonna have to do it again and again until we get it right." He had a smile on his face that is forever etched in my memory. He told me that I was not in this alone, we did this thing together, and we are going through it together. I mean it literally when I say his words were like music to my ear. He said that I would come home the following weekend, and we were going to tell my parents. He would tell his parents without me. "While we are telling your parents," he said, "I will ask for your hand in marriage." I knew that this man was my soul mate, and I would spend the rest of my life as Mrs. Fred Winslow!

I was happy, yet sad that I had to deliver this news to my parents. I hoped that Fred was not faking just for me. The following weekend, I went home. Mama, Daddy, and my brother George picked me up from the bus station. Fred was working overtime, already planning for the unexpected delivery.

On Saturday evening, when Fred arrived at our house, he came in playing with Mama as always. He had dinner with the family, and we all sat down to watch television. Mama made popcorn dripping with butter at Fred's request. She really liked him and I hoped that would help make our news a little less painful. George retired for the evening, and just as Mama and Daddy were getting ready to leave the room for the night; Fred asked if we could have a word with the two of them. My heart fell to the pit of my stomach. Mama sat back down, but Fred had to ask Daddy to sit down. Mama blurted out, "I hope you kids are not going to bring that marriage stuff back up again.

We have gone through that you know!" "It's important," Fred said, taking a deep breath and clearing his throat. I could sense his nervousness as he began to speak. He began, "The first thing that I want you to know is that I love your daughter very much, and she loves me. You know we asked if we could get married, but waited because you wanted her to go to college first. We understood your concerns, and we waited. Now we find that we must address it again, because she is pregnant!" "Oh my God!" Mama squealed so loud I almost jumped into Fred's lap.

Daddy just sat there and never parted his lips. There was no reaction from him, and still to this day, there has been no reaction or comment about the matter. I felt that he could tell I would have passed out had he spoke on the matter, or was he so hurt that he could not speak? Maybe he thought that mama was reacting enough for the both of them. "Now look what a mess you two have made. Can't you just hear the whispering around the community, and oh goodness, the church!"

Daddy got up went into the kitchen and brought mama a glass of water. "Don't you have anything to say, Daddy?" Mama asked. "Drink your water baby," Daddy sighed. I could not look at either Mama or Daddy in the eyes. I was hurting the two people whom I wanted to be most proud of me. Now, they would never be proud of me, unless I could create a miracle of some sort. I could hear mama sniffling, and I knew she was crying. I glanced at Fred to see if I could get confirmation from his expression. He was looking at Mama with such pity. "We are so very sorry to disappoint the both of you, but I want you to know that she will stay in school and finish."

Mama cried more at that statement, and because I could not speak, I kneeled and crawled to her feet. I laid my head in her lap as I did when I was a little girl and sobbed. It was all I could do; I could not speak! I would not have blamed her if she had pushed me aside. In some way or another, I kind of thought she might do just that, but she didn't. I do remember her touching my hair, kind of patting me like I was a puppy! I knew that I was not out of hot water, but anything was better than nothing. I felt somewhat relieved. I had acted like such a coward and let Fred do the talking, because I could not speak without falling apart. Fred had told me to let him handle it, and I did just that. Fred and I were so in love!

The Sunday before I returned to school, I saw all of my sisters and brothers at dinner at mama's.

I could tell they all had been told. Mama to Ann everything and Ann could not keep a secret to save her life. She told the others, but they would not say anything unless I did. We had eaten and I was preparing to go back to school as soon as Fred came to take me to the bus station.
Ann came into my room and asked me if I had something to tell her. "Nope not a thing" I replied.

She could not handle that, so she called all of the other girls into my room. They came running but they did not know why. "Our little sister done got herself pregnant ya'll" she stated. Tisah said, "Oh, leave the girl alone. You always are meddling."

Meddling, Ann replied, as she walked out of the room. "The truth is the light"! Nadelle yelled out to her, "If I recall correctly, you were in the same fix a few years ago, sister of mine! We all laughed, as Faye and Tisah high fived Nadelle Are you ok Savanah, don't let her get to you, Faye said concerningly. "I am good," I responded, "the hardest thing was telling mama and daddy." Tisah questioned, "did they fuss"? "Naw I said, mama was upset, but I let Fred do the talking. I was about to shit on myself"! Faye said, "you know you can still do this school thing, and we will all help you with the baby." "Thanks guys," I responded.

Just then, George came into the room to tell me that Fred had arrived. Nicholas, came in behind George, put his arms around me and said. "You are still my sister, and I love ya Savanah!" I took a deep breath, and thanked him. "Now go before you miss your ride," George said. "That's one ride, I don't want to miss. Tell Fred I am coming, I said as I hugged George goodbye. He picked up my bag and went to put it in Fred's car. I said goodbye to everyone and we were off to the bus station.

Upon arriving the bus was running behind schedule, therefore Fred decided to drive the one and a half hour to take me back to school. He spent the night with me, took my clothes to the house that morning and dropped me off on campus. During our time together that night, we planned our wedding for January 6, just seven months before I was to deliver. I completed the semester, as if nothing was different. We needed extra money for the July 13th delivery date, but we kept Fred's visits at once a month, and I continued to go home once a month. That meant that Fred still had two free weekends every month without me. It wasn't that I didn't trust him; I just wanted to be with him every chance. We decided to have a very small wedding with just the immediate family because we did not have the money to support a lavish wedding.

It did not matter to me; just to become Mrs. Fred Winslow was enough! We spent our wedding night in a small hotel in El Dorado, Arkansas. I could not have been happier had we stayed at the Marriott! Although there were a few whispers about me being pregnant back at home, I was not showing until toward the end of my fifth month.

The gossip wasn't as bad as Mama predicted, she finally admitted. Everyone at church was kind, but I could see the curiosity on their faces. One after another came to me to say hello and to congratulate me on my wedding, but their eyes could not fight off the urge to glance at my stomach.
Mama had told me it would be that way, but "you are not the first, and you won't be the last girl to get pregnant," she said. I wanted to hold my head up and not down in shame. What did I have to be ashamed of? I was proud to be Mrs. Fred Winslow. As soon as I was back at school, I went to the registrar's office to change my name. They told me that I had to wait until my marriage license had been recorded and mailed back to me. I flashed my little ring in the faces of all of my friends at school, and no sooner than my marriage license was back in my hands, I changed my name.

Savannah Marie Winslow had a nice little ring to it. Fred and I decided that after the baby was born, I would get on birth control pills to ensure that I didn't have another baby until this one was at least four years of age. By that time, I would have finished college and have worked at least two years.

I really never knew I could get them before I got pregnant because most people I knew did not take them. They were relatively new and people in my circle did not go beyond the use of condoms. I did not have to be a rocket scientist to know; I had to find a more reliable contraceptive. I made it through the second semester of my sophomore year growing tired of being pregnant. My friends were so supportive; I don't think I would have made it so well without them. We still had fun and laughed a lot, like the silly girls we were. It was only when they went dancing and I had to stay home, that I felt really pregnant.

When I was alone, I spent that time with my baby. I talked to it and really felt as if it understood in some small way, how optimistic I was about its future. I wondered whether it would be a girl or boy, but it did not matter; I was going to be the best Mom ever. Fred got a little more excited as the date got closer, and finally admitted that he really did want a boy. Since he wanted a boy, I wanted him to have just whatever would make him happier!

I welcomed the month of May! I would be twenty years old next month, and in July, I would be a mother and Fred a father. We talked about what great parents we were going to be to this baby. We spent the full first weeks of July, before

the baby arrived with his parents. They were delightful people after I really got to know them. They were all somewhat bashful and kept to themselves, but I grew to understand them as time passed. They were awesome after I got to really know and bond with them. The baby was due on July 13, so we went back to Mamas so that when I went into labor, I would have her right there.

I was a little afraid, but I knew that if other girls younger than me could do it, so could I; I just wanted my mama there with me through it all. Almost all children are typical, when facing fearful events in life. We feel that mothers can make things turn out better. I wanted my husband to be right there by my side, but I desperately needed my mama! She would be there as she had been with my sisters before me. Fred went to work, and I went to play cards with one of my friends from high school. Gina and I had played together since elementary school when they moved into the community.

We had been so close that I knew we would be friends throughout our lives. She had married Roy, her high school sweetheart, directly after our high school graduation Fred and Roy were friends also, and had played basketball together on the high school team. I reflected back on our high school days when Gina and I would run to meet Fred and Roy in one of the empty classrooms, in order that we could kiss quickly before we all had to board the buses for home. I had perfected the art of kissing with Fred, and I did it relatively easy. Maybe Jimmy intimidated me too much!

It was already 12:15 a.m., July 12, and I wanted to be home when Fred got there. Mama had put his food back for him to eat after work. We had gone to bed, and Fred and I were just lying there talking. Suddenly, I felt wet, and I reached my hand down between my legs to see what was going on. I was indeed wet and so was my panties, gown, and the bed was slightly damp. I told Fred, "I guess I must have peed on myself because everything is wet."

I got out of the bed, went to the bathroom, wondering how I could have peed and not know it! I cleaned myself up, changed my clothes; Fred and I changed the bed linen and settled back in for the night. After a few minutes, I had the same sensation and reached my hand down there again, only to find the same thing had occurred.

Now it was time to go wake Mama up, because I did not understand what was happening. Mama laughed when I told her I had peed on myself twice, and I didn't feel like I needed to go. She got up and went to the bathroom with me, examined my gown and chuckled, "Your water broke." "My water?" I asked her all confused! "Yep, we're gonna have a baby pretty soon," she said, smiling as if she was pleased. She asked me if I had any pain that felt like the cramps from my menstrual period.

I did have a slight bit of cramping, but she said it was not enough for us to go to the hospital so early. "Why didn't you tell me I was going to lose water?" I asked. "I thought you knew all about it since you decided you were ready to have a baby," Mama said, still chuckling. She gave me a sanitary pad to put on to catch any leakage and said, "Wake me up if the cramps get worse over into the night. You are gonna be just fine, so don't worry." Mama said as she turned to go back to her bedroom, "What is my grand baby's name gonna be if it's a boy", mama asked? "Bryan," I said.

"You go to rest. Baby Bryan will be here before you know it and you'll wish for rest!" I wanted a boy for Fred, and Mama had said it was going to be a boy since when I was seven months pregnant. I thought they both would be too outdone if it turned out to be a girl. I slept through the rest of the night, but upon rising, I had more cramps. Mama called the doctor, and he told her to bring me when my pains were ten minutes apart. The cramps would come and go, but they remained twenty to twenty-five minutes apart almost all day. Around 5:00 p.m., the pains were at twelve minutes apart, and Mama was ready to go. She wanted to go when the cramps reached twelve minutes because we had an eighteen-mile drive to the hospital.

At the hospital, they prepped me for deliver by giving me an enema and shaved off every drop of pubic hair I had. I was shocked when the nurse started shaving me; nobody told me they would do that. At the hospital, the vocabulary changed. My cramps became contractions, and I was in labor. I was not dilating as I should have been and Mama started to ask the nurse questions. They started talking about assisted birth and using forceps. It occurred to me that I had spent so much time studying and listening that I failed to educate myself properly for my baby's birth.

I had listened to my sisters and friends who had babies already and thought I just about knew it all. Of utmost importance to me was tracking the growth of my baby from the beginning. I had a book that showed its development in every stage, but I never worried about the delivery itself. I knew it would hurt, but others had done it and lived, so could I. Now the contractions were coming faster and stronger, and I did not like he look on Mama's face. Fred even looked worried! I could stay in the prep room until I was ready for delivery. Mama and Fred could stay with me.

After about three hours and it seemed like ten vaginal checks, they decided it was time to move to the delivery room. They wheeled my entire bed into the hallway and opened the double doors that said employees only. As they were taking me through the doors, the nurse told Mama and Fred that they could go to the waiting room. "What"? They can't go with me?" I asked the nurse. "No, this is as far as they can go with you, but don't worry, you will be just fine," the nurse replied.

I couldn't believe that, and I immediately started to cry. Fred and Mama watched me, and I watched them as I looked back over my head, the doors slowly closed. I felt more alone and scared than I did when I first discovered that I was pregnant.

Surrounded by strangers I had never seen before, the contractions grew much stronger, and I had dilated. The nurses were kind but firm, until they transferred me to the delivery table, put my legs in the stirrups, and buckled my arms against the table so that I could not move.

I did not bargain for all of this! Too many things were happening that I was not told about. My sisters were telling me so much, but they left out a whole lot of things. I began to complain that the pains were hurting too much. The nurse gave me a shot and suddenly; I felt tired, drifting in and out of sleep with each contraction.

I thought that they probably sedated me just to shut me up, but afterward, I found that they had to sedate me, because they would indeed use forceps to assist me with the birth. When I woke up in recovery, a nurse was doing something to my stomach and asked me if I knew I had a baby. I felt my stomach, and it felt like Jell-O. I could tell there was no baby there anymore. She could not tell me if it was a girl or boy, but she did tell me to go back to sleep, and when I was awake again, I would be able to see it and hold it. I was so sedated that I went to sleep immediately.

Just as she said, when I woke up the next time I was much more alert. I was in a semiprivate room, and could hear my roommate crying. The curtain was drawn between us, so I just listened, wondering why she was crying so much. Finally, a nurse and a member of the clergy staff came in order to pray with her. Her baby had died, and her heart was broken! As they started to leave, I asked the nurse to come over to my side of the curtain, and she did. I whispered, "I want to know if I have a girl or boy?" She also informed me that she did not know, because she was traveling through the hospital with clergy today. She said, "One of your nurses will be in shortly, and they will give you all of that information." I later heard my roommate getting out of bed; she was no longer crying! She went to the restroom, and as she came back to bed, she peeked around the curtain at me. "Joyce!" I said in amazement that I knew her. She smiled in spite of her pain, and said, "You don't know what you have yet?"

"Not yet," I whispered, hoping that she would not start crying on me. "I guess you heard that my baby died." I shook my head, "Yes, I am so sorry!" She shrugged her shoulders. "I don't understand, but maybe I will later." I did not speak; instead, I nodded my head in agreement and smiled slightly. She disappeared behind the curtain, and neither of us spoke for a while. Suddenly, I said, "Joyce, you know I have been thinking.

I woke up one time in the recovery room and asked the nurse about the sex of my baby, and she said she did not know. The nurse who came to see you with clergy said that she did not know either. Do you suppose my baby died too, and they don't want me to know yet? Maybe that is why they put us in the room together," I suggested fearfully, "Oh no, I don't think so." She got up and went out of the door! When she returned a nurse was with her. "Mrs. Winslow, I will be right back with your baby boy," the nurse smiled and left the room. I thanked Joyce for helping me get the opportunity to see my baby, and I could not wait! Mama and Fred were on their way back to the hospital, and I would ask if the baby could stay with me until they arrived.

The nurse walked in holding my son ever so carefully. As I finally laid eyes on the blue blanket, I knew it engulfed a beautiful little bundle of joy. I was in love from that very moment to this day. By the time Mama and Fred arrived, I had memorized every detail about this baby. I counted his toes and fingers. His little mouth was so tiny, and his nose was pointed like his daddies. They told me that they stayed until after the baby was born last night, and I was resting in recovery. They saw the baby that same night.

He was born July 12, at 11:50p.m, just ten minutes before my due date. I could not believe how accurate my doctor had been in predicting the date, but I remembered nothing about the actual birth. I had all the battle scars to prove I had that baby! I was in the hospital for four days and was surprised that instead of Fred coming for me and the baby, Mama and Daddy came. When I asked where Fred was, she said that he called and asked them to pick me up; and said to tell me he had to run out of town and would return tomorrow night. "out of town where?"

I asked. Mama said she didn't know; he had called her yesterday after he left the hospital. I did not know what to think; my husband was supposed to be there to take us home. Although I was consumed with my new baby, I was still puzzled! When he returned, I wanted some answers! He went to Dallas, Texas, with the husband of one of our friends. Jacob needed him to ride with him; there was no one else available to help him drive.

Jacob had worked the midnight shift and was too sleepy to drive that distance safely. Although it was a flimsy explanation to me, I accepted it. My husband was back, and that was all that mattered. His parents came to see the baby and me the day-after Fred returned. They thought he was beautiful also. They debated on which of their five kids, Bryan looked most like. Fred told them to stop the debating, "He looks just like his old man, me!"

Bryan was five weeks old, and it was time for me to go back to school. I told Fred I wanted to wait until after the baby was older. He told me, that I had no other choice, because if I did not return to school, my mama would never forgive him. "I promised her you would stay in school remember," he said. He decided that we would go away for a few days with Jacob and Doris to Dallas. Doris's family lived. Mama kept the baby, and off we went! I had never been to Dallas, so I was excited that I was getting a real treat. Once there, we went straight to Doris family's home.

It was such a large house and her mother insisted that we stay and not get a hotel. Fred left it up to me, and I accepted the invitation. After all, we needed every dime we could rake and scrape, with me going back to school and his trying to maintain things at home. We would spend Thursday night through Saturday night with them and return home on Sunday.

Our room was on the opposite end of the house as if it was built for such an occasion. Doris's sister Gloria had just had a baby also. It was a boy that looked So much like our baby. I told her that our babies could have been twins, they looked so much alike. She smiled and continued to talk to her mom about keeping the baby while she went with friends. Since we were not going out, I told her that Fred and I would watch the baby until she returned. She was a single mother, and I wanted her to have a little freedom. As I held Samson Fredrick, I missed my own baby so much. Again, I told Fred that I could not get over the striking resemblance of the two babies. We purchased fish, and barbeque, so the entire weekend was a feast. We had lots of fun, but three days went by like the blink of an eye.

On the return trip, I thought of ways to approach Mama with the idea of my staying home at least one semester. I was sure she would agree that the baby was too young for me to leave him. She had told me from the beginning of my pregnancy that she was going to keep the baby until I completed college.

When I got the nerve, I approached her with my idea of returning to school the next semester, and staying home with the baby, but she disagreed! I could not believe she wanted me to leave my baby and my husband behind. Other girls went back to school after having babies, but the babies were not so young, I argued. She insisted that if I quit now, I would never return. "I can take care of this baby for two years. I took care of all of my kids and did not kill anyone. Baby, you are halfway there." I told Mama, under no uncertain terms was I going to leave my baby and my husband behind.

In my own heart I knew, had I quit then, it was an immense chance I would never return to the university. Certainly, I would miss my friends, but I was a mother and a wife, and I felt my family needed me more. Mama was totally distraught, but my mind was made up! I called my friends from my hometown who attended school with me and informed them that I would not be returning to school. They, too, were disappointed! Willie was my Best guy friend, and he was acting almost as offended as my mama. When they saw that my mind was made up, we agreed to meet for lunch the day before they were to return to school.

Our little town was so small that we had no place to sit down and eat together without traveling eighteen miles. We opted to go to the school cafeteria and buy lunch. There, we could sit down together and because the cafeteria workers did not get off until 2:30p.m, it gave us plenty of time to visit. I was reluctant because my mama worked in the cafeteria at our school. I was feeling awful for letting her down a second time in just over a year's time. We had all sat down to eat, and we were actually having a great time. The students were back in class, and we had the cafeteria to ourselves. I was sending messages back to other friends at school, when one of the other cafeteria workers came running hysterically and said to me, "Girl, you need to come back here and see about your Mama."

We all jumped up and headed for the kitchen, following the lead of the messenger. Mama was back in the storage room where the supplies were kept, crying and praying all at the same time. I still headed for Mama but Willie stopped me just before I approached her. "Wait! She is praying!" She was on her knees praying a prayer so different from other prayers I had heard her pray. This one was louder, almost as though she was screaming at the Lord, or maybe me! "Everybody is going back but my baby, Lord has mercy!" She asked God to intervene, "Make it happen right now Lord, I pray in the name of Jesus." I had no immediate response because I was speechless! Speechlessness was quickly replaced by anger!

I could not believe that she was acting this way. It was so embarrassing! When I looked at my friends, they all had tears streaming down their faces. I thought, What is wrong with everybody? Am I the only one who cares about my baby and my husband? What did Willie know? He was not a husband, and he had no babies! None of them had husbands, wives, or children, but they knew what was best for me! They all pitied Mama, and I could feel from their reactions, they blamed me for her pain. I felt trapped, angry, confused, and embarrassed that she would act like this in front of people.

To tell the truth, I was upset with them all! I walked over to Mama feeling so defeated, and told her, "If you will just stop, I will go back to school! I will go pack my things and go back today." Mama gathered her composure and struggled but eventually stood from kneeling, dried her face, held me in her arms for a moment, and was ready to finish her workday. Mama had begun having problems with arthritis in her knees, and she was even using them to help manipulate me back to school.

Now, they would hurt all night and Daddy would be rubbing her knees with liniment. She told me to go home and pack, but she would be late getting home. Willie and the others were so happy to hear that I was going back to school and Willie volunteered to come back to pick me up after he registered the next morning. My friend was going to drive 125 miles back home to pick me up? I wondered if he and Mama were in cahoots. I went home with my tail literally tucked between my legs to tell Fred how Mama has shamed me and that I was going back to school after all.

I could see that he was just a tad disappointed, but he thought it best so that he could stay in Mama's good graces. He was convinced that I was not going back, because I had convinced myself that I was going to stay out one semester until the baby was older. I told him that Willie was going to pick me up the next day, and I wanted him to spend as much time with the baby tomorrow as possible, before going back to his parents' house. He promised to visit Little Bryan several times each week so that the baby would grow knowing that Fred was his daddy. I would come home every other week now to see them both. Fred would not have scheduled visits, but would come from time to time. I saw Fred off to work and began packing my things. I had really mixed emotions about the whole ordeal, but I was going back to school like my mama, and all of my friends wanted me to. When Mama finally arrived, she had so many bags; I had to help her unload the car.

She had gone shopping for me and purchased so many beautiful outfits. I always had pretty things, but I was exceptionally proud of these pretty new outfits. I thought that I would be wearing those same clothes I was wearing before I got pregnant and hoped that everyone would have forgotten them. I tried on all of my outfits, and each one of them fit perfectly. I never knew how mama managed to always pick my clothes so well. I made mama a promise to show Bryan my picture every day and tell him that I was his mama. She said that she would do just that! The last thing she told me before I got in the car was, "Baby, I promise you that one day you will understand why it is so important to me that you get an education. I know you love your husband, but sometimes love is not enough!"

"What are you trying to say Mama?" I asked. "I am just saying, if for any reason your marriage doesn't work, you can take care of you and this baby," Mama replied. The next afternoon, I said my good-byes to my little family, to my parents, and my younger brother, George. I went back to school with heaviness in my chest that to this day, I cannot describe. After a couple of weeks, I was back in the swing of things. Just like last year, we would do all of our homework in the evening after classes grab a bite to eat, and go straight to the card table. Sometimes we would play cards from 7:30p.m to 1:00a.m I called home regularly to talk to Mama about the baby and then to Fred's parents' to talk to Fred. After a few times of calling Fred, I sensed a big change in our relationship, and it scared me to death.

I would call him, and many times he would not be at home. I began questioning him as to his whereabouts. He would give me an answer, but they did not always make sense to me. When I would ask Mama how many times Fred came to see the baby in the week, she would say, "Oh, he came one time, on Thursday," and sometimes she would say, "Well, he didn't make it this week." If I asked him the same question, he would say, "Well I didn't go this week because I worked overtime, but I am going to see my son three times next week." It never happened! As time progressed, if Bryan saw his daddy once every two weeks, he was lucky

At home for Thanksgiving break, we had Thanksgiving at his parents' house. He had left home with Dale, but I saw Dale's car pass back by the house a couple of hours later with only one person in it. When his brother came home from town, I asked him if he saw Dale in town. He had indeed seen Dale, and he was in his car alone. It was 11:30pm and Fred was still not home. As I lay across the bed that night looking out of the window, I wanted to see who would drop Fred off at our house. At 3:34a.m, everything was quiet, and I hadn't seen a car in twenty minutes or so. It was warm outside, and with the window up, I was having trouble keeping my eyes opened. Suddenly, the lights of a car slowly approached and stopped just short of the house. It sat there a minute. I heard the door of the car, and then it proceeded on past the house. Under the street light, I could see the station wagon and the driver all too well. It was Marilyn from the chicken poultry. My heart sank into the pit of my stomach! My face felt warm, and I was filled with both anger and pain. It looked like they did have a relationship outside of work.

It took Fred about twenty seconds to appear, walking into the driveway. I quickly closed the curtain and assumed a sleep position. He came into the house, ever so quietly, as if he did not want to wake anyone.

In our room, he did not turn on any lights; he undressed and slid ever so carefully in bed. I snuggled up to him and began to tickle his sides, "Where have you been, Sir," I asked? He answered, "Down to the café with Walter and the guys." He was holding his body slightly frigid. "So did Walter bring you home" I questioned? "Yea now go to sleep," he said with a chuckle. I laid there for a minute thinking, "No, he didn't just tell that big ball-faced lie." I sat up, placed my back to the wall ever so carefully, put my feet against his back and pushed him off of the bed as hard as I could. He landed in the middle of the floor about three feet from the bed.

Bryan squirmed in his bed, from the loud thud his daddy made when he hit the floor. I did not want him to wake up, not yet! Fred's mother heard the loud thud and came to the door. "Is everything OK in there?" she asked? I answered, "Oh yes; everything is just fine now Mrs. B, as I playfully referred to her." He got up off of the floor and asked, "What you do that for?" Our first major argument was conducted in complete whispers. I told him that I was doing everything I could to insure a better life for the three of us, and I did not appreciate being lied to. We talked all the time, about the importance of our life together, and he seems to be doing things to alter our plans as much as he could. I told him that if he had changed his mind about me and the baby, let me know now so I could make some adjustments.

I knew that I wanted this marriage more than anything in the world. He said he wanted the marriage the same as he always did. "Then why are you running around with Marilyn?" I asked. Everyone at the chicken poultry thought something was going on between the two of them last summer. "That woman means nothing to me! You and Bryan are my family, and that is that!" He finally expressed something with feelings. Fred had never been a big talker, but he didn't have to talk when he wanted to express his love. It was the way he looked at me, touched me, treated me, laughed when we acted silly, and his attentiveness that I fell in love with. I had taught him to dance while we were still in high school, and he was a fabulous dancer. People used to stand back as we mesmerized them with our moves. This man is who I love with all of my heart and soul, and this marriage is going to work, I told myself over and over again.

After Thanksgiving, he seemed to have been making an effort to get things back on track He called me at least twice a week and was spending much more time with Bryan since I left home this time. In December, I went home for the holidays and decided that if Fred went out, even for an hour, I would go also. Sure enough, he told me that he was going to have a beer and would be back in an hour or so. I had learned that an hour really meant two or three hours, and when I was at home for Thanksgiving, a couple of hours turned into almost all night long. I waited until he was practically to the car and yelled, "Wait, I think I will go too." The look on his face was priceless; I ran out and got in the car. "Bryan was sleeping, so I told mama that I would be back in an hour or so." I didn't want to leave him very long.

Mama kept him all the time, and as his parents, we needed to be back in at least an hour and a half. When we walked into the joint, as it was called, his friends and some of their wives and girlfriends were sitting around tables in the little hole in the wall of a club. They all seemed so surprised to see me, far I seldom showed my face in juke joints. Phyllis was somewhat a friend of mine, and we sat and talked while the guys were over near the pool table. We had been there about fifteen minutes when someone called Fred's name from the outside. It was Craig calling but when he stepped in the door, he kinda froze when he saw me. You didn't expect to see me here, did you? I thought!

Fred had answered him, but he made it a point to say nothing else until he walked right up to him. Fred looked at me from the corner of his eyes and told Craig he will be out there in a few. Craig went out of the door, and I watched Fred closely even though I continued to converse with Phyllis. Soon Fred came over, sat next to me and joined our conversation. I guess he sat there for about five minutes then excused himself outside, saying he would be right back. As soon as he disappeared from the doorway, I told Phyllis, "Let's walk out of here for a minute. I walked outside and Fred was talking to Marilyn, who was leaning against her car grinning like a Cheshire cat. I said not a word as I walked toward them. I could see Marilyn's uncertainty about how to handle the situation. I had a drink in my hand, dashed it in her face and commenced to beat the living hell out of her.

I don't know what came over me, but I gave her one good butt-whipping. Fred came toward us as if he was going to try to separate us, but I turned to him quickly and told him that he had better get back, and don't touch me! He backed off with a surprised look on his face. After a few days as I replayed the events of that night in my mind. Fred probably backed off because I looked like a replica of the character in the movie "The Exorcist." The other guys standing around finally broke us apart, but not before I gave her one last kick in the stomach that melted her body around my foot.

My cousin, Ray, was there and after things had settled down a minute, he said, "Girl, I did not know you had it in you. Man you kick ass!" I asked Ray not to say anything to anyone in the family, and he agreed not to say a word. I knew that if I asked Ray not to say anything, he wouldn't. Fred stood there as if he was afraid to open his mouth! I said, "Let's go," but before I left, I told Marilyn, "There is more where that came from and actually that was just for you and Fred trying to be so slick. Don't you worry; he and I have some talking to do also." "I got you because you're old enough to be his mama, and you both played me when I worked at the chicken poultry last summer."

You know how you do things and wonder why afterward? I don't know what came over me. It was something I should have been able to control, but I couldn't. I went after that woman to try to tear her head off with my bare hands. I yelled at Fred all the way back to Mama's house. He stopped the car down the street to try to calm me. "Now my family is going to hear all about this!" I told him. "Not because of me, because of you and your little flings. I love you too much, but if I don't have to have Flings with guys, neither should you. That doesn't spell love, Fred, "it spells lust!"

Within two days, Mama and Daddy had the news. My sister Ann Went to town; she was the only one in the family that brought news about the rest of us back to our parents. The rest of the brothers and sisters worked things out among ourselves, and kept most things to ourselves. On Christmas Day, Fred, the baby, and I went to Mamas for dinner; my older brother called me into the back bedroom, "Hey, are you OK?" "Yeah why wouldn't I be?" I asked. "Well, Ann was talking to Mama about a fight you were supposed to have had with Marilyn

Young!" "Yeah," I told him, "I got it under control." He gave me the spill about my being too much of a lady to be rolling around out there in the street for any reason. I told him how much I agreed and that I didn't know what came over me. "It would not happen again," I guaranteed him. He then said, "They tell me you handled yourself real well though," smiling as he turned to walk away.

We had Christmas dinner and opened all of our presents. Baby Bryan had the most gifts that year! Everyone passed him around from lap to lap. He was a beautiful baby and loved to smile at anyone who talked to him. I was doing the dishes with my sister, Tisah, and she told me that mama was going to talk to me about that fight I had. I told her that I was sure that mama would talk to me about the fight, especially since Ann opened her big mouth. "Yeah", she said, "you know she can't hold water on her stomach". I dreaded talking to Mama because I had no idea what she would say. "you know better than that and blah blah . . ." Tisah said mocking mama as she laughed. We finished the dishes and I took the garbage out which gave mama her chance to corner me. After dumping the garbage into the container, I turned and she was standing behind me. "Oh my goodness, you scared me Mama," I said holding my chest.

Mama began, "Now look here, let me tell you something, you better stay out of people's faces about that man; you hear me? "Down there fighting like some street woman!" Everybody is not Marilyn Young; you might not be so lucky the next time! If you can't trust him, ya don't need him!" I could not believe my ears, Savanah!

You are up there in college, trying to make something of yourself, but stuff like this- ruins your name." As mama turned to go back into the house, she said "I want this to be the last time I hear about your fighting, Do-you-understand-me?" "Yes, Mama," I said softly, ashamed as I could be. Her eyes watered and her voice was trembling as she spoke, and I had hurt her, yet again! I did not like hurting my mother, but I was not going to accept the treatment that my aunts, neighbors, or any of those women whom I watched get beat down when I was growing up. As a child, I looked around me and all I could see were women who were putting up with men who treated them like cold leftovers. I swore I was not going to be one of them, and I was not! I knew that this had to be my last fight, because I did not like the feeling I had afterward, and I did not want to hurt mama.

I was soon back at school to finish the second semester of my junior year. Things had settled down. I was working really hard now, because the classes were getting more demanding. I had to spend extra hours in the laboratory, and studying became first in my life. We had cut out most of the card playing and dancing that we had time to do as freshman and sophomores. Fred had continued coming to the university once monthly this semester, and I would go home once a month also.

Every two weeks had to be enough, because my schedule was challenging and our money was tight. Even Daddy and Mama still helped tremendously. I went straight home from school on Wednesday because although we went to the lab on other nights, Wednesday nights were mandatory. Effie, one of my classmates lived in the same house with us. We had most of our classes together, because our majors and minors were the same. This class was microbiology where we were tossed a microorganism, and had to test it and tell on our final exam the name of our unknown microorganism. Finding the unknown was 50 percent of the grade, and believe me, only about 70 percent of the class found their unknown. Thank God I was one of them.

As I walked out of the house going to the lab, the phone rang; it was Evelyn, a girl I knew from home, who had close ties with Linda. Linda had always liked Fred and had never tried to hide it. Evelyn wanted to know what I was doing, and I told her that I was going to class. She wanted me to call her after class because what she wanted to talk about would only take a minute. I thought probably she was going to talk to me about her and her boyfriend, because when I was home for Thanksgiving, we had a long talk about their relationship. When I finished lab, I was so tired that after my bath, I talked to Fred, and I went to sleep. On Thursday evening, I had a few minutes to spare, so I took the liberty to return Evelyn's call.

I first apologized for not calling the night before as I had promised. She and I talked just in general first, and then she told me that she had something that she needed to tell me about Fred and Linda. Immediately, I felt like throwing up! This characteristic has been a pattern throughout my adult life, beginning when

I became pregnant. It was as if I knew what she was going to say. I told her to hold, and I ran to the restroom pulling the phone with me. I sat on the toilet and listened to what I never dreamed I would hear. I used the bathroom so much you would have sworn I had taken a laxative.

Linda was pregnant with Fred's baby! I could not believe my ears were hearing such "bullshit"! She went on, "It's been going on for some time, but she throws herself at him. He doesn't want her! He's just doing what men do." I managed to ask her if Fred knew that Linda was pregnant. "Yes, he found out during the Christmas holiday." I stayed in the bathroom so long that the other girls came knocking to see if everything was ok. "I am OK, just go away," I told them! I knew they were listening through the door. That is just what girls do, even me. So I took slow deep breaths through my nose and breathed it out through my mouth as I listened to words that made my world disintegrate!

Nobody can tell me that a heart does not hurt. It does, and I am a living witness. My heart was broken into what seemed like little pieces. It actually hurt so much I could feel the pain. It was March; she was five months pregnant, and somebody else had to call and tell me. "Let me tell you something else you just have to know," she said. "I am so sorry to hurt you, but I am taking this chance on our friendship being able to weather this storm in your life. He is at fault, but she is too, for putting herself out there. He tried to pressure her into getting an abortion and gave her the three hundred dollars to pay for it. She went shopping with the money and said she could not do it." "Evelyn," I said, "I have to get off the phone now, but I will call you back tomorrow or the next day." Evelyn said, "You can tell him I told you, I don't care about him. I care about you! If I could have gotten someone to bring me to the campus I would have, but I want you to work through it there and not here." "OK, Evelyn, I have got to go now!" Evelyn told me she loved me; I think,

I told her I loved her too, but I am not quite sure, because pain is a funny thing! Some things can hurt you so severely in life that much can be blocked out psychologically. I can feel really inadequate when friends say, "Girl, you remember when . . ." and I draw a complete blank! Without saying no, I just laugh! That implies that I remember but I can be completely clueless! I tell you this story the way I remember it, however things may be altered some, but very little. I have heard that people on drugs lose track of a portion of their lives, well, so is it with people who have experienced excruciating heartache. I sat there in the bathroom and cried as softly as I could, hoping the girls on the other side of the door would not hear me. I stayed in the bathroom for a while, cleaned myself up, and opened the door to all the girls standing there. They heard the majority of the conversation, and they all surrounded me in a big group hug.

I cried endlessly all through the night. I would fall asleep and wake up and cry some more. They told me it was time for me to start getting ready to go to class the following morning. I told them to go ahead, I was not going today. My eyes were swollen, almost shut! Effie said that she would take good notes and bring any assignments that I missed. I lay in bed all day, only getting up to use the restroom, and to throw up what little they forced me to eat for breakfast! How Fred could do this, is all I could think about! I drifted in and out of sleep during the day as I had that night before. It was Friday, but Wednesday, Fred had told me that it would be impossible for him to come to visit. He was having car trouble; at least, that is what he told me. I would not believe anything he could possibly have tried to tell me at this point.

The car being broken was probably the excuse he was going to have for giving her the three hundred dollars that she used on herself. Effie did her assignments on Friday night, and she did my work for me on Saturday. They all felt so sorry for me, I could tell, and I was feeling ashamed. I was ashamed that I could be so much in love with someone who apparently cared so little for me and Little Bryan. If this pregnancy stuff is true, then my marriage is over before it had a chance to begin.

I did not rush to talk to Fred; I couldn't! I was afraid to ask the question! How do I fix my mouth to say the words that might have to be said? Although ashamed, everyone in our house at the university was used to drama in their relationships. It was Effie two weeks before and Alice several weeks before that. It was my turn, and I had a real problem, with a real reason to cry. My situation made theirs look like a walk in the park. I made it a point not to talk to Fred that weekend; however, my every thought was about him. He did not call me, so I did not call him, but my imagination was running wild. He was back home sleeping with either Linda or Marilyn, maybe both. Sunday was a slow dreary morning with heavy rains in the late evening and night.

Cassie always made Sunday dinner because she was the best cook in the house. I ate much more in one sitting than I had eaten the last three days all together. All I had heard since Thursday was how I needed to eat, but until Sunday, it just felt that something was caught in my throat, and the food would not go down. Fred called on Monday evening after my classes, and I cried immediately upon hearing his voice. I had gone through the day without shedding a tear and had planned not to shed a tear when I spoke to Fred. I had thought of all the things I should say to him, but could not think of any of them once I heard his voice. I felt stupid for letting him hear me cry. He asked over and over what was wrong, thinking something was going bad for me at school.

I told him that we would talk about it later. He told me he loved me and could not wait to see me. I said ok, but I thought, you liar, and hung up the phone. He was used to my saying, "I love you too," but not today. He called again on Wednesday, but when Effie told me it was Fred, I would not go to the phone. "What am I to tell him?" Effie asked. "Tell him whatever you want, I don't care," I scoffed! She went back to the phone and told him that she didn't know where I went because I was there a few minutes ago. She suggested that maybe I had gone back to campus for some reason. He told her that he would call back later. He called again on Thursday evening, and Cassie gave him the same spiel. I weighed myself, and I had lost six pounds in one week. I was five feet, six inches tall, and weighed one hundred twenty-three pounds, now I was one hundred seventeen pounds.

As I walked home from class on Friday and turned the corner onto the street where I lived, fear filled my whole being! Fred's car was parked in front of our house! My first urge was to turn and go back the other way, and for maybe ten or twelve steps I did turn back, but there has to be a discussion at some point, and it may as well be now. I did not want to confront him in front of the girls. We were all nosey when it came to one another's relationships. They would have heard every word, even if it meant they had to listen through the door or go outside near the window, I stopped and gathered my nerve! By this time, my heart was beating fast and simple perspiration became full-blown sweats in a matter of seconds. As I approached the house, I could see Fred sitting in the swing talking with Cassie. It was not uncommon to hear music playing because Cassie studied with music playing. It was a beautiful day, and signs of spring were a welcome sight.

We lived two blocks from campus, and those walks to class when it was cold seem like a mile. In front of the house, Fred saw me coming. I reminded myself that I needed to hold myself together and not cry, because although the pain was still present, I was angry even before I listened to any spill from him. He knew that Evelyn loved me, and she would not call and hurt me that way if there were not some truth to it. I understood that she wanted me to work through it while away, because had I been home, I would have walked up to Linda and asked point blank! Fred sat there with a smile on his face and stood when I walked up the steps. I avoided eye contact, and as he started to kiss me, I turned my head for him to kiss me on the cheek. He drew back and looked at me as if to say, "Oh. It's like that?" His cologne smelled so good, but I did not recognize the scent. I told him that I was going to put my books down, and I would be right back! When I returned to the porch, he had this puzzled look on her face! He told me that he had been calling me and wanted to know why I hadn't called back. I told him that I had been busy with my class work; in fact, I had work to do this weekend.

He was hoping that we could spend the weekend together, and I could still do my work. I agreed, grabbed a few things, and off we went. We went to our favorite little hotel where we had become known very well. We picked up food on the way, but we traveled in virtual silence. Once in the room, we ate our food in silence, and I immediately started the one short assignment which took all of an hour to complete. He was watching television as I worked, and I wondered if he knew that his little secret was out. Once I finished my homework, I gathered my sleeping clothes and headed for the bathroom. He stepped in my path, and said, "Hey–hey, what is wrong? You know that I know that something is wrong, now let's talk about it!" "When I finish my bath, we will talk Fred," I whispered.

He wanted to know if I was finished with my homework. When I told him I was finished, he said that he thought that I had tons of work to do. "No," I replied, as I slid past him into the bathroom. As I took my shower, I was thinking of how I would begin this conversation. I would not lash out at him, because I did not want things to go haywire from the start of the discussion. I would remain calm and just simply ask him the question.

From there, I knew the conversation would flow according to his answer. I could not plan it, but I knew I needed to control myself from the beginning. By the time I came out of the bathroom, he was undressed and underneath the covers. "I just got out of the shower three hours ago, so I made myself comfy," he said with the most beautiful smile. At that moment, I could not imagine myself without it, but a baby is a bit much to accept. "OK, Fred, I am ready to talk," I said as I climb into bed. "Let's sit up so that we can, no, let's sit at the table." I wanted to be eye to eye so that I would not miss anything. I wanted to observe his body language and every little flinch, all the "I am-lying indicators." I began, "Fred, I have been wrestling with something in my mind for over a week now." "I knew something was going on! That is why I am here," Fred replied.

As I looked into his eyes, he could see the urgency, and it seemed that he was a little afraid of what was to come. "Do you want to tell me about Linda's baby, or do I need to tell you?" I asked. Fred just sat there staring back at me for several seconds as if I was a hypnotist, and he was hypnotized! His shoulders rolled forward, and his head dropped slowly as if air was being expelled from his body. That one question had knocked the wind right out of his sail! I gave him time to get himself together. Even though I feared his response, his voice broke as he spoke "Baby, that girl doesn't know whose baby that is. She tells other people that the baby is Bill Henson's! I never wanted this shit to get to your ears, I am so sorry!" I fought back the tears as I listened to my husband tell me about yet another fling. He proceeded, "I know you are upset, and I admit you have all the reason in the world to be, but babe; she doesn't know! I promise you, that I don't think that it is mine.

I slipped one time with this girl, but it has been too long ago for the baby to be mine. She said that the baby was due in July, so the timing is just off. It cannot be mine! I gave her the money for the abortion that she said she wanted, but she didn't get it." I grew increasingly unhappier with every word he spoke, and I was livid, for having to go through such, as his wife. "You spent our money to try to correct your wrong, and it still doesn't get corrected? So where is the money?" I asked. His eyes began to water as he told me, "She spent it!" I sat there and looked at him, as I thought, "how stupid"!

Was I not worth his just being able to smile and casually walk around women who wanted him, like I did to the guys on campus that asked me out? Was I quickly turning into the kind of woman whom I vowed not to be from childhood? I told Fred, "You know what Fred, I am tired, and we are not going to finish this conversation tonight. I am going to sleep, and you can do whatever you want, but make no mistake about it, by no means will you touch me sexually! I will be highly insulted if you even try! I don't know what to say about you, and I don't know what to think about this marriage and where it can go from here. I won't even ask if you used a condom, because if this girl is talking "pregnant", you didn't use one! Everybody you sleep with, I sleep with them also! If you get some disease, I stand a good chance of getting it as well." In the softest voice I had ever heard him speak, he whispered, "I am so sorry, baby!" "Yeah, you are," I said as I turned to climb in bed. I know that he knew I meant business! I awoke a couple of times during the night, and I was in Fred's arms, but as soon as I was conscious of it, I removed myself.

On Sunday, it was time for him to return home, so after having lunch, we drove back to my house near campus. We said our goodbyes outside. I was so disappointed in my husband; it was sickening, but I still loved him more than I loved myself, and Bryan needed his daddy. April and May were the longest two months, but I made it through. My grades did fall some, but one "A" and five "Bs" wasn't so bad. He stuck very close to me the entire summer without incident. Bryan was growing so much, and he and his daddy were buddies.
Fred played baseball with a league that summer, and Bryan and I went to several of his games. He was such a good player who most people thought would and could do something with that talent. Being from such a small place, we knew nothing about where to start even trying to get him close to the major league. At one game, everything was going just great when, Linda, big belly and all, stepped into the park. She always had a way of looking at me as if I had poop on me! I felt awful! How many of these people had she told she was carrying my husband's baby? As she proceeded through the crowded stand,

she chose to sit right in front of Evelyn and me. Evelyn could feel my uneasiness and said, "Don't be bothered about her, she just wants to be seen."

Every time Fred would score, she would jump up and scream for him. I really wanted to just knock her brains slam out of her head, but I knew what hitting a pregnant woman would cost me. He saw her sitting there, because he often looked in the stands at me especially if he had done something outstanding. I continued giving him the thumbs-up sign, and clapping, but she was doing enough cheering for the both of us. I sat there and did nothing! He paid her no attention at all during or after the game. He came straight to the stands and gave me a quick smack on the lips as I told him, "Good job, babe." He reached for Bryan, and my little family and I left the park together, the same as. we had come. I could see her staring us down, but I pretended that she was invisible. On July 27, I got the news that she had her baby. It was a little girl. Although our marriage was still suffering, I did not say a word about the baby, and neither did Fred. Maybe it wasn't his child after all!

Summer was over so fast, and it was time to go back to school. How I wished I could stay home, but that was out of the question. I had made it this far; one more year and I would be home with Fred and Bryan. I would get a good job, our whole lives would be transformed, and I was soo . . . ready! I went through my senior year without too much drama. Once I found out Linda had asked Fred for diapers and Formula money for the baby. I don't know whether he gave it to her or not, but I had decided that if it was in fact Fred's child, I had to try to find it within myself to accept it.

Maybe after I was out of school and working, we could give her a little money here and there. I kept telling myself that I was stupid for even thinking like that, but I had to either accept it or reject it. I was trying to talk myself into accepting it. I had heard nothing else about Marilyn and guessed that she finally decided it wasn't worth another ass—kicking.

In April, a few weeks before graduation, Fred called me and told me he had cashed his check and lost his wallet. He could not send me the money I was going to need to pay for all the activities and fees for graduation. I called Mama and Daddy, and they sent me the money. Fred had to play catch up with the next few checks. He had to pay the car note and pay the first and last months' rent, on the house that we were getting ready to lease. We partied the entire night before graduation. Although I did not drink too much alcohol, we drank beer, played cards, and danced all night long.

That was my third real hangover in life! The first was when I was about ten years old. Daddy bought some home-brewed beer home, and I liked the taste. My brother and I stole little sips until we sipped upon a drunk. The other time was at my Uncle Alvin's house. My cousins, who were two and three years older, could handle the moonshine, I could not! My whole family turned out in big numbers for my graduation! Although tired, we were up and ready for the twelve o'clock Ceremony. Mama was as happy as she could be! She finally had a college graduate in the family! She hugged me so tight after graduation, smiling jovially, and said, "Lord, it was a struggle, but you helped us through it all. I thank you!" She said, raising her hand toward the sky! I thanked him too. I was all packed and ready to go home after graduation. Fred loaded our car up and Mama and Daddy brought their truck. Back at home, I spent the first week putting up curtains, cleaning, and arranging furniture. I had told mama to pack all of Bryan's clothes and I would pick him up on Saturday.

We were getting ready to start our lives, all living under one roof! Fred was kind of sick the week after graduation, so I suggested that he saw a doctor. He insisted that he would be alright and disregarded the suggestion. After we had been in the house just one week, Mr. Harris came by to collect the rent. Confused, I woke Fred so that he could talk to him. To my surprise, Fred paid him the first month's rent and said he would give him the rest the following week.

After Mr. Harris left, I asked Fred why he had not paid the full first and last months' rent. He told me that he was playing catch up. I thought, he would have caught up by now, but he had not. I found it strange that, since he only had a car note and it had been several pay days since he lost his check, "there fly in the buttermilk somewhere". Either way, I was home now and would be handling the money and the bills. I would make sure that everything was paid on time. I went to Mama's house to pick the baby up on Saturday morning. Once there, I sat and talked a while before heading back home. When I was ready to leave, I asked mama where the baby's bag was. She was very slow to answer. "Well, I have been busy and have not had time to pack." "Well, that is OK, I can pack his things," I said. So I emptied his draws and pulled his little dress outfits out of the closet. Anything that is dirty or left, I will get later. I told Mama how much I appreciated her taking care of the baby all this time. She just casually said "uh huh!" I knew my mother well, and something just was not right! I loaded Bryan's things in the car and came back for him.

Mama had him in her lap by the time I returned. She was saying goodbye as if he was leaving forever. "Mama, he is just moving six miles up the road, don't think he is gone for good. He will probably be here every weekend at least every other one or so." I slowly and carefully made my exit, because I could feel her feeling that he should stay there with her and Daddy. I told her to come by and see what I had done to the house as soon as she had a chance. She kind of nodded her head, as was we walked out of the door. Baby Bryan seems to take to the new place relatively well that first night. He woke up in the middle of the night crying, and I moved him into the bed with Fred and me. I thought that best, especially the first few nights if he continued to wake up. He usually slept through the night, but he could have been a bit confused waking up in a totally different place. Once he was in our bed, he fell right back off to sleep. A feeling of warmth came over me as I sensed his comfort with me and his daddy, without my mama and daddy being in the next room. He would have his second birthday party at our house this year. He had a big yard to play in, and I let him explore late in the evenings after it cooled down a bit. I wanted us to start going to church as a family but not this Sunday, I was really tired from fixing up the place.

On Sunday evening, after letting Bryan play in the yard, I looked out and saw my daddy's truck pulling into the driveway. I was excited because they would get to see what I had done to the house. As Mama walked in, I could see that she was pleased with my decorating skills. Bryan was so happy to see them! His little eyes just lit up and he ran to them. Mama picked him up and went from room to room smiling and nodding in approval. Even Daddy said it was nice. "I didn't know you had it in you girl," he said. "Oh, Daddy, you know she did all of my painting and decorating since she was fourteen," Mama said. "Yeah, Daddy, who did you think picked the curtains and moved the furniture around every time mama decided she wanted a change?" I asked. Daddy replied, "I thought your mama did it!" Mama responded, "That's because it was usually done while you were at work." They stayed a while and when I realized that they were getting ready to go, I told mama to let Bryan go play and then they could slip out, because I was sure he would probably cry to go if he had to watch them leave.

Mama wouldn't have it, she said that she would not slip off and leave him, and if he wanted to go then just let him go. I really wanted him to spend a few more days with us before going back to Mama's Just as I had thought, as they got up to leave he wanted to go with them. When I started to take him from her, he pulled away! "Oh let him go, you can come and get him in a couple of days, he's used to us and you just can't expect him to adjust to you all in a day." My feathers fell, but I gave in and let him go. I told Fred after they left, "I don't know, but I have a funny feeling that Mama doesn't want us to have our baby." "Well baby, they miss him but everyone will be adjusted in a few Weeks," Fred muttered. I wasn't so sure about that!

Willie dropped by the house and said that he wanted us to plan a class reunion for our high school class. "We've only been out of school for four years, so why not plan it for next summer, which will be five years," I asked. "Well", he said, We can do that too, but let's have a semi reunion with those who live around here. Then, we all can plan together". I hesitantly agreed, but I could not understand the urgency. It had barely been a month since we all graduated from college. Nevertheless, he and I called every classmate that lived in the area, and we all met at my dad's café and actually, it turned out to be a wonderful party. There were only thirty six graduates in our high school class, and most had moved away after graduation. There were sixteen classmates present, and Willie stayed with me until everybody left. He had purchased a bottle of Bacardi Rum, and once the party was over, he stayed to help me clean up. He gave the rum to me and said that we would finish it once he returned from a trip he and his wife were taking. It was to be the honeymoon they didn't have. He and Shirley had gotten married a month before we graduated, because they had both secured a very good job prior to graduation.

On Saturday morning, I was awakened by the phone ringing; I slowly reached for it to discover that it was Beverly. I knew it must be important, because she would never call that early. She would never be up that early! I strained to see the time and it was 6:33a.m. "Hey, I said as drowsy as could be. But the words that came from the other end of the phone, woke me instantly. Willie had been killed in car crash! "No, no, no," I cried so loud it woke Fred! It could not be true, I thought, Oh my God! Willie and I had gone through elementary, high school, and college together. He was so instrumental in my staying in school, that sometimes I thought he and mama teamed up on me. My friend was gone! Fred's friend was gone, and we mourned together. One of my former teachers made the obituary and I was asked to speak of him as a friend at the funeral. I did not know how that would be possible. She told me to go to the funeral home and view the body during visitation hour, and it would help me to be able to do so. It hurt so bad! Thinking back on how persistent he was about having the pre-reunion party, maybe he felt something was going to happen. I cried off and on all day. He was my confidant, my sounding board, so what would I do without him. I remembered the many times he would come home from college just so that I could come to see Fred and the baby.

I think he took some of Fred's secrets to the grave with him! At the funeral, I did speak of him as a friend, but it was not easy. He looked as though, all I had to do is call his name and he would wake up. I knew that was hopeless, but I had to try! "Willie, Willie, I miss you already! I will never forget you." I cried! I thought about him so much, and I cried often, A couple of weeks after his death, I was sleeping ever so lightly. I felt the side of my bed go down, as if someone had sat next to me. I felt his presence and I felt a little fearful. Knowing that he would not hurt me, I called his name. Ever so softly, I heard him speak. "Don't be scared, "I am ok, I'm ok"! I felt the bed as he stood to leave, and I thought, "amazing"! I missed my friend, but I began to heal that night. I thanked God for allowing me to share his life. He was one of the most decent young men, I have ever known! I lost touch with Shirley, but I heard that she made a full recovery, and eventually remarried.

One Sunday, shortly after we moved to our new place, Bryan and I were in the yard, and I met my new neighbor, Patricia. I had heard someone playing piano earlier, and I thought that the sound came from that house. I asked her if she played piano and she said she did. I loved piano music and she played extremely well. I reflected on when mama had given me piano lessons, but I guess I wasn't cut out for it. I was truly afraid of my music teacher because she would hit me on the fingers with her pencil when I make mistakes. She wore bifocals, and when I would look up at her, her eyes would magnify through those glasses. Patricia was beautiful, with long black silky hair. Our heights and complexions were almost identical, and we had an awful lot in common. She was from one of the neighboring towns and had recently married a guy whom I had gone to school with. As the days and weeks passed, she and I became close. We had fun getting to know one another to the point that we were friends.

Mama and I were playing a "give-and-take" game with Baby Bryan; I would go and get him and two days later she would come back and take him away again. I would ask mama to let him stay this whole week each time I picked him up, but it never failed, two days later she would be in the door ready to pick him back up again. I was really getting upset, but Fred thought nothing of it. Since Patricia's husband and my husband both worked the night shift, we began spending more and more time together. There was no wonder we became great friends! We soon began sharing information about our relationships with our husbands and I especially shared with her the tug of war my mama, and I were having over Baby Bryan. Fred and I enjoyed our new home, but he was becoming more distant as the days went by. We had begun spending more and more time with our neighbors, but Fred sometimes chose not to be sociable. I knew he liked them very much and I could not figure the reason why he would sometimes want to stay home.

While out in the driveway with Bryan, I saw this car driving slowly past our house as if they were looking for an address or something. I did not think anything of it until it came through a third time. A young lady whom I did not recognize was driving, and she seemed to be more focused on me or my house than any other address. I wondered why she didn't just stop and as for help. Several days later, I was in the yard, when the same car did an almost identical repeat as a few days before. This time upon the last drive by, Linda was on the passenger side with the baby in her arms, sitting up where I could get a pretty good look at her. I supposed she must have been lying down, and probably was in the car a few days ago also. We lived on a dead-end street; therefore, there is no way the driver could have picked her up anywhere.

Shocked does not describe what I felt as they drove through a third time! I was Fred's wife, and I did not know how to handle this kind of disrespect at age twenty-two. I thought that as his wife, I should be exempt from these kinds of insulting acts. Fred was asleep in the house, so I waited until he woke up. Why was she doing this? Was she trying to see Fred or just trying to get to me? Had he kept his distance, none of this would be happening! Was this Fred's baby? A million thoughts just flowed into my mind as I waited impatiently!

When he finally woke up, I confronted him about Linda's driving by the house like that. He said that he was not communicating, nor having anything to do with Linda and felt that she was probably trying to get into my head. "Well, mission accomplished," I said as the tears began to trickle down my face. The total contemptuousness was getting to be a bit much. Rent for July was late again because according to Fred, something was going haywire in the front office, and only a few people got their checks. He said that his check the following week would be for two pay periods. Mr. Harris was a nice man, but I could see his disgust when I told him we could not pay until next Friday. I told him what Fred had told me about the payroll department. We had never had real bills other than a car note, but I wanted to pay my bills the same way that I had seen my parents pay theirs. I never remember my parents having collection calls or being unable to meet their obligations. I was encouraged when I received a call that same day that I had landed a job working with handicapped children in a local school district.

One week of work convinced me that this was the job for me. The children were six through twelve years of age with major and moderate handicaps; therefore, I had to prepare different lesson plans for each of them. The teacher before me had developed goals for each child to work towards. My job was to try to help them accomplish those goals. Because each child had their own individual lesson plan, I grouped them accordingly. I loved my job, and my principal was the greatest ever. He would do any and everything to help me help the children to be successful. Some of my kids were just learning to drink from a cup at age six; others were engaged academically at different levels. Some wore diapers, and others could use a standard restroom equipped with rails to assist them. It all combined to make my job challenging to say the least. I had a total of thirteen children, and the district had allowed me three teacher aides to assist me in my duties.

The classroom setting was pleasantly decorated with the assistance of one aide who was an expert in that area. The bulletin boards of which I took total credit, complimented the decorations so well, providing a great homely atmosphere for learning. Other teachers would tell me that it took a special person to be able to handle a class like mine, but although a challenge, Milton, my deaf/mute friend from childhood, had help to prepare me for the task ahead. My first handicapped friend had moved away, and was married with a family. Every summer he would come back, and we would come together and reminisce about the days we spent dancing and his teaching me something that was so vital to my current job. Now that I was in full swing at work, Fred began to cash his checks and come home with less and less money each pay period.

Before long, my checks became the basis for which our bills were paid, and it looked as though I was going to be the major bread winner. Arguments with him developed over the money that he was providing for the household to no avail. Although Fred's weight fluctuated, he became visibly thinner. I was despondent because things were not going as I had believed they would in this marriage. Fred was more different than I had ever seen, and the change after I started working happened so fast that it was unreal. We had planned Thanksgiving at his parents and Christmas with my family, but he refused to show for either of the holiday festivities. At his mother's house for Thanksgiving, the family asked me questions that I had no answers. I told them that I thought that he was working too hard, and it was getting to him.

I suggested to his dad that maybe if he would speak with him, he might be able to get some idea of how we as his family could help him. His dad agreed to speak to him, but later in the week, he came to our house while Fred was at work and said Fred told him he was being trained for a new position that was stressful! "Just keep an eye on him and let us know if we can do anything else to help," he said. I thanked him and hoped that he was right, but why had he not told me about the position? At my parents' house on Christmas Day, everyone wanted to know where Fred was. Is he coming later? Between my graduation in May and the following May, I made one excuse after another for him. I had lied over and over trying to portray an excellent situation that truly was in shambles. We were supposed to be happy!

After all the promises, nothing had changed, and I was a nervous wreck, enduring what no wife should ever have to endure. When he began staying away from home, sometimes the entire weekend, I finally came to the conclusion that he just didn't love me anymore. One Monday morning in August, after he had been away from sun up to sun down, both Saturday, and Sunday, he came home. He looked tired, and I could tell he had not shaved or bathed! I literally crumbled! I supported myself with the door frame as I could feel my knees buckle. How could a man who was always immaculate turn into a bum? I begged him to stop it and to tell me what was going on. He cried just as hard, and as much as me, saying that I was the love of his life, and if he lost me he would die!

I had never been so confused, trying to make sense out of all the mixed signals Fred was sending. He showered, then shaved and wanted me to lie down next to him in our bed. The whole idea repulsed me, but I did it. He seemed small that day as he lay curled up in my arms as I had in his so many times before. I watched him as he slept so hard that he snored. It was out of the ordinary for him to snore. Only if he was extremely tired did he snore. I wondered where he had been, and what kind of fool I was to still love this man. I had always prayed, but I would begin, and my mind would not focus, wandering, consumed, lost, in a state of bewilderment.

Thanksgiving and Christmas came and went again with no change, and I grew wearier by the day. I am having to face the fact that my marriage was not going to last this way. At work, I hide my grief, until the day I became consumed in thought and broke down in the classroom. I must have scared my aides to death. They all came running to me, trying to figure out if I had hurt myself, or if I was ill. Upon realizing that I had lost control; I ran into the bathroom. Two of them came in behind me, while the one watched over the classroom. That day, I let go of all that was bottled up inside. I had to tell someone what I was going through, or I was going to burst wide open. They comforted me the best that they could and told me things would work itself out. I knew in my heart that was not true. I faced a reality that day, whatever reality was. I could not fix whatever was wrong with Fred and my marriage.

I had failed as a wife, and he had failed as a husband. I had been relieved through having a good cry before, but a good cry coupled with breaking my silence offered a different type of relief. I told Tisah all about my marriage, and I was not so surprised that she was not surprised. Everybody probably knew that the marriage was in trouble. She did what she could to console me, but she could do nothing to fix my heart. The following Saturday, I went to the grocery store to get a few items for dinner. I started down one aisle and there in person, was Linda and her baby girl! I was startled to say the least! My first instinct was to leave the store, but I decided against that. I moved to the next aisle thinking I had escaped direct contact with them. Soon, Linda was behind me in that aisle.

I then moved to another aisle, and so did she. This girl was following me around in the store. When I moved over an aisle, so did she and the baby. I felt much li8ke a caged bird, with nowhere to escape. As she walked close behind me, I could hear her talking to the baby, who was reaching for everything on the shelf. "Stop Mama," she said several times! I wondered if she was intentionally following me, so I reversed directions and went back to the aisle I had previously been on. She came right behind me to that aisle also, still talking to the baby. "Chrissy Winslow, will you stop!" Oh my God, no she didn't give her daughter my husband's last name," I thought! I was traumatized by those words that cut like a sword. I could feel my eyes watering and I prayed. "Lord please, help me control myself and not cry, and help me know what to do in this situation!"

I gathered all of my strength and proceeded to check out. Within seconds, Linda was right behind me. She parked her shopping cart walked in front of it, and positioned herself at my back, pretending to be buying chewing gum. She was so close I could hear her breath, and the baby pulled at my hair. I took a couple of deep breaths, turned to the baby and said, "Hello sweetie; you want to play with me!" I reached my hands out for her to come to me. Chrissy leaned toward me with outstretched arms, and I took her from her mother. While the cashier totaled my groceries, I played and talked to the cutest little girl with such an enormous smile. I looked her over really good, to see if I could recognize any similarities to my son, or his daddy. I did not see Fred, but I could see that she looked much like her mother. When the cashier had finished, I passed her back to her mother, paid for my groceries and went home in tears. I packed all of my and Bryan's clothing, and necessities and left, what was supposed to be our quaint little love nest, behind.

I still loved my husband, but I felt like the biggest fool in town. He had turned me into the woman that I was not destined to be. After I left, Fred came to my parents' house and asked me to come home. "Things would be different," he cried! I wanted him, and loved him with all of my heart, but I did not believe him. I could not fight for my marriage all by myself! It was as if a powerful vacuum had sucked all my strength away. We talked on the phone several times that week, but I could not go home. I wanted him to miss us, but he insisted that we could not work on our marriage in different households. He came to visit with Bryan and me again on Sunday to inform me that he was moving over five hundred miles away. He said that he could not exist in our little town, without Bryan and me. I stood in my sister's yard and watched my love, my heart, drive away, leaving me distraught and Bryan fatherless.

Somebody Should Have Told ME!

Chapter Three

On Monday, I stopped by the bank to pay my car note, I went in the trunk of the car got my purse, but the two one hundred dollar bills I had tucked away for my car payment was gone. I panicked! Where could the money be, I know I put it there. I remember Fred getting my keys going to the car to get a copy of the insurance card that I had received in the mail. I told him that I would keep his car insured for one month. I also remember hearing him close the trunk of the car and thought he must have left something in my car. When he came back into the house he had nothing other than the car insurance card. I then thought that he was just checking to be sure he was not leaving anything, Fred had taken my money! Oh my God, as if he hadn't done enough!

Over the next few days and weeks, I went through the motion of living, when my soul was devoid. I became so depressed that I could barely function. During the next days and weeks, Bryan would call out to him as if he was in another room, and I would become unimaginably sick. I suffered tremendously, and I wondered if I really could live without him. I knew that he was in the state of Kansas, but I didn't know where, or how to contact him. Was he punishing me for leaving him, or did he just not care as he demonstrated when we were together? What about his son? My teacher aides helped me through what, to this day, was the most difficult period of my entire life. I told them what to do with the children, and they did it gladly. They followed each child's individualized plan, only coming to me for clarification. I would go in the bathroom and cry as softly as I could, several times a day I purchased house three lots over from my parents' home so that we could share in Bryan's care. I tried hard to keep friends and family from knowing I was hurt so deeply. I stopped going to Sunday dinners at Mamas because I didn't feel like putting on a facade. I stopped going around my friends, telling them that I was still decorating and that Bryan needed me, although it was mama that took care of Bryan the majority of the time. I stopped going to church; simply wanting the pain to go away, but it seemed to have come to stay.

I knew that my baby needed me but, sometimes when he would talk to me, I would be so consumed in thought and pain that he would have to pull on my arm or clothing to get my attention. I would take him in my lap when I could not speak, and hold him to my chest, hoping he could feel my love! There was an old abandoned road up the street from my parents' house. Every evening after school, I would stop there and drive deep into the woods to pray. I felt closer to God out there and could usually gain the strength I needed to pick up my son, and the food mama had begun making for us each afternoon. We used to walk that road picking berries when we were children, so I felt safe. In the country, when I was young, we didn't have the fears that people experienced in city living. I knew that mama was aware I was struggling, though she never said it. I would try to eat, seldom consuming over a couple of spoon of food, and I could tell I was losing weight. I had always been quite skinny, so I had none to lose. I played with Bryan for a while before his bedtime each night, when he was home with me. Some days when I was down that old country road, when I prayed, all I could say was "Lord have mercy on me!" It was until much later in life that I realized, that I am sure, I had what is typically called a nervous breakdown. Although I stayed away from family, I could not escape my nieces. They were more like sisters to me. Because they loved me they just wanted to be where I was, and nothing was going to jeep them away. I often told them that I was sick, but they knew I was suffering. It was much easier facing them because they were easier to deal with.

One Saturday morning, I was awakened by the doorbell and was surprised to see Patricia standing at the door. I had not talked to her over two months, but she rushed in as though we had a date planned. "Girl get yourself dressed; we are going shopping," "Shopping, "I whispered. She grabbed my robe from the foot of the bed, pushed me into the bathroom and said that she would have my clothes out of the closet and ready when I come out.

I stood in the bathroom for a minute trying to gather my thoughts! She called through the bathroom door, "Come on now, hurry, we are gonna be there at 9a.m. when the doors open!" I brushed my teeth, turned the shower on and crawled in. Submerging from the bathroom refreshed, she had my blue jeans, my favorite shirt, a pair of panties and a bra lying on an already made bed. She called from the kitchen, "Go on girl and get dressed, I am just washing up these dishes." I didn't want anyone to see my house in disarray, but it was too late. She was all over the place! I lotioned my body, hurriedly dressed in the now saggy jeans and went into the living area. "Come on girl, don't clean house, I can do that!" Although she was finished, I led her to the sofa and sat her down. "Now why are you here?" She sat there a few seconds before she said, "I came to get my friend back! I miss you and I think you need me, so here I am! I love you girl!" I told her that I really did not feel like going shopping, but she would not take "no" for an answer. "I talked to your mom last night, and she is as worried about you as I am.

You are blocking everyone out, even your sisters. We have all let you have your privacy, but now it is over." I stared at her, but I could not think of a response to that. Tears slowly streamed down my face as my release began. "People are talking about us aren't they?" I asked. "Girl, people talked about Jesus, so who are you?" she replied. "I can't get it together," I said as I broke down, and I began to talk to her. "I am hurting so much. Girl, I wanted my marriage more than anything, but it's gone and I don't have my husband and Bryan doesn't have his daddy," I sobbed louder, as I continued, "I guess he just didn't love us enough to act right and do as our vows said do. I was supposed to have his babies, and suddenly, this girl is pregnant and he has a daughter." "I know," she said as her eyes got watery. I poured my heart out to her that morning. She listened without prejudice as I went on and on.

By the time I finished talking it was 10 am, and we were an hour late for the sale. "Pat, I am making you late for the sale, so you go on," I said with a giggle, I did not know I had within me. "No you go, re-do your makeup, and there is not going to be any more crying until later, much much later, OK!" Patricia drove and we spent the day shopping, and I ate more than I had for quite some time.
After our meal, we had a glass of wine and then another. We had finished the whole bottle when she began: "Listen girl, I want you to know that I know you have been hurting, and enough is enough." She stared me dead in my eyes and asked me to look at her. "You can't stop living!" You are so pretty, and if Fred was for you, he would be right here beside you. I don't know what the future

might bring. You and he may get back together after he gets himself together; or you might never, but you are twenty-three years old and you're trying to die too early!" I could hear the genuine sisterly concern in her words and I knew she was telling the truth. The wine was making her words slur just a little, but it was numbing my pain. I ordered another bottle, and we stopped by her house. She got on the piano as she did when she was upset with Mike, and she played and we both sang songs from Aretha Franklin, Bob Dylan, and Otis Redding. Mike was at work, so we decided to listen to music on the stereo and danced until we were completely sober. She had to go to church and play for the choir on Sunday, so she dropped me off at home.

Once back inside of my four lonely walls, I realized that I felt better than I had in three months. I bowed beside my bed and thanked God for the relief I was feeling at that time. I walked to Mama's and told her that I wanted to take Bryan home with me tonight. He was sleeping, but I lifted my baby from the bed and carried him home with me. I watched him sleep and thanked God for him. I was his mother and he was my son, and we would be together until God decided to take one of us away. Until then, I needed to cherish every moment that we had together. The next morning I was still feeling somewhat relieved but I could feel depression lurking.

I decided that I needed to get out of the house and go to the family dinner at Mama's house. I dressed Bryan in one of his new outfits I had purchased for him while shopping, and I dressed in one of mine. I put on makeup a little heavier to camouflage my weight loss, and went to Mamas. I thought it would draw attention to my face and away from my frail body. Everyone was so happy to see me; we laughed and joked as if I had not been absent from our dinners in over three months. After I had been there about thirty minutes, Daddy came through the backdoor. "Hey, Daddy," I said, as I laughed at my sister Nadellie's joking around. "Hey, baby, where have you been?" he said as he hugged me pretty tight.

I took it to mean that since he was seldom home when I stopped by Mama's, he was glad to see me. He stood and looked at me a little too closely for my comfort. "What?" I asked hesitantly? "Do you feel OK?" he asked. "Yeah, I feel fine, Daddy," I said trying to brush him off. He then replied, "You need to start eating, 'cause you don't look so good!" He might as well have drop kicked me, I was speechless and so embarrassed! I turned and ran out of the house, got in the car and drove home as fast as I could. As I ran out, I heard my mama chastising him for his carelessness. "Daddy, I have told you about your mouth," is all I had the chance to hear before I was out of the door. Nadellie came behind me and as I got out of the car, and ran into the house, I saw her car turn into my driveway.

She walked in without knocking and sat down in the living room. I was in the bathroom, trying to compose myself before going out to talk to her. I had blown my cover, showing them my weakness. I could not hide it anymore; I a wreck! I walked out of the bathroom and took a seat beside her on the sofa. "I am sorry," I told her as I wipe away a tear. "Ms. S," as they lovingly called me, "it is OK to hurt and it is OK to cry, but don't pay Daddy any attention! He is just outspoken like that, you know him." I did know Daddy, and I know he was expressing concern even if it hurt. Daddy loved me, but he had always spoken before thinking of the impact his words had on others. Mama had been trying to impress that fact on him all of our lives.

Nadellie and I sat on the sofa, and she put her arms around me and held me just as she had done when I was a little girl. She went on to tell me that we were family, and they all wanted me to know that they loved me. She still wanted me to get out of the house and start socializing again. She had seen Jimmy, and he had told her to tell me he wanted to take me to dinner. He had done his time in the service and was back home. "I heard that he was going to make a career out of it," I told Nadellie. She squelched and shrugged her shoulders. That was the last thing I wanted to hear! Jimmy had gone to the same university two years prior to me and was disappointed that I was so spellbound by Fred and would not date him anymore. While walking to class, I saw him on campus; he asked me if it was true that I was pregnant. After I confirmed it, he stood there looking afar, then turned and walked away without another word. He wrote me a letter before he left, and gave it to one of my classmates, to give to me. When he found out that Fred and I were getting married; he quit school and went to the Army, a few months short of his graduation.

The note read, "The baby you are carrying was supposed to be mine, and you are supposed to be my wife. I can't say that I hope you are happy, because I don't want you to be. Take care of yourself and I love you still." He said nothing about leaving for service; he was just gone. He didn't tell his parents until the day he was leaving! When I found out, I was so sorry for him, because I had always known that he cared for me. I worried that, had he told me what his plans were, maybe I could have changed his mind and convinced him to stay in school.

You cannot tell your heart who to love, it just happens. I was undeniably head over heels for Fred. I prayed that the Lord would take care of Jimmy and allow his safe return to his family, but that was all I could do. I was glad to know that he had returned home safely and was out of the service after doing about a four-year stretch.

It was another three weeks before I had the occasion to run into him at the store. We hugged and talked for a few minutes, but before I could get into my car; he asked me for my phone number. I gave it to him, although I really didn't want to. I actually had a little guilt about his leaving school like he did and did not have the heart to say no. I told him that if he called, to please call on weekends, because my plate was completely full during the week. That meant that I could keep him at bay, and he would only have two days out of the week to call.

He called on Saturday morning, and we had a pleasant chat, but he did ask me to dinner. Since I made an excuse for that weekend, he told me to tell him when I would be free to go. I was in an awkward position, so I told him that I would call him and let him know. I could hear the disappointment in his voice, so I just said, "I promise to call!" I didn't want to go out with him. I was still very much a married woman, and still very much in love with a husband who seemed to have fallen off the edge of the world.

I took Bryan to visit Fred's parents that evening and asked his mother if she had heard from him. She said he had called only once since he had been gone, but her brother who lived in the same city saw him quite often. She wanted me to know that he was doing OK, but something in her voice said that it was truly over for us. She was evasive in her answers to my questions, and I wondered what she knew that I didn't. Bryan and I had gone to sleep watching TV and were awakened by the phone at three o'clock in the morning. It was Fred! After five months, his voice was better than music to my ears. Mrs. Winslow had caught up with him and told him to call home. "How are you, baby?" I asked.

"I'm OK, what about you and my little man?" he replied. I told him that we were doing all right, but we missed him. "Oh," he said, "you both are better off without me." I asked him why he had waited so long to call and told him how Bryan walked around for weeks calling his name, after he left. I wanted to know what he was doing, if he had just thrown his son away, had he missed me, did he care at all, what was his phone number? I had questions that needed to be answered, but he really had no answers.

He soon told me that he would always love me, but he needed to get off of the phone, and that he would call us again real soon. Just before the phone disconnected, I heard a woman's voice saying, "No, don't hang up now! Are you talking to one of your bitches?" That messed me up! What? Nobody talks like that unless there is a relationship going on. There was no caller ID as of yet so, I had no number, and I couldn't call back! He had to be living or spending the night with someone with whom he was intimate! I was hurt but equally as angry! I thought about driving up there, but I wouldn't know where to start looking for him. I couldn't drive up there anyhow, because I did not know anything about traveling or driving cross-country. None of my friends knew anything about driving cross-country, and even if one or two did know, they had no time to go because they had to go to work the next day. I was hopeless, helpless, and mad as hell!

I decided that night that I was not going to fall that deep, ever again in life. No man would ever hurt me like that again! I would never give my whole heart and soul to another man, not in this life! Any man who looks my way had better come with his billfold in hand! If they come and go, I would have plenty to show they had been there. If one touched me, or my child, the war was on! Don't lie to me, I won't lie to you! If it's a game, let's play! If it is for real, show me! Be straight up with me, and I will be straight up with you! If it walks like a duck and talks like a duck, then it's a damn duck, and so be it. Nobody was worth this kind of heartache, and this was not going to happen again. A month later, I had not heard from Fred! I had begun to visit with friends and family occasionally, but I still made pit stops up the little dirt road to be alone with myself and God.

Jimmy called me and asked me to go to dinner with him again, and I did not hesitate to say I would go. At dinner, we had a great meal and sat and talked over a few glasses of wine. He explained to me that he was devastated in learning of my pregnancy and truly believed that my marriage did not work out because I was supposed to be his wife. He wanted me to know that he still wanted me as his wife. He said that he could love my child just as if it were his own and that I should think about that really hard. Could it be that I was not supposed to marry Fred? Then why did God allow me to love him so much? Why did I not love Jimmy then or now? Yet those words haunted me in my totally confused state of mind. He sent me flowers and candies, and wined and dined me until I thought that just maybe he knew what he was talking about.

One Friday night in November when we were returning from dinner and a movie, there had been a terrible accident. No one could move going either direction! It was two o'clock in the morning, and we had sat in the line of cars for already over an hour. He asked me if I trusted him enough to spend the night in a hotel. I told him that I did, and he managed to turn the car around in the road, and we went back to El Dorado, got a hotel room and talked into the morning.

I told Jimmy I had to get home early for Bryan, but that was a lie. I had to get home before Mama, Daddy and our little community woke up to see me getting out of Jimmy's car so early in the morning. Before going to sleep, Jimmy wanted to know if he could kiss me, and I allowed him to do so. That was the closest I had been to a man in months, and it felt good. I asked him to be a gentleman, and he was just that. I slept in his arms that night, like I had in Fred's for so long. He wasn't Fred, but it was the best I had felt in so long that I welcomed it. Afterward, I felt guilty for having slept with him and vowed not to do that again, until I was completely over my husband. Even though no sex was involved, I still was another man's wife. Jimmy would call every other day or so now, even managed to come by a few times. On a Thursday night in early December, Jimmy had to drive his mother to Memphis, Tennessee, he would be back on Sunday, and would pick up food from my favorite restaurant and stop in for a visit.

When he did not show up by 6 pm as expected, I felt that something must have caused him to be late, and maybe he would not make it by my house. I went onto prepare for work the next day. As I stepped out of the shower, Jimmy came by with flowers and food. When he knocked, I could not imagine who would be visiting that time of the night. It was 10:30p.m, bedtime, and there was work tomorrow. Jimmy had experienced some car problems, and they were late returning from the Memphis trip. I allowed him in, placed the flowers in a vase and shared the food with him while still in my robe. I finished first and sat on the sofa. When he emerged from the kitchen, he sat on the floor. "Don't get comfortable, you have to go so that I can be ready for work tomorrow, but thanks for the meal, it was great," I said. He laid his head back on the sofa, looked at me from over his head and smiled, "All that's missing is dessert." He turned and began to kiss my thighs knowing that there was probably no pantie underneath my robe. I was still partially wet from showering when I answered the door. Well, I did not stop him! I was clean, horny, and my lips just refused to speak the word "no". He got his dessert and I made love to both he and Fred. Either way it spelled relief! It was the best feeling I had felt in what seemed like ages. It felt so good, that I let him come by and do it again the same week! I thought myself a "hussy", but who cared, certainly not Fred.

By Christmas, Fred was gone for almost a year. It was the loneliest Christmas I had ever known. Donald, one of our classmates, came home from Kansas and dropped by to see me. He told me that he had seen Fred several times since he moved there. I didn't want to seem over eager for information, so I casually asked questions. He told me that the only thing he wanted me to know is that I should go on with my life. I then had no choice but to ask if Fred had a girlfriend. Donald would not say whether he did or didn't, but he thought it best for me to go on with my life, just my baby and me. He promised he would stop back by before he left going back to Kansas after the holiday. I was undecided whether I wanted to give him a letter for Fred, but I did want to give him new pictures I had made of Bryan and me.

While I was having dinner at Mamas with the rest of the family, Jimmy dropped by to bring presents for Bryan and me. He had a gigantic rocking horse that sat on a frame with springs for Bryan, with two other gifts that were wrapped. He helped Bryan open his other gifts. One was a little car that made real car sounds and a toy gun that made real gun sounds when you pulled the trigger. He told me that I had to walk with him to the car to get my gift, and my sisters went crazy. They elbowed one another and whispered to one another playfully as we walked out of the door. I casually turned to give them one of my famous "go to hell" looks before walking out of the door. He emerged from the car with three boxes. One box was small, one medium, and one large! I opened them in the order that he presented them. In the large box was a coat, quite stunning, and just my style! The medium box had fifty, ten-dollar bills in it, and my mouth fell wide open as I counted! "No you don't have to do this!" I said. I had hurt him once, I was not about to do it again.

"Jimmy, listen now, I don't know where this is going with us, so I don't want to take your money," I said. "Can't you use it?" he asked. "Well sure, I can use it but I can't promise you that this will work out between us. I am still very much in love with my husband. I know that I have been sleeping with you but if my husband were to return tomorrow, I just might go back to him!" "Hush, and open the other box," he said. He took the money to my car, put it under the seat, locked the doors, and made sure I had my keys. As I opened the last box, his demeanor changed as he said; "Now this box, I will keep with me, until you are ready for it, and you will be ready soon." A bit confused, I open the small box only to find another box. I lifted the top of the smaller box to behold the most beautiful pear-shaped diamond engagement ring, I had ever seen.

"Oh my God, we are moving a little too fast here!" I told him! "A little too fast! A little too fast for who?" he said. I looked at that gorgeous ring, but I was still wearing the little diamond that once completed my world. I was not ready to pull it off! Jimmy was so sure that I would get there real soon! Fred did not call the entire Christmas holiday, so I was completely discouraged, It seemed my son had truly lost his father. Donald stopped by on his way back to Kansas, and I then begged for information! He sat there for a moment contemplating before he began. "Fred is on drugs really bad, and yes, he lives with a woman you went to college with." He said quickly all in one breath. "What," I screamed, "Who?" Her name is Betty Wilson. "Oh my God, Betty Wilson, how does he know her?" He said, "Fred met Betty at a party, shortly after he arrived in Kansas.

She fell for his good looks immediately, but now she has realized that he is doing drugs, and the relationship is rocky." I was completely blind-sided and without words for a minute. "When did he get on drugs, Donald?" I asked. "Oh, he was on drugs when he first arrived. He was on drugs down here, before he came to Kansas." I sat there totally bewildered, but thinking back, that explained why Fred was acting the way he was before our separation. My mind reversed, back to the day he lost his whole paycheck, and why the deposit for our house was not completely paid when we moved in. I told Donald, "That would explain why, after I started working, I had to pay the bills, with little assistance from Fred." "There is more, since I have revealed that much, I am going to tell you all of it," Donald said. I braced for the impact, as Donald continued. "Are you aware that he has another child?" Donald asked softly. "Oh my God," is all that I could say, surprised that even Donald knew about Linda's little girl.

"Yes, he has another son, born the same week as your son." Donald declared! I just sat and looked at Donald. He paused to allow me time to digest all of this new information. "No! Donald, the child by Linda is a girl," I said to correct him. "No, Savanah, he has a son whose name is Fredrick." Fredrick was the name that we planned to name our second son, should we have one. Now he has named a son by somebody else, Fredrick! "Who is the mother of his son?" Donald took a deep breath and then said, "It's Gloria." "Gloria! Gloria who" I asked? "Gloria Bennett," he said, as he cleared his throat. I was wiped out! "I thought Gloria only had the one child!" I told Donald. He did not know how many children she had, because it had been years since he had seen or heard from her.

All of his information came from Gloria's cousin who lived in Kansas. He was at her house when Gloria called one day, and was shocked that Fred had weaved himself up into his own web. They talked about whether I knew; both were satisfied that I did not. Donald said, Penny, Gloria's cousin, asked her, why she didn't tell me. Gloria was a little younger than me, but she was probably more mature. Her answer to her cousin's question was that she did not want to hurt me. She thought that I had enough problems without her adding to them. Donald said that Gloria said, "After all, Fred had chosen to marry you, which meant that it was you who he loved!" I sat there and looked at Donald a few seconds thinking, "I would beg to differ."

I picked up the phone and called Doris. I asked her how many kids Gloria had. She confirmed that Gloria only had the one child. I was so confused! If the baby was born the same week as my son, it had to be the same baby I kept while she went out, when we were visiting, a few years back, I thought!

Now I really started to think of the trip Fred and I took with Jacob and Doris. I had expressed to everyone in the house, including Fred that Gloria's baby and my baby looked like twins. I called Doris again and asked her when was little Fredrick's birthday. She told me that it was July 14. "Doris, we have been friends for ten years and I love you, but I need to ask you a question that requires a truthful answer."

"Oh man, here we go," said Doris, as if she knew what I was about to ask. "Is Fred, Fredrick's father?" Doris hesitated, and I anticipated the response! "Yes, he is Fredrick's father!" "Doris, why didn't you tell me?" I asked as my voice began to crack! "It really wasn't my place to tell you, and I hope you understand. I've thought about it for years, what would I say if you ever asked? Well now you have, and it just wasn't my place to tell you," she said. I told her OK I would call her later, and goodbye!

I cried and cried as Donald comforted me the best he could. Now I realized why Fred went to Dallas while I was in the hospital directly after Bryan's birth. My mama and daddy had to pick me up from the hospital, so that my husband could go to Dallas and be present at his son's birth. I must be the laughing stock of the entire town! Samson Fredrick was the baby's name. He was given his middle name after his daddy, Fred. How cold hearted my husband was! He did not deserve me nor Bryan! Donald soon got ready to leave but questioned whether he had done the right thing by telling me. I told him he was right to tell me, that I appreciated him. I wanted him to go, because I needed to go to my secret place, up the little dirt road. Every dream I had ever anticipated, my hopes, every bit of trust, and all of my convictions were no more.

I went to my secret place and was there from probably 2:00p.m in the afternoon until it was so dark I could not see my hand before my face. I thought about many things that evening and I made some major decisions. Life from this point on would be about me and me alone. Nothing and nobody in this world other than my baby was more important. My mental meltdown was at its peak! I didn't see Jimmy for several months because I was right back where I started emotionally! The news of the third baby and all that went with it had set me back to the day I watched Fred drive away. My anger had turned to plain mad, but for some reason, I could not understand, I still loved Fred. I was so sad all day every day, felt so worthless, guilty, indecisive, restless, and I lost interest in things that I truly enjoyed doing. I was tired, couldn't eat, but I never wanted to commit suicide, although, I did feel at times that I was going to die. I didn't see how I could live under such conditions.

The more I tried to pull myself out, the deeper I seem to sink. I kept telling myself that it's all about me. I stood in the mirror and talked to myself, telling myself what I needed to do, and eventually, I decided I had to do something. I took one of Jimmy's calls one day and allowed him to come over. The only people I had allowed in my home since the last devastating news were my sisters and brothers and my friend, Patricia. I would try to hide my suffering, but they knew. Before Donald gave me the details, I was beginning to put on a little weight, but that and more was now gone.

I thought, if I just divorced Fred, I would feel better and less like a complete fool. I visited my secret place and prayed more than ever now. I was fighting death with all I had within me. I filed for divorce in April, and by Bryan's fifth birthday in July and directly after my twenty fifth birthday, I was a single woman. Donald had given me his address, and I had Fred's divorce papers delivered there. He would see to Fred getting them, I was sure. I was right, Fred called and I was able to confront him with some things. The only thing I truly wanted to confront him with was the son by Gloria. "So you are divorcing me huh," were his first words after I answered the phone. He had no answers just questions. "Who told you that shit?" he asked me. Everything about him was different. He did say that he was sorry things worked out like they did and promised that he was going to stay in touch and come to visit his son. He wanted me to know that he still loved me and always would.

"It is no longer about us, Bryan needs to know you as his father," I said. I didn't say anything about his living with Betty, nor did I bring up the drugs. I did not want to give him any idea that Donald had told me anything. I wanted him to know that he had ruined the most beautiful thing in this world, our marriage. Our son was without his father because he could not keep his penis where it was supposed to be. I allowed Bryan to speak with him, and he delivered a lot of empty promises.

On the day my divorce was granted, I sat in the court room and listened as divorce after divorce was granted. When it was my turn, I walked up to take my place beside my attorney. It was the last case called by the judge that morning. It was a rude awaking just learning that there were so many divorces that day. Some people acted as if it was just a casual affair, others seemed as distraught as I was feeling. One couple broke the grimness of the room for a short time, by asking the judge to allow them one last kiss prior to pronouncing them a divorced couple. The judge told them, he'd had strange request before, but that request beats them all. He heard their case, and just before he hit the gavel against the desk to pronounce them a divorced couple, he said, "Well are you ready for your last kiss as husband and wife?"

They both told him "yes" and proceeded to kiss each other, as if they would be unable to ever do it again! The judge took one minute to tell them that this was not something they had to do. He found it such a strange request that he refused to grant the divorce and reset the hearing a full month away. He said the only thing they needed to do, was to show up and the divorce would be granted. They did not seem disappointed at all; they laughed with the Judge and left the courtroom together.

When it was my turn, it was over so quickly. My attorney said a few words to the Judge about the case and I could barely breathe as the judge hit the gavel against his desk and said, "Divorce granted." He casually got up from his seat and walked away! "What? That's it?" I asked my lawyer. "I'm divorced?" I asked. "Yep, that's it," he said, as he sat packing his briefcase to leave the courtroom. There was no one to protest or fight over anything as if no one cared! I stood there for a moment, trying to digest what I had just heard. He looked up at me and said, "That's all, I will mail you the final papers after they are recorded," the attorney said. I turned to walk out of the courtroom, but I could not go through the tall brown double doors that lead to the hallway. I didn't know why I couldn't go, but my feet felt as if I was standing in a ton of cement. I sat down on the last seat to gather my nerve. Soon, my attorney was standing in front of me. He stood without saying a word.

When I noticed him, I looked up at him. His face was different; it was filled with pity, as he placed his hand on my shoulder, and said, "Take as long as you like, I'm going back to my office." I don't know how long I sat there, but I would guess maybe thirty minutes. I didn't cry but I realized that I was leaving something very important to me there in that room. It was my marriage! As I walk through those doors, I was closing a chapter in my life that still meant everything to me. I loved that man more than I loved myself. I had left him and longed for him, suffering more than I ever dreamed possible, but I knew it was best. He had to know that I would have learned that he was on drugs sooner or later, and he had to know I would one day learn that he had another son. He took the easy way out! I knew in my heart that I could not go back. When he came to me and told me that if I was not going to take him back, he was moving away, I let him go. The night before he left, we made love, but somewhere deep within me, I knew that it was over.

I could not take him back after all that had taken place now anyway. I was trying to do something with my life but, everything I had planned involved Fred and Bryan. Like Donald said, it was time that I go on alone. I could not see any signs that he was going to do anything other than run women, smoke dope, and have babies by other women among other foolish acts. I was still Mrs. Winslow, but I felt like Mrs. Lonely with a broken heart, and had to learn to live again!

Once I arrived home, I went straight to my jewelry box and placed my wedding ring in the very bottom. I picked up the phone, called Jimmy and asked him to take me to dinner. He agreed eagerly to do so! We went to dinner and another movie. He noticed that I was not wearing my ring at dinner and I told him that my divorce was final today. His brows raised in amazement as he took my hand to get a look at my finger without the ring. He kissed my hand, and said jokingly, "Now there's room for another." "Not so quick, Buddy," I said. We laughed and besides the little sick feeling I had in my stomach, we had fun. He had wanted us to spend the night together, but I did not want to. I jokingly told him, "You've got to give a girl a chance to enjoy her newly found freedom."

When I got home, two of my nieces were spending the night at my house, and Bryan was there with them. He was fast asleep in my bed when I arrived. I looked at my son, and I felt sorry for him. He lay there looking so much like his daddy, and I knew that though I might be able to survive the demise of the marriage, I would be reminded every day of Fred Winslow. I said my prayers and went to bed. I crawled in the bed and cuddled up with my son and thanked the Lord so much for him. He would not leave me; I would be his mother forever. I was going out with Jimmy every weekend now, and he was beginning to get more assertive. He kissed me for everything! If I smiled at him just so, it deserved a kiss. I still thought of Fred, but I kept pushing the thought in the background because that phase of my life was over.

Our first sexual encounter after the divorce was quite nice. I did not feel like a hussy, nor did I feel like I was cheating. Jimmy had some really good qualities, and he poured it on real thick about the Lord bringing me back to him. Sometimes he could be so serious that it was frightening! Sometimes I believed him. Maybe that is what God wants for me, I thought. Sex was becoming a quite frequent part of our relationship. Within two months after I had taken off my wedding ring, he kept trying to put another one on my finger. One night, he asked me to just try it on to see if it fit. I put it on and it fit perfectly! That beautiful pear-shaped diamond looked great on my finger. He asked me to wear it overnight, and we would discuss whether I would keep it tomorrow. The next day, I planned to give it back, but giving it back was going to be harder than I expected.

I called Jimmy to come over so that he could pick up the ring, and he came, but he wanted me to keep it. I told him that it was impossible for me to wear it because it was too soon to consider getting back into a marriage or even an engagement. I told him I had to let the spider webs in my brain clear out some. He felt that it was time for us to move forward, because Bryan needed a father figure in his life. He wanted to become a part of his life as soon as possible, so that he could grow up with him as the father figure. He said he had always loved me, and it was the first time in his adult life that he had felt so complete. "There's nothing like the truth, I have loved you since elementary school, you know it," he said.

"People would think I had lost my mind, and you know that," I said. "Who cares what people think," he said, "not me!" "Look Jimmy, I enjoy your company, and yes, as kids, we were going to grow up and get married! We are not kids now! I care for you, but I don't love you! Let's stop talking about this marriage thing right now. We should not address it for another year, and if then things have changed, maybe we could get more serious about the idea. Let's date and have a little fun together, OK!" Like a child, he dropped his head and did not say another word to try to convince me any different. He reached out for the ring, and I put it in his hand. He turned and walked out of the door, and I felt bad for him. I heard his car leave my driveway in a hurry, and I knew he was upset with me.

Jimmy was not quite as tall as Fred and far less good-looking, but I was flattered that he wanted to be a father to Bryan and even a husband for me, and he was a nice guy. Spoiled by his parents all of his life, he was not used to hearing the word "no"! I could tell that he had grown up some, but I attributed that to the discipline he learned in the army. I was getting ready for bed and was planning to watch two movies until I was sleepy. Bryan was at Mamas, since it was her night to have him. I had spent some time up there with him, and I hope that no real damage was being done with us splitting him down the middle. Jimmy had been gone about three hours, when the doorbell rang. My cousin Don was standing there telling me to come with him because Jimmy had an accident just down the road a piece. "He is asking for you!" he said. "Is it bad?" I asked. "I am afraid it is," he told me. I throw on some clothes as fast as I could, and Don drove me to the accident. A crowd of people had gathered by the time we got there; and, emergency response was pulling away with him headed for the hospital.

We rushed back to the car and headed for the hospital about twenty miles from where the accident occurred. As we drove by the scene, I was sure that Jimmy was hurt badly after getting a look at the cars. It was a head-on collision, and both cars were destroyed in the front. Jimmy was not wearing his seat belt and had been thrown forward hitting both the steering wheel and the windshield. As we drove further, I question Don to determine if he left Jimmy at the scene of the accident alone or was there some other person with him. "What were Jimmy's exact words when he asked for me?" I asked. He told me that he was the first person on the scene, but before he left coming to get me, three other cars had stopped. Felicia was there, and she had to run to a nearby house to call the emergency response. "What did he say?" I asked again. "He really didn't say anything but your name. He repeated it over and over again, so I took it upon myself to come and get you," Don said. "Do you think he is hurt bad?" I asked, thinking about how hurt he seemed to be when he left my house. "He's hurt a bit," was his response.

I could tell that Don was being evasive in his answers about Jimmy, and I really hoped he was not hurt too bad. I thought, I certainly didn't want him to die, because it would be my fault that he had the wreck. It had already been my fault that he went to the Army. Maybe had I married Jimmy instead of Fred, everything would have turned out differently. I was afraid to go into the hospital, when we arrived. What if we went in to find that Jimmy had died? "We had found that the people in the truck that Jimmy collided with were going to pull through." There being in a truck, and because they were wearing seat belts, may have contributed to their being saved.

In the hospital, we found that Jimmy was in the emergency room getting ready to go to emergency surgery. He had several broken ribs, some internal injuries, and a concussion so severe that his brain was swelling. I could hear his mother crying before I could get into the emergency room waiting area! The doctor was telling them that he was most worried about the swelling of the brain. They needed to stop the swelling, so they were going in and would keep us abreast of any changes. His mother, father, and I stayed at the hospital that night until he was out of surgery.

We had a little time to catch up, since I had not seen them since Jimmy first went to the Army. His mom was getting ready to retire, but his dad was going to continue for another two years. His mother looked at my hand and said, "Oh, he didn't get a chance to give you the ring?" I didn't know what to say, because I was not aware that they knew anything about it. I babbled a bit before I could say, "Well, no, I guess not!" "I hope my son pulls through this, because I want him to be able to put that ring on your finger and marry you." I smiled as I thought, He did put it on my finger, but I gave it back!

I prayed that he would come through this and be normal. If this did not happen, I would feel awful! He came through the surgery, but the doctor let us know that he wasn't quite out of the woods yet. They relieved pressure on the brain and had sewn the top of his skull inside of his stomach, for the time being, to preserve it. I had never heard of such a procedure before. They would be able to tell us more within three days, but until then it was going to be a waiting game. They would keep him in a comatose state, because he was not opening his eyes and talking to us did not mean that he wasn't getting better. I feared that he may not make it. I prayed at least ten times every day, every time I had the chance!

Although it seemed like a month, on the eighth day after the accident, Jimmy woke up! He did not talk, but he would squeeze my hand whenever I asked him. The doctors were very sure that it would be a long recovery period, but he would probably make a full recovery. He was able to speak within a day or two after he regained consciousness! His mother was coming out of the hospital when I was going in. She stopped and talked to me for a minute. "Girl hurry on in, he has asked about you ten times today I know! I had to go clean out his car today, and bring a few items he wanted," she said. "Can you understand him well?" I asked. "Yes, he's talking really well," she said, "but you have to listen carefully because he doesn't have the strength to speak loudly. It's just above a whisper, but I thank God for it." She raised her hands to the sky and said, "Thank you, Lord," as she turned to be on her way.

In his room, I was happy to see him looking so much better. I listened as he spoke softly, "I thought someone might get your ring, but mama found it, still in the car pocket." "I am happy that she found it," I affirmed. I watched him slide his hand underneath his covers and come out with the ring still in its box. "Will you marry me please? I know that you are suffering with the issue of your marriage to Fred, but you will learn to love me just as much as I love you.

Please help me by putting the ring on and wearing it proudly." "I know there is a chance that it may never happen, or if we get married, it may not work, but that is a chance that I am willing to take," he said, now struggling to breathe and beginning to shake, "it will give me something to work toward as I go through these next surgeries and rehabilitation." The surgery necessary to remove then replace that portion of the skull that they tucked inside of him was going to take place tomorrow. I reluctantly took the box, put the ring on my finger, and there it stayed until he completed in patient therapy two months later.

Once he was home, he went to therapy two days each week. His mother drove him back and forth and took excellent care of him during the healing process. I visited him on Saturdays and Sundays for two hours or so. By this time, the word was out, and the entire town thought that we were getting married. I admit that he grew on me some but probably not enough to consider marriage. I was not missing Fred or crying nearly as much; Jimmy's attentiveness had helped me in that area, but sometimes I would still visit my secret place. It was always peaceful up there, and I felt so close to God every time I went, and when I needed to talk to him, that was my closet.

Everyone was congratulating me on my engagement, and I reluctantly said, "Well, we shall see!" I know to this day that I should have waited before I allowed myself to become involved with Jimmy so early after my divorce. I did it because after all of the pain, it made me feel better, and to feel better is what I wanted most. It only served to create more confusion in my life! I was so vulnerable that I began to really feel that because I married Fred, knowing that Jimmy loved me, it was indeed possible, that I was being or had been punished by God in his effort to direct me to where I was supposed to be. Jimmy was walking around with no residuals and certainly looked better as he continually pushed for us to set a date for our wedding. I didn't want a wedding! After several months of holding Jimmy at bay, Jimmy and I went to purchase our marriage license. They would expire in thirty days, and I had to do some real intense soul-searching.

The local newspaper put all marriage licenses issued in the paper, and once people saw that we filed for marriage license through the county clerk's office, they began asking about the date. Was I sending invitations? Where was the wedding going to be held? I had no answers, and I can imagine that many thought that I was a stone nut. Mama had a fit, "That boy is different since he went to the Army. You don't want to do this! It will be like jumping out of the skillet into the fire, Savanah," Mama barked. "You are not ready for this, and he is not the one for you." I told her that I was not going to go through with it, and I think she believed me. Mama never really liked him anyhow! I think it was because of his aggressive disposition, growing up.

He had more than any of us kids, and he flaunted it. I guess I didn't mind as much as she and some of the other kids and adults, because he always shared his good fortune with me. I guess he started buying me meaningful gifts for my birthday and Christmas when I was in the sixth grade. Mama never made me give anything back, but she did talk about doing so. His mother would drive him up to our house; they would come in together, for him to give me the gift. She and Mama were friends, and they worked closely with the auxiliaries of the church.

Two days before the thirty-day expiration of our marriage license, Jimmy and I talked again about our getting married. I told him that I did care about him very much, but I still had a ways to go before I could marry anyone. I told him that I wore the ring and I did love it, but that he should give it to someone else more deserving. I pulled the ring off once again, and reached over to his hand and put the ring in his palm. "I am sorry Jimmy, but I am trying to protect the both of us!" As I talked to him, the first tear I had ever seen him cry, came rolling down his cheek. I felt terrible! All I have ever done was cause this man pain! "Was I being heartless," I asked myself.

My mind traveled back to our conversation on campus, leading to his enlistment in the Army. I had his heart trapped, like Fred had trapped mine. Fred did not deserve me and I did not deserve Jimmy! Why did things have to be so complicated? We never talked about it, but I had always felt that had I not let him leave so upset the night of the car crash, he would never have been speeding, causing such a terrible accident. Now, I had not only hurt him, but I hurt the husband and wife who barely escaped the accident with their lives. His tears were falling so fast now! I walked over to get him a Kleenex. Still standing, I pulled Jimmy to me, put my arms around him and gave in to him. He was feeling for me what I had experienced so intensely for Fred! What an ugly feeling! "I don't want a wedding; so if you marry me at the justice of the peace, we can do it tomorrow," I said to Jimmy. He now cried and laughed at the same time; he was happy! I was making him happy, and I was so confused!

I don't really know what I felt. Now, I was getting ready to defy my mother's wishes again! I did not tell Mama or my brothers and sisters. I was caught between a rock and hard place it seemed, with no way out. We had a quick and quiet little ceremony at the justice of the peace office. His secretary was our witness, and it was a done deal. I was Mrs. Jimmy D. Price!

I didn't know what or how I was going to tell my mama. I knew I was on my own this time, because I did not have Fred to help me through it. One thing for sure, I did not want Jimmy to go with me. Mama had a way of letting you know exactly how she felt about things without saying a word. If I was going to try to make this marriage work, I did not want her and Jimmy to get off to a bad start by having words. I waited until around six-thirty Monday evening to go to Mama and daddy with my news. I wanted both of them together so that I would not have to repeat myself. Daddy did not get home from work until 5:00 p.m. As I walked in, Mama was in the kitchen and Daddy was taking a bath, so I waited for him. Evidently, she had peeked out at my house before I came over because she asked me, "Don't you have company?" "Yes, Mama," I replied. "Well, why are you up here, leaving folk in your house?" "Wait until Daddy comes out and I have to tell you something, Mama," I said. "Where is my baby?" I asked. "He had gone to the store with Nadellie.

You know he swings every ride that comes by; I have never known a child that likes to ride so much," Mama chuckled. Daddy was in the kitchen by this time and was headed to the table to eat. I told them that I just needed a quick moment to tell them something, and I would be on my way. Daddy sat down at the table, and Mama followed suit. "I don't know whether this is good news or bad news, and even I still don't know what I am doing, or why, but I married Jimmy today." Mama grunted as if she had been punched in the gut! Daddy looked at me a minute, as if he was trying to digest what I had said! My heart began to race because I could feel that he was getting ready to say something in disapproval. "Girl, are you serious," Daddy said in disbelief.

"Yea," I replied. Mama just sat there shaking her head saying, "My, my my, oh my my my," repeatedly. Then she said, "Well, we are really getting ready to see what you are made of. That boy is spoiled rotten; his mama and daddy did that. He is not used to the word "no". "He pushed you until you said yes, so get ready," Daddy said. "Your Mama told me you said you were not going to do this foolish thing!" he said, as he shook his head in disbelief! "Ready for what, Daddy?" I asked. "Ready to be told what you can do, when you can do it, and just how much of it you can do," Mama chimed in. "Look, baby," Daddy said, "I don't say much to you, because Mama and I know how hard it was for you when you left Fred. We know it was even harder for you when he left town. We are your parents who have watched you grow to this point in your life. You cannot fool us!" "You don't want this, and if you don't know it now, you will later. He always has wanted you, but Fred came along and swept you out from under him. He hasn't forgotten that and he is gonna try to make sure nothing like that ever happens again.

He's gonna try to keep you too close, when you always have been a free spirit. You can't be closed in, you will suffocate," Daddy added. "Why didn't you tell us before you did this?" Mama asked. I replied, "I knew how you would feel about it, and I know how the both of you feel about him.

He thinks that my marriage to Fred did not work out, because I was supposed to be his wife from the beginning. He has been good to me since he came home from the Army, and I think he has matured some, but we shall see. I started not to tell you, but that would not have been fair. We plan to get a house in town or maybe build one a little later, but I won't do anything until I see where both of our heads are." Daddy added, "Savanah, for the sake of God, don't have no baby!"

I smiled and said, "For my sake, I promise you, I won't." Bryan came running in, and I was so happy to see him, not only because I had not seen him all day long, but because he had given me a break from the hot seat I was in with Mama and Daddy. It still was not as difficult as I had predicted. I played with my baby boy for about thirty minutes, gave him his bath, and dressed him for bed. "Where are you staying tonight my prince?" I asked. "I am staying here tonight, Mommy, I stayed with you two nights and Mamo will be sad if I stay tonight," he said. "OK, son, I told him, as I kissed him and tucked him in for the night. My son had learned what he had to do to keep my mother and me from fighting, and he seemed fine with it. It did not matter whether he was fine with it or not, that was the way Mama wanted it, and I could not change it.

Upon returning to the dining area where Mama and Daddy sat still in dismay, Daddy looked tired, and I wondered if he actually was, or if I had caused him to look older than he did when I first gave him the news of my marriage. I kissed both Mama and Daddy, and asked them to pray for me! I told them that if it wasn't what I wanted, I would not be with him long. I also told them, Jimmy was aware I had reservations about the marriage, and he was also aware that if it felt wrong for me, I would remove myself. Mama stood up and hugged me really tight and said, "God bless you! We will respect what has happened, and we will be kind to him; but be watchful, and take care of you!" I turned, walked out of the house and went home to my husband. Jimmy had told Bryan several times that he wanted to marry his mommy, and when I went to Mama's to dress him for school the next morning, I told him that I married Mr. Jimmy. "So is he my daddy now, Mommy?" he asked. "Well, kinda like your daddy, but we will let him remain Mr. Jimmy for now OK," I told my son. "OK," he said. I told my son that he still had his own daddy in Kansas, but he worked so much that he couldn't see him often. "When is he coming to see me again?" he asked as I put on his new little red raincoat. "Soon, baby," I sighed. I was tired of lying to him!

I survived the first week of marriage with Jimmy. He wanted sex twice a day, both morning and night. I wasn't used to that, because both Fred and I worked. Once every other night or so was good for me. Toward the end of the first week, I was having third thoughts, because I had second thoughts from the beginning. I would lie awake at night after Jimmy was asleep and watch him snore. "How did I allow myself to get in this mess?" I asked myself. I had not been able to go to my secret place for a while now, but I needed to go there if not but for a few minutes. I was uncomfortable when he pawed over me possessively, different from when we would make love before. It had been only one week, and his whole disposition was changed. It was like he said to himself, "I own her now!" If he only knew what I was feeling and thinking!

I was standing on the porch when I glanced up at the passing car and did a double-take. I would know that car anywhere, but was surprised that Fred still had it. It was getting pretty old, but it still looked great. My heart raced at the thought of him being that close to us. There were so many unanswered questions, and we never had the closure that all relationships need before one can move on. I wanted to see him, but I knew that Jimmy would not hear of it. Faye, my older sister, saw him that same afternoon, and she came to the house to get Bryan to take him to his father. I told her to take him, but she should not leave him alone with his dad. She argued that Fred was his father and should be able to visit with his son alone. I encouraged her to remain there with them and to bring Bryan back when she returned. Jimmy listened intensely, so I could not tell her that I had been told about Fred having a drug problem. I didn't want Jimmy to know that, because I felt that he would condemn Fred even more than usual. Jimmy was kind of self-righteous and always needed to prove he was better than Fred. I told Faye that if she could not do as I asked, I would take him to see his dad myself! She thought it best if I took him because she just would not have known what to say if Fred said for her to leave Bryan.

After she left, I told Jimmy that I was going to take Bryan to see his dad, but just as I thought, he wasn't buying it. He suggested that he take Bryan to visit with his dad. That definitely was not a good idea! I went to Mama and told her to call and tell Fred's mom, that he could come visit Bryan at her house, and he did. I stood in the kitchen window and watched my son playing with his daddy. I wanted to be there too! Everything within me wanted to be with them. I don't think I wanted to have sex with him, because I would have been too afraid since he had been out in the drug world, and God only knew who he had sexual encounters with. Yet I wanted to look into his eyes and see what he was feeling. I used to have that ability when we were in love. I wanted to talk to him and ask him if he was truly on drugs when he moved away, why did he allow me to be such a fool? Why did he allow me to keep his other baby while the mother went out to party? Deep inside, I knew the answers, but I needed to talk to him face-to-face just one more time. I needed closure so that I could go on with my life. I told Jimmy that I needed to speak to Fred and was going to walk up to Mama's house where he and Bryan were visiting. I got no response, so I walked out of the house and over to Mamas. Jimmy did not have an approving look on his face, but I was drawn like a magnet.

Fred saw me coming but continued to play with Bryan, and as I got closer, he gave Bryan the ball and told him to practice his dribble so he could talk to his mama. I approached him carefully, knowing Jimmy was probably watching me out of the window. I was standing face-to-face with the man, I was sure, I still loved him. I struggled to keep my composure as I asked Fred how he had been doing. It was apparent to me that he was struggling to keep his composure as well. "So you are married?" Fred asked as his voice trembled. "You didn't want me," I responded. "We have to talk, babe, can't we talk now?" he said. "We can but . . ." He did not allow me to finish. "I have so much to say," Fred said. "I know Jimmy won't go for it," I said as I detected a little jealousy or something in Fred's expression. "Can I come to the school tomorrow after the kids leave and speak to you there? I won't keep you long," Fred responded so seriously. "OK, you can come," I whispered. "Three-thirty?" Fred asked. "Yes, three-thirty is good!" I had a date with Fred! As I walked back home, filled with anticipation about tomorrow's meeting, I resisted the urge to look back, knowing Fred was probably still looking. I wondered how Jimmy was going to handle my speaking with Fred. I opened the door and Jimmy was standing there with the look of fury in his eyes! He wanted to know why I had disrespected him by going to speak with Fred. I explained to him that I simply wanted to speak to him about Bryan first and then a couple of things that we needed to address in order for me to move to the next level in my own life.

Jimmy threw a fit, saying that there should be no other issues to address because I had already moved on to the next level. I was married to him, and as his wife, he would not allow me to see Fred or have any dealing with him. He roared, "All the two of you have in common is a child." I told him that I would always need to discuss Bryan with Fred, it was my right as his mother and Fred's right as his father," but I thought to myself, after tomorrow things would flow more smoothly! That was a new side of Jimmy that I had not seen. Maybe he was upset because he knew that I still had a strong and very real emotional bond to Fred.

I never lied to him about my confused and uncertain feelings for Fred, even though I married him. He said that I would learn to love him, but I wasn't quite sure. He saved a bit of money while he was in the Army and paid the bills for the month even though he was not working yet. It certainly did help me; I used my money to catch up on a few things that had been lagging.

After school, when the kids were on the bus, and I was going back to my classroom, I saw Fred's car pull into the parking lot. My heart began to beat fast, and my palms began to sweat. I ran to the mirror and straightened my hair and makeup really fast, and sat at my desk to appear busy. I had told my teacher aides that Fred would be coming, and they wanted to stick around to get a glimpse of the man who shattered my heart. They would be conveniently leaving as he came into the room. The door to my classroom opened, and he stood there, not as well kept as he always was, but still very handsome. My aides told me that they would see me tomorrow, as I told him to come in. Once we were alone, I felt nervous and hoped that Jimmy did not come to the school. I knew that I would never be able to explain that what was happening had to happen in order for me to heal. I merely existed, traveling aimlessly through life for the last eighteen months or so. Fred sat down in one of the students chairs in front of my desk.

"Well, where do we begin?" I asked. Fred pulled off his hat and said, "We begin with me telling you how sorry I am for all the pain I have caused you and my son. I have acted so irresponsibly in every way in this marriage, well, what was our marriage! I don't blame you for divorcing me, Savanah. You had every right. I had a lot of pressure on me, from the time that I allowed myself to get involved with Linda. "That was a big mistake if I ever made one," Fred whispered. I was drinking that night, and Ray needed a ride to the little café in the curve on Eighth Street. When I dropped him off, Linda came over to the car and asked me to drop her off at her house. It had started to rain a bit and her house was on my way home. I saw no harm in it, even though something within me said I shouldn't. When I arrived at her house, her brother, Cedric, was sitting on the porch. He called me to come to the porch where he had a fifth of Crown Royal. He fixed me a drink, and I drank that one then another.

I was missing you so much that night, and I really didn't want to go home. I was already hiding Fredrick from you, and Gloria was riding me for money that I did not have! Oh, I thought, he is trying to tell me about his son!

I passed out right there on the porch they tell me, and Ray and his younger brother Sid help me to bed in their house. Sometime that morning, I woke up being touched and fondled, in my mind it had to be you. It was still dark, and I didn't have my bearings. I woke up in the bed alone, feeling like crap from a hangover! I did not realize where I was, but remembered I had made love to somebody or I had a very realistic dream. I had no underwear on, so I immediately decided it was no dream! I jumped out of bed and started to dress, trying to get out of there, when Linda came into the room. The words "Oh my god" expelled from my lips so fast, realizing it had to be Linda that I made love with.

She started trying to hug and kiss me, and I pushed her away. She was hurt that I wanted no part of her that morning, when I had made love to her a couple of hours ago. Her parents were out of town, and both brothers were drinking before bedtime, so she had freedom to roam during the night. I just wanted to get away and forget the whole thing. I did get away and stayed away, but it popped up again about six weeks later, when she told me that she had missed her period. I told her that if I had anything to do with it, there would be no baby. She knew that I was married, and she had taken advantage of my being drunk and tricked me into making love to her.

Three weeks later, she called my parents' house over and over until my mother insisted that I find out what she wanted. It was to tell me that she had been to the doctor, and she, in fact, was pregnant! Talking about a sucker punch, I felt too warm, as if I could not get enough air. I met her at the park and told her that she had to have an abortion, because I had no intentions of being a father to her baby. She called me a few days later and told me that she was going to have an abortion, and it would cost three hundred dollars. I hurried up and gave her the money, hoping that she would take care of things and we could put it behind us. I have never been an advocate for abortion and thought that I would never have wanted a child of mine to be aborted.

All I could think about was what you would think and do behind it." Fred got up and pulled his chair closer to my desk, and continued his speech. "She took the money knowing good and well, that she had no intention of having an abortion. I guess, I don't know," he struggled to find the words. "Once she decided to keep the baby, I lost my mind. I hated her for what she did, but now, I realize that it was my entire fault, not hers. I put myself in the position for her to be able to get that close to me.

I should never have gotten drunk; therefore, my lack of control allowed things to go haywire! Now, I just keep running off at the mouth not allowing you to get a word in edgewise." I sat there and looked at him, because he was supposed to have more to say. I then told him "It is OK, proceed!" "Savanah, you will always be the love of my life, and I will beat myself up for losing you, for the rest of my life, but I have to know, are you happy?" Shocked at the question, I fumbled for words. "What kind of question is that?" I asked. "You answered my question with a question." Fred said again, "Are you happy?" I became agitated that he had the nerve to ask me if I was happy when he had put me through so much pain. I knew the answer was no, but I wasn't going to give him the satisfaction. I still felt in my heart that I would never be truly happy again. I went on the defense and said pointblank, "So you have a son in Dallas, huh?" Fred stood and walked over to the window, staring out into the wooded area behind the school. Now the room is filled with silence, and neither of us spoke for at least two minutes. When I asked that question on the phone after Donald gave him the divorce papers, all he said was, "Where did you get that shit?" The custodian walked in, but backed out saying, "Take your time, I have a lot of other rooms to do before I have to come in here." I thanked him. Fred turned and looked at me as if he pitied me for what was to come next. "I do, have a son in Dallas that I never meant for you to find out about. I have been so wrong and such a fool, I had everything, and let it slip right through my fingers."

He looked at his hands and rubbed them together as if applying lotion. I sat there, remembering the baby that looked so much like my own. I remembered telling everyone in the house how much that baby and my baby looked alike. They all had played me for a fool. "You left me in the hospital and could not come and pick us up, because you had to go to Dallas to be present at another baby's birth." I stood because I was getting ready to unload! This was too much! Here come the tears again! I fought them back as long as I could. Had I held it any longer, I would have busted wide open. "You have made a complete ass out of me and our marriage. You have made a mockery of the trust I had in you, and it hurts so bad!" "Am I happy Fred? Hell no, I am not happy and I don't ever think that I will be happy again in this life. You may as well have taken a gun and shot me between the eyes! You are a prime example of what people call a motherfucker," I said.

Fred came toward me, and I backed away, putting my hand out for him to stop. "Don't you touch me, don't you ever touch me again! You are Bryan's father, and I want you to be in his life, but I want to hate you. I want to live to see the day that I can say it and mean it," I stammered. I felt myself out of control, so I looked at Fred a second and I had to know the answer to one last question. "Now tell me about the drugs," I said with furiousness all in my voice. Fred dropped his head and tears welted in his eyes, "I have made a mess of my life, Savanah, I have made a mess of your life and our son's," his voice just above a whisper. "It was so much going out of control in my life, with the baby by Linda, then the one in Dallas, I was stressing so badly that Winston gave me a blunt to smoke to calm my nerves. I did not realize that it was laced with something, plus it had crack cocaine crumbled inside of it." Fred sat down in the chair and cried like a baby.

The urge to put my arms around him grew almost overwhelming, but I did not. I walked over and took a seat next to him and placed my hand on his back. I rubbed his back consolingly until he calmed down a bit. Here I was feeling so sorry for myself, and his pain was greater than I could begin to imagine. I looked him dead in his eyes and told him that I couldn't quite identify with his pain, but I know that he did not intentionally mess things up. I told him that I had been so much in love with him, that it blinded me from seeing the big picture.

For the first time, I was able to think outside of the box. "Let me tell you what I want for us now, Fred," I whispered. "I will pray for you as I pray for myself, but you have got to go for help once you return to Kansas. Check yourself into a program, and stay there for as long as it takes. I don't care about your job; you can get another after you take care of yourself. Don't worry about me and Bryan for now, because you cannot be a good father until you can be whole again. Find the Fred that I fell in love with and hold on for dear life." "I have never nor will I ever love anyone as much as I love you, Savanah," Fred said, as he wiped away his tears. "I can see that I have made you change. You are tougher, and I hope it will somehow help you in the future," Fred said with a slight smile. "Will you do as I ask?" I said as I smiled back at him. "I will," Fred replied. "Now go, please!" "I want to take Bryan to the park tomorrow before I leave, if it is OK with you," he asked.

"He is your son, just take care of him, he is all I have." "I know," he replied. I turned my face toward the wall. I have to know Fred, "Did you take my money?" "I did," he dropped his head, but here, Fred went in his pocket pulled out a one-hundred-dollar bill and gave it to me. "That is half," Fred said with an embarrassed look on his face. Then he pulled out a ten-dollar bill, handed it to me and said, "With interest," and once I give you the other hundred-dollar bill; I will give it with interest as well. I am so sorry and I know you can see I am quite embarrassed to have to admit to you that, yet again, I hurt you.

I know that I have done so many wrong things, and will carry it with me the rest of my life. If I thought you would have me back after all that I have done, I would fight that Jimmy tooth and nail, and take my family back. If you ever decide that we can try again, please call me," Fred said, handing me his phone number. "What will your girlfriend say if I call, I mean for you to talk to Bryan?" I asked.

"My girlfriend," Fred shook his head, "it's a long story, but I would not call her my girlfriend. If by chance I am not there when you call, just leave a message, and I will get it. She knows the deal. Do you think maybe someday you will forgive me?"

"I have forgiven you already," I said with a smile, then turning my head to look out of the window. I whispered, "Now go please, but Fred, get some help! You never know what the future may bring, one day maybe years from now, we might be a family again. One never knows what life has in store. Either way, we need to be friends because we have a beautiful son." Fred replied, "I will get help, and hope for the rest, someday!" It's funny how things that are painful you avoid some way or another. I was letting Fred walk away again, but I refused to watch him leave. I heard his footsteps as he slowly walked toward the door; he stopped for a second, then proceeded to open the door, walked out and closed it behind himself. I had myself a good cry, went to the bathroom to wash my face, re-apply makeup, so that I could go home and try to sort out the mess; I had allowed myself to make of Jimmy's life and my own.

I thought about Jimmy on the journey home, and I decided that I would try to make it work, since I started it, I might as well finish it. I also thought about Fred, and for once since I left him, I had inner peace. The relationship and marriage as we knew it was over, and it was OK. I needed that talk so much! I stopped by my secret place, and for the first time, I did not cry. Instead, I thanked God, for sending Fred back just long enough to set me free.

I asked for guidance in dealing with my and Jimmy's situation. I needed to know what God wanted me to do. When I arrived home that evening, Jimmy was waiting. I suppose I seemed too happy or my newly found peace showed too much. I was smiling and talking to Jimmy about casting our votes in tomorrow's election, and he wanted to know where I had been so late. "I stayed after school for a while," I responded. I was approximately two hours late and still had to go to Mamas to get our dinner, and tonight, I was going to bring Bryan home with me. I needed him to be there, close to me tonight.

I must have been a little too happy, because after we all had eaten, and Bryan was fast asleep, Jimmy asked me again why was I late. I looked up at him and his eyes were piercing as if he could see through anything I might say. "I stayed over at school because I had some things to do." Jimmy wanted to know what exactly I had to do. I wondered if he had driven by and seen Fred's car, so I didn't lie. "Fred came to the school, and we talked," I said softly, anticipating his reaction. "You talked to him yesterday, and that wasn't enough was it? No, you had to talk some more and God knows what else!" Jimmy shouted. I could not believe he was insinuating that I might have had sex with Fred!

"We were at school, Jimmy, what else could we have done other than talk?" Jimmy was standing by the hallway door, and I was standing in the family room "Here we are talking about spending our lives together, and you have already started doing things behind my back," he said angrily! "It was so innocent, Jimmy, but every relationship has to have closure, and that was our closure," I said. "I won't have a wife of mine running around behind my back, Savanah." "I'm not running around behind your back, Jimmy. I just had to have some of my questions answered, so that I could go on with my life." I went to the kitchen to wash the dishes. Jimmy sat in front of the television, and I could tell he was furious. I was standing with my back to him putting the plates in the cabinet. Suddenly, it seemed as if the roof had caved in on me. I blacked out immediately, probably before I hit the floor, but awoke dazed as Jimmy carried me to the bedroom and laid me on the bed. I was disoriented and did not know what had actually happened, but I could feel him taking my clothes off. The blood felt warm streaming down the side of my head.

It was as if a dream was being played out before me. I am hurt, I thought as I tried to clear my head and understand exactly what was going on. Why is he crawling on top of me if I am hurt? I thought. He spread my legs and visually inspected my vagina, smelled it, fondled it I suppose, until he was satisfied that I had not had sex. I was powerless to resist, or fight, but I knew I was being violated. I did not cry, but I wanted to know what happened. I was being violated with my son asleep in the next room. Immediately, my mind wandered back to my childhood when Mrs. Evans was so brutally assaulted by her husband. I was living the life; I so desperately vowed not to live! "What did you do to me?" I asked. "Baby, I was crazy. The vase was sitting there, and I just hit you because I was upset, he said. I will buy you another, I promise," he stammered. "You hit me on the head with my vase, Jimmy, how could you?" I repeated over and over, as the tears rolled back into my hairline along with the blood.

He had broken my favorite vase over my head, now he wanted to help me! After going through my hair to see the damage, Jimmy said that the cut was tiny and would not require stitches. He put pressure on the area to stop the bleeding, placed an ice pack to reduce any swelling that might occur, and gave me two tablets to help with the pain. I now believed the rumor, that he had treated Lucille in a similar fashion once when she made him mad. Lucille was a girl whom he dated when he was still in college before he enlisted. After my head had cleared a bit, I got up ever so slowly. Jimmy ran my bath, and I went into the kitchen to assess the damage there. The vase was shattered, and blood was on the floor where I fell. Jimmy made sure Bryan was ready for school the next morning, while I lay in bed in bewilderment. I took two sick days from work.

The next few days were a strain for me. I worked with pain in my head, and I could barely turn my head. My neck would not allow my head to move from side to side, nor could I stand to tilt it up or down. I continued to take the pain medicine three times daily, and the stiffness and soreness slowly subsided. I told everyone that I had a bad crick in my neck, and if it did not get better soon, I would go to the doctor. I did not talk to Jimmy for two days and barely spoke to him for several days after that. Jimmy pleaded and begged forgiveness, because he didn't want to lose me, he said. Well, little did he know, he was all but gone already. The marriage to Jimmy was over, and I was completely turned off with him. It was not all his fault; it was mine also! He wanted it, and I didn't, just like I wanted my marriage to Fred, and he wasn't mature enough to handle marriage. I was too far away from him, and by the time I got out of school, he had spun himself a web that he could not work his way out of. I was too young to understand the danger there was in getting pregnant, even though Fred married me, and I truly feel that he loved me, getting pregnant was the wrong thing to do.

I woke up early on this particular Sunday morning; Jimmy was asleep, and I watched him sleep, as I had done several times before. When I began the new relationship with Jimmy, I was searching for help. The pain I was feeling over the loss of my marriage was dulled when he made me feel good during sex. When I was hurting, I let him make love to me repeatedly, and because it made me feel better, I became dependent upon his body. His love seemed honest and pure, and I thought that I could exist in that state of being. I didn't want to marry him, but I didn't want to lose him either. Although I was honest with him about my feelings, it was wrong and unfair for me to let him talk me into marriage. I had seen his possessiveness in its fullest bloom, and I didn't like it. We had only been married four weeks, and I wanted out. I could not hate him; I just didn't want the marriage anymore. I knew I had to let Jimmy and Fred both go in order that I could heal and find a way to move forward with my life. I allowed him to rush me, pressure me into this marriage. Now I just have to find the right time to talk to him about it. My mind was made up, and I was not going to let his whining and crying, stop me from undoing what never should have been done. I don't know whether I deserved what I got or not, but for both of our sake, it was time.

When Jimmy went back to work, I was exceptionally happy because I did not want it said that I left him while he was down and out. On Friday after school, I will talk to Jimmy and ask him to leave. I would file for divorce on Monday. I made his favorite meal, allowed him to eat and enjoy it. He took a shower and sat down to read the paper. When he was finished, I asked him if we could talk. He said we could, and I began, "Jimmy, I am sure you realize that we jumped into this marriage all too quickly. I wasn't ready for it so soon after my divorce." I tried to be ever so careful with my words, because I did not want him to attack me again.

I continued, "We should have dated longer, and it would probably have worked out much better. I need the space to heal, Jimmy! As long as you are here, I can't heal." I could feel the tension building in him as I continued. "I will be filing for divorce on Monday." Jimmy's eyes watered as he began to lose control. "Divorce my ass; we are not getting no divorce, Savanah." Jimmy paused; it seemed in an effort to compose himself. "We got married to spend the rest of our lives together, and that is what we are going to do. Sure, I have to work on my anger, and I told you that I was sorry that I did not trust you to do the right thing when you met with Fred, but I am your husband, baby, I love you." "You, don't understand, Jimmy, I have to do this for the both of us. It did something to me inside when you broke that vase over my head. If you can do that in anger, what else are you capable of doing to me?" I then told Jimmy, I wanted him to go still. I told him that I was leaving for a couple of hours, and I wanted him to be gone when I returned. I walked out of the door, got in my car and left.

As I was pulling out of the driveway, an all-too-familiar car passed. Linda was driving, and that cute little baby girl was in her car seat in the back. She waved and smiled, and I couldn't help but wonder how that gesture was intended. I had to get used to it and move forward, past the hurt it all caused me. Fred had left me here with all the unpleasant memories, and it felt so unfair that he could wake up every day without being confronted with all the demons he created. I went shopping for almost exactly two hours and returned to find that Jimmy was still there and had not packed a bag. He only had a few outfits and personals to pack because I encouraged him to leave the majority of his things at his mother's house until we finished building our home. My house was small and closet space was a problem. Construction was going to begin in three weeks, and I had to end this farce of a marriage before I got in any deeper. A house would further complicate an already too complicated situation.

I called the bank and canceled the loan. I had known the president of the bank all of my life, and he told me that it would not be a problem because no funding had exchanged hands nor had construction began. When I walked in, Jimmy was sitting on the sofa, having what appeared to be a few too many glasses of Crown and Coke. I figure he began drinking soon after I left, and I knew that whenever he was disturbed, he would drink the first two or three drinks really fast. After that he usually would sip to the point that he was mellow but not drunk.

Whenever he drank, his skin would appear to be a little shiny, as if the alcohol caused his pores to produce too much oil. Not knowing what was going to happen, I placed my keys on the bar near the door, so that I would have easy access if I had to run. I went into the bedroom, to place the blouse I purchased on the bed. I went back to ask him if he was going to pack and leave today as I had asked. He jumped up, turned the coffee table over and began to rant and rave about saving his marriage. Afraid of what might happen, I told him I would not file for the divorce on Monday, if he just agreed to leave.

I suggested that maybe we could have dinner together once a week to touch base on our relationship. "We have only been married five weeks," Jimmy scoffed. "Who gets a divorce after living together for five weeks? What will people say about us?" "I don't care what people think about us, Jimmy, I know what I am feeling, and I have to be alone right now," I said. He stood and stared at me long and hard, and I became more fearful of what might come next. I turned and walked in the dining room, but remembering the vase incident, I kept an eye on him at all times. He came in the dining room and tried to pull me to him, but I resisted. With that, he went crazy and shelved me into the wall. I ran to the other side of the table, and a chase around the table began. He tried to reach across the table to get me but fear caused me to act swiftly. Frustrated because he could not reach me, he turned the table over on its side causing the glass centerpiece to break, splattering it into small pieces. I ran to the bathroom and locked the door behind me. He came to the door and beat on it repeatedly, telling me to open it. I refused, unsure of what he might do next!

My heart was beating so fast realizing that I had nowhere to go if he happened to get in. Suddenly, he was kicking the door and running into it with his body. I could see the door facing pulling away from the wall. The door hinges were coming off with every attempt, and the door was certain to fall on me. I jumped over into the bathtub, laid down, and closed my eyes, anticipating the big bang.

In an instant, the door fell so hard across the tub that I could feel and hear the enamel popping off of the tub. Jimmy fell with such force when he fell on top of the door. I could hear him struggling to get up, so I used my back to lift the door and turned it sideways causing him to slide to the floor. I was on one side of the door, and he was on the other. It just so happened that I could slip out of the door, slowing him down by turning the door over on top of him, making a desperate dash for the bedroom where he kept the gun in the headboard of the bed. Knowing that he was close behind me, I grabbed the gun and turned around pointing it directly at his upper body. I told him not to come any closer, or I would shoot. He stopped, but continued to talk to me.

"So you want to kill me and spend the rest of your life in jail, huh?" he asked. I had already decided that if I had to shoot, I would aim for his lower extremities. I continued to tell him that I would shoot if I had to, so stay back. I anticipated through his body movement and his eyes that he was going to make a dash for the gun. He did, and I fired as low as I could. He pulled me to the floor with him as he fell. I maintained control of the gun, as I struggled to get from underneath his body. My first instinct was to get my keys and get out of there. Panic set in really fast as I stepped over him and ran to get my keys and purse. I grabbed my keys, but my purse was not there. I needed my purse! I was afraid to go back in the bedroom, not knowing whether I had killed Jimmy or not. It took every ounce of strength I had to gather the courage to go back into that room to get my purse. As I peeped around the corner, I could see Jimmy moving and was so relieved, but I still had to go.

I leaped over him, grabbed my purse from the bed and started to step back over him to get out of the house. As I did, he caught me by the ankle. I snatched my leg away from his grip, as I heard him whisper, "Take me to the hospital." I proceeded to the front door, but stopped, turned around, went back, and helped Jimmy to his feet. I kept the gun in my hand just in case I had to fight again, but I needed him to live!

There was so much blood on the carpet, and I knew he was hurt badly. I helped him to get into the car, and as I glanced up toward Mama's house, I was thankful that my parents and my son were still gone. I put the gun between the door and myself, just in case Jimmy tried anything, I could get to it. I drove him to the hospital in complete silence, but praying that he would not die.

Once there, I went to the passenger side and helped Jimmy out of the car and into the emergency room. As I entered the door, one nurse realizing that he was seriously injured came toward me to help with him. Suddenly, she turned and ran the other way as fast as she could. The nurse sitting at the desk looked puzzled as she watched her coworker run from us, but upon standing, she seemed to have frozen in her tracks. "What is wrong with you people, can't you see he needs help" I screamed? Although frozen in her tracks and looking stunned, the nurse's eyes focused on my left hand. As I followed her eyes, I realized that I had brought the gun inside the emergency room with me. I immediately said, "Oh, I am so sorry," as I laid the gun on the desk. "I won't hurt you, I am just so upset; will you help him please?" Still watching me very carefully, she came from around the desk and helped him into a wheel chair.

I told her that I was leaving but would be back shortly. As I turned to walk out, the first nurse who ran away from me and several doctors peeped around the corner to see what my intentions were. I was all covered with blood from helping Jimmy and would go home clean up and return to the hospital. I prayed aloud all the way home that Jimmy would live, and that I did not have to go to jail. I worried that I would be fired from my job, making my life and my son's a complete disaster.

After I cleaned up, I immediately returned to the hospital only to find the police waiting for me. I called his parents and my sister while I was gone, and soon my entire family and his were there. When I walked back into the emergency room, the nurse fingered me to the police. Two of them came over to me, identified themselves, and asked me what happened. I told them the whole truth! They wanted the weapon, but I had left it at home. They took me back home to get the gun, and while there, they saw how the house was in disarray. My arm was turning black and blue where he held me when he shelved me into the wall. I had scrapes and cuts from the incident in the bathroom. Splinters in my hands, showed distinctly the battle I encountered with the door. I had a large bruise under my chin that I suppose happened in the bathroom as well. The officer took pictures of the bruises, and every room that we fought in was a wreck.

They said, after seeing the coffee table turned bottom side upward, and the dining table lying on its side and all of both tables contents spread all over the floor, "You had no other choice in this matter, we can see." They told me that they were not going to arrest me, because it was clearly self-defense. I did have to go before the judge and tell him my story, and the pictures and their report would be in court to help assure that the judge conclude this as self-defense. They told me Jimmy had told them he shot himself cleaning the gun. His statement would be in court as well, to let the judge know that even Jimmy knew I had no other choice and did not want me prosecuted. They dropped me back off at the hospital where I found that Jimmy was in surgery. My sisters and brothers were there with me until almost morning. Even after Jimmy came out of surgery, it was morning before I could see him. I stayed with him every night until he recovered enough to be released. I had all of his clothes packed and delivered to his mother's house, and took him to the door, returning him to his family permanently.

My principal never brought the subject of the shooting up to me, and I wondered how I could be so blessed! Although, we did not discuss it, I called him into the office to do so. I knew he and his wife were both fond of me, but I also knew he had heard about the shooting. In the office, he saw that I was distraught. Knowing that I had to go to work, he just said, "Look, I don't want you to speak to anyone on this campus about what happened. I already know why you did it. You let me handle it, and you keep quiet!" I did just that, and it all went away. It would be years before I stopped reliving that tragic incident within my mind.

I had the carpet replaced in the bedroom because I did not want to see any signs of the struggle that took place there. I purchased new bedroom furniture and began to recapture some of my life, spending much more time with my son and my family. I thought of Fred quite often and talked to him every now and then. It took a while for him to get his life back on the right track, but it finally happened. He remarried several years later, and had another son and a daughter. His new wife has gone through many changes with him, just as I did, but she stayed the course. I was happy for the both of them. Two years would pass, before I ever entertained a thought of dating. Oh, I was asked out many times, but I would say no. I was not ready for any involvement! My son was growing up with most of his father's features, and I was finding happiness all by myself.

Chapter Four

It was a Saturday, two and a half years after Jimmy, and I was cleaning and raking the fall leaves in the yard, when this shiny blue coupe came driving by extremely slow. A man was driving, and he looked long and hard. I could not, for the life of me, imagine that it would be anyone interested in meeting me, because I looked a mess. I was all bundled up to protect my body from the chill. I had put on gloves and a skull cap, and leaves were piled as high as I was tall, for burning. The car became a passing thought as I continued my work. I would finish raking and burn the leaves. We could do that in the country, unlike in the city. I had forgotten about the man in the shiny car when my cousin, Bill, turned into my driveway. He wanted to tell me that the man in the pretty blue car would be back through in an hour and wanted to meet me.

He explained that he had seen me several times but was never close enough to speak. I wasn't quite sure if I was ready to meet anyone, because all of the drama was behind me, and I liked the peacefulness. I went through almost eight years of turmoil and welcomed this sweet peace! I could not stop cleaning just to meet the man, so I continued to work. Surely enough, about an hour and a half later, the shiny blue car turns into my driveway. Bill and this handsome man both got out of the car and came over to join me at the burning pile. What a handsome man he was; maybe I should have changed clothes, I thought. Bill introduced us as I blushed all over myself. His name was Samuel, and he was from a moderately small Louisiana town, which was only thirty-five miles away.

After the not-so—formal introduction, Samuel took the rake and pushed the outer edges into the middle of the pile to complete the burning process. I thanked him and told him to stay back so that he would not get his clothes all smoked up. He was dressed so nicely, and smelled so good, but smoke would ruin all of that. "I know a little about fires and raking," he said looking absolutely scrumptious. After a few minutes of small talk, he and Bill left, but I had his face permanently etched in my mind. "He is a man, mature and seasoned," I thought.

After they left, I went about my day getting the yard and the house as clean as a whistle. I washed clothes and prepared both my and Bryan's clothes for the week.

I had started back going to church on a regular basis and looked forward to having nothing to do on Sunday evening after our regular Sunday dinner at Mamas. We finished dinner, and by 4:00pm I was home. I had just walked inside when there was a knock at my door. Thinking it was Bryan or some of the other kids; I opened the door without finding out who was there. There on my porch stood Samuel! "I am sorry to come by uninvited, but I left last weekend without getting our phone number, so I drove all the way back up here this weekend to ask you if I could have your number please."

I hesitated, because I wasn't sure I wanted a relationship. The smile and the look in his eyes told me under no uncertain terms that this guy is interested." Seeing the hesitation, Samuel said, "Well I really don't want to impose." "Oh no," I said, "it's not that, it's just that I have been through a lot and I am really not seeking a friendship right now." "Well," said Samuel, "I can understand that, so is it OK if I come every Sunday about this same time until you decide that I can have your number, or until you are ready to give it to me?" I found it so amusing that I said, "OK then, if you wish."

Samuel laughed a big hearty laugh and said, "OK, Ms. Savanah, see you next week, same time, same station." I smiled and said goodbye, wondering if he truly would show up a third time, next Sunday. He did show up the following Sunday at just about the same time. I again had just arrived home from our family's Sunday dinner. When I opened the door this time, I was truly surprised and flattered that he actually came back just to ask for the phone number. "Hello, Savanah," Samuel said flashing his big smile, and beautiful white teeth. "Hi Samuel," I said with what I am sure was a smile to match his. "Would you like to come in for a few minutes?" I asked.

Samuel stepped inside, and I showed him to the sofa to sit down. "Nice place you have here," said Samuel. "Thank you," I said, "I still have lots of work to do to this place. "So," still smiling, I said, "you came all the way back here today to ask for my phone number again I suppose." "I did," Samuel responded, still smiling. "Now suppose I don't give it to you today, will you be back next Sunday?" I asked. "I will," replied Samuel. I went in my purse, scribbled my number on a note pad and passed it to him. "Thank you," Samuel said as he looked at the number and tucked it in his shirt pocket. "Now if you lose it without memorizing it, it will be even harder for you to get it the next time, and that is a promise," I said. "Oh don't you worry your pretty little head about that number; it is already committed to memory," Samuel chuckled.

"When can I call you?" he wanted to know, kind of serious like. In a little more serious manner, I responded, "You can call weekdays between 8 and 10 p.m., and anytime you can catch me on weekends." "Sounds good, so should I go and leave you to prepare for work next week?" asked Samuel. "Well, if you would like to stay maybe an hour or so, you are welcome," I smiled. He responded, "I think I would like that very much." I made him a drink, just so that I could have one myself to settle my own nerve. It seemed like such a long time since I spent any time around a man. Two years really was a long time for a young woman to be without male companionship.

We talked about several things that day, both asking and answering questions that helped us to get to know each other better. Samuel called every other day through the week; on weekends, he found a way to make every Sunday evening his day to visit.

The more the pattern was set, the more I grew to expect it. I explained to Samuel, my need to take things slowly, and how important it was to me that our expectations for this friendship were stated. As the days, then months went by, I began to see Sam more often. Over the two years that I was without a man, I tried to establish myself as Bryan's mother more and more. Some weeks, I was able to trick mama into his staying at my house four to five nights, but she almost always managed to turn the tables on me. Some weekends over that two-year span without a man, I would visit old friends from college, just to get away from home. I had more good friends in Pine Bluff, Arkansas, than in my own hometown. I had a couple of cousins, of which I was very close, that made Pine Bluff their home after college.

I could go there anytime and feel right at home. Kaye and I were closer because she and I were close to the same age. We were a lot alike in some ways as well. She had already been married and divorced a couple of times also. On that subject, we had plenty to talk about. I had a good friendship with a man from Pine Bluff. He was U.C. Cummins: charming, interesting, and a whole bundle of fun, but our friendship was purely just that, friendship. We never took it to the level of committing ourselves as lovers; however, friends we shall forever be.

Sam's coming into the picture "kinda" slowed my visits to Pine Bluff. On Saturdays, he would take me to the movies, out to dinner, and shopping. He paid for anything and everything I purchased, with no second thoughts about it. We had been seeing each other for months by the time spring came around. As the sap rose in the trees, so did our nature and sexual desire. In the back of my mind somewhere, I still knew I needed to take heed. We were spending so much time together, and he was so good to me. Still, I had experienced love gone wrong, and I didn't want to taste its bitter sting ever again. I had to maintain an image within the community, and for several months, he would be parked at a neighbor's house, walk to my house, spend the night, and leave before daylight. When I think about it now, we were only fooling ourselves; everybody else knew the real deal. I remembered my plan, the promises I made to myself when I was going through changes trying to get over Fred's and my separation.

My plan of action was as follows:

1. Any man I dated was going to take care of 50 percent of my needs. Sam did better than that.

2. I refused to be used and discarded like old trash. I didn't know quite how that was going to turn out yet.

3. Once I discover infidelity without a doubt, it's time to go. I would not compete with any other female for my boyfriend or husband, she was welcome to him and I would bow out gracefully.

4. At the end of one year, either of us could decide the relationship did not warrant any more time. One or the other could end the relationship. Time is of utmost importance, and I had none to waste. If we both wanted to stay in the relationship, it was time to make a commitment. By that I mean, as Beyoncé says, "put a ring on it."

5. I would hold on to my heart until it was snatched away by the right man. If

Mr. Right turned into Mr. Wrong, "goodbye"!

6. When the good in the relationship played out, and it became apparent that it would not return, it was time to go.

7. I would not be abused, physically, mentally, emotionally nor sexually.

Sam and I talked about my image, and he remedied that by asking me to marry him. I said yes without too much hesitancy, yet I was truly nervous about the whole thing. He was so charismatic and smooth that I am sure he did not believe I meant business when I told him under what conditions I would abandon the relationship. Our wedding was a quiet little secret ceremony in which we both were a little excited about.

It was his second marriage, and my third. We made a great-looking couple, and people often complimented us in that area. We thanked them and smiled, but as good as we looked together, looks can be deceiving and looking good together will not save a marriage. The first year of marriage was really great, and we started spending time with other couples in town. We would play cards and have a few drinks, cook, and feast, then see who could tell the best jokes. It became the highlight of our weekend, and we called it good clean fun.

That year in 1973, Ann lost her baby daughter "Tina" in a car accident. Ann had married Dave five years before Tina's birth in 1952. Tina was their third child all of which were daughters. They divorced four years after Tina was born. Tina had become pregnant at the age of 16 by a boy in the neighborhood. She was the very first of any child to die in our family. I could not believe that she was just with me the night before, and now she was gone.

Being the youngest aunt in the family and only seven years older than "Sarah" her oldest daughter, nine years older than the middle daughter, and eleven years older than "Tina". They were always at my house. Even in pouring rain, I would look up and there they were. I could not keep the two youngest girls out of my clothes. There were things that I allowed them to wear and things I did not want them or anyone else to wear. They would climb through my window when I was gone and wear some of my better clothes. I would fuss and did hit them a few times. It did not good whatsoever. I would have no idea that when I was not looking one or the other would unlock the window.

It had always been a habit that on Saturday or Sunday, I would organize my wardrobe for the week. All the clothing that I had sent to the cleaners were lined up in the order that I planned to wear them. The girls knew my routine and would wear any of that week's item of clothing that they liked, usually a pantsuit or casual shirt suit, come home from school, climb back through the window and put it back into the plastic as if it were clean. On the day that I had planned to wear it, I would discover that it had been worn. It often upset me and I would give them a piece of my mind, and make them stay away for a week or two. Then they would gradually find their way back into my house. I loved them too much to keep them away.

Once my dad saw a paper sake pushed underneath the edge of the café. He pulled it out to find that it was a pantsuit of mine. They tucked it there until they had the opportunity to smuggle it back into the house. They could see me when I visited mama's house, and that would be their chance. Samuel came to the school to tell me that we needed to go to the hospital because Tina was in an accident. He did not tell me the severity of the accident, although he acted upset. I kept asking him if he thought she was going to live, and he said "sure,

just pray!" Those words coming from Sam meant big trouble to me. Seldom did he speak of prayer in that context. I worried all of the way to the hospital.

Once there, we met family members crying, but going outside to smoke a cigarette! "Is she dead", I asked, almost at the point of tears myself? Curtis, a cousin said, "no Savanah, but it is really bad!" In the emergency room waiting area, Ann was distraught and crying uncontrollably. I needed to find some hospital staff member to tell me what was going on with Tina. As I got closer to the emergency room, I could hear screaming! It was Tina! I rushed toward the sound of her voice as hospital staff tried to stop me! I wanted to tell her that we all were out there waiting for her. I wanted her to know she was going to be alright. Tina was very scary and I knew she must be more terrified than ever before! As I approached the area, I saw her feet, but the nurses and Doctors around the table she lay on prevented me from seeing her clearly.

Two nurses and a man dressed in hospital attire wrestled me back into the hallway. Samuel had come around to see where I was, and as they pulled me back into the hallway, he wrapped me in his arms and held me tight. "I just wanted to tell her we were here, she is so scared! Oh please God, I screamed!" A doctor came to me with a glass of water and two pills and said, "here take these, they will help." To this day, I have no idea what I took. He asked Sam if he was her father. He said no, but led him to Ann in the waiting area. I am told that when Ann saw the doctor coming she was so fearful about what he was going to say that she covered her ears and said, "I don't want to hear it," thinking Tina had already passed away!

The doctor gently pulled her hands from her ears and said, "No, no, it is not what you think, we are doing all that we can for your child. She has severe injuries, but first we are going to take the baby by caesarian section. Then we will work on the ruptured spleen. Staff is working on her as we speak. I do need you to know that if she lives, she will more than likely be a vegetable." "What do you mean a vegetable," Ann questioned! He answered saying "she will be bed ridden, unable to do anything for her. Her injuries are two severe." Hearing that, Ann passed out! The Doctor told the family that he would return after each procedure, and let us know how things were going. The doctor attended her on the spot. She came back around within thirty seconds.

He told us that he was sending her something to help relax her. The same man that gave me the pills gave her the same two small white pills. After delivering the baby, the doctor came back and told us the baby was dead. We were sad, but we still prayed for a miracle for Tina. Soon after that, the doctor came back and told us she was gone. All I heard was loud cries from the family. I am sure that almost every family member was there. Some waited outside but all of Ann's sisters and brothers were in the waiting area to support her. Before we left. A nurse brought us a plastic bag with her clothing. For some reason, my favorite blue pantsuit was gone and I did not care. They had cut it off of her when she first arrived at the emergency room.

At the funeral, I refused to view the body because I wanted to remember her as she was before. Ann visited her grave every day for at least a year, but gradually slowed her visits after we kept after her to do so. She would never learn to accept it that way, but we knew that she would never get over it fully. When a mother loses a child, it leaves a void that can never be filled. Even

after the funeral, I wondered about her. Did she know that we were there? Did she know how much we loved and missed her? Was she alright in general?
If I suffered over her death, I could imagine what Ann was feeling. After a month, I still needed the answer to those questions and I went to our pastor. He prayed with me and told me to ask God to give you confirmation. One night as I slept, I dreamed that I was sitting on a log in the woods. She came walking up to me with the biggest smile, and acting just as silly as she did when she was alive. As she approached, I began to tell her things that had happened since she died. I noticed that she was there but I could see right through her.

Then I noticed that everything that I was telling her she would say, "yea, I know"! I asked the question, "How do you know"? She said, "girl, just because I am dead does not mean I don't know what is going on". She smiled and faded away gradually. When I awoke, I knew it had to be a dream that seemed so

much like reality. I was in my bed, not sitting on a log in the woods, but I had my confirmation. She was ok! Ann eventually married again, and had two sons by Charles. He was truly a ladies man who had a baby by another woman as well. If his car was broken, he would stand next to the road and his women would pick him up. It did not matter if Ann was looking, he did it anyway. She finally divorced him and has never remarried. She dated one man for thirty years, made his breakfast every morning, and his dinner at night. He spent the night every night, but never left clothes or any of his belongings there.

After thirty years, he walked out on her and never looked back. She was distraught and never understood fully why he changed so drastically, almost overnight. We had told her that she was giving him her good years and if he had not married her after ten years, he more than likely would not ever marry her. Her response to that was," a half of man is better than none at all"! I never addressed it again. We were sisters, but our mindset was so different. She is now seventy six years old and realizes that she wasted all of the good years she had left, chasing a dream! As my marriage to Samuel progressed into its second year, I began to notice his wandering eyes.

I let it go on for a while, but finally called his attention to the fact that I was noticing how he looked at other women. We were getting ready for vacation when we got a call that my brother George and nephew Harry had been in an accident in Tulsa, Oklahoma, and both were in critical condition. My mother and my sister Nadelle, were both hysterical when they heard about the accident. We had to go immediately! Sam had just purchased me a new luxury Cadillac, so we put it on the road. Sam was in business for himself and could not go with me and my family to Tulsa.

He stayed behind and played with my girlfriend "Nettie," and God knows who else in my absence. We traveled back and forth between Arkansas and Tulsa for three months until both the boys were recovered, or at least able to return home. When I was home, I watched as Nettie placed herself in Sam's path every chance she got.

I still said nothing! When I was in town, Sam and I still attended the couples' get-togethers. Nettie drooled over Sam and the things he did for me. She and her husband were a part of our little weekend house party group, but she spent more time trying to make herself available to my husband, than anything else all night. He never initiated any kind of play at her in my presence, but every time he would go to the liquor store, grocery store, or anywhere, she wanted to go. Her words would always be, "Sam let me ride with you, I need to check something out." Everyone in the group noticed and some called it to my attention, thinking that I could not see what was happening for myself. She was the type that wanted everybody's man but her own.

I never said a word to her, but I told him, if he could be interested in something that had functioned just like a door knob, have at it! He wanted to know what that meant, and I politely told him, "Everybody has had a turn!" He laughed until tears just rolled out of his eyes. I had no doubt that he would have sex with her, because before it was over, I found out what I had believed ever since we first became intimate. He was addicted to sex, and wherever he could get it, he would. As time passed, there were other incidents that occurred with other women. Some, I had no doubt because I caught him in the hotel with one of them, just three years into the marriage. That was the turning point in our marriage, and it was over very soon thereafter. I loved him, and it hurt, but I have never hurt to the extent that I did when Fred and I separated. Once you hurt that way, you never hurt to that same degree again.

I think Nettie was more disappointed than I was when I caught Samuel in the hotel with my brother's girlfriend. You know how you can just see it in someone's face; Nettie was fit to be tied! When I was sure that I had the strength to walk away and not look back, I did just that. The marriage was good! It could have been wonderful, and although he cheated, I knew he loved me without a doubt. The sexual addiction would have caused me to have to endure too much over a period of years, and I was not willing to do it. Cheating was on my checklist, and it was time to go. After three years of marriage, I filed for divorce and upon it being granted, I quit my job, rented my house to Sam, and moved approximately ninety miles away, to pick up the pieces from yet another failed marriage.

It was about six months after Sam and I married that I discovered that he was not paying into social security for himself. So many times, I urged him to start paying so that he would have something to retire on. He always said he would, but never did. I had him write social security to get an estimate of what he would receive if he became disabled that same year. We found out that he had not paid enough quarters to be eligible. I hit the ceiling because, it meant that I would be stuck taking care of him in our old age. Sam was living for right now, and the money that he should have been paying into social security was too much for him to sacrifice.

He needed it to be Mr Big Stuff! He made good money, but he spent every dime on me and living the fast life. Was I going to take care of him in his old age? I didn't think so! I was finished with getting caught in the crossfire with his affairs. I felt that had I not gone away, I just might have gotten into trouble. He was not worth my life, my getting in trouble with the law, or the sacrifice of not being with my son. I had to go, and Nettie or anyone else could be the clean-up woman in Sam's life.

I relate painful experiences to that of a scratched record. In the 60s, our music was played on 45 and 33 speed vinyl records, followed by eight-track tapes, cassette tapes, and now CDs. Records had to be handled ever so gently in order not to scratch them. If one happened to get a scratch, each time the needle on the phonograph (record player) reached the scratched spot; it would skip, leaving out a word or two. The scratches on those records could not be repaired and is relative to pain from a broken heart. To be remorseful does not heal pain, but it does have a somewhat positive effect on the individual you hurt when you offer your sincere apology. I wanted a whole new start, with new people. I could not see Linda passing by with the baby, nor could I see Nettie drooling over Sam. I could not see the disappointment in Jimmy's eyes when I glanced over at him in church.

Once and for all, I was going to have my son to myself, and I would be a good mother. I had purchased a cocker-poo puppy, (half-cocker spaniel and half poodle) and named her Fritz. She was white and as fluffy as a kitten. Everyone said she looked more like a cat than a dog, so I named her Fritz, after "Fritz the cat"! I would leave her at Mamas with Bryan until I was ready to bring them both home with me. He would come at the end of the school year. His homework was getting to be too much for Mama and Daddy to help him with. Mama completed ninth grade and Daddy finished seventh grade.

Somebody Should Have Told ME!

Chapter Five

When I visited Bryan, I would see Sam standing underneath the carport or doing something outside, especially if he saw my car at Mamas. He would find something to keep himself busy outside until I would leave going back to Monroe. I would still attend the Sunday family gathering. One Sunday in early February, it was cold, in the thirty degree range, I answered Mama's phone, and it was Sam. He said he needed to see me, so I went to the house I once called home to see what was so important. He asked me to come home and told me how much he missed me! He offered what I knew to be empty promises that he would do so much better. I told him that I missed him as well, but I could not come back home. He should have done better before I left, and I would never have gone away.

I told him to move on with his life. After that, he seldom would be home, and the rumors of him, Nettie and his other women were flying high. In April, Sam and I talked again. I told him that I had heard that he was keeping company with the old doorknob. He laughed! I was reminded of the way he smiled at me that first day I saw him at my door. He said, "Well, I will tell you like this, when you can't ride in a Rolls Royce, you settle for a Chevrolet." And so, this Rolls Royce left him to continue riding in that Chevrolet. Nettie was one of those country women, totally uneducated, but worked all of her life on a decent plant job. She now has an unexpected dependent.

Too bad she did not do her homework! Every time Sam and I see each other, he tells me how he wish things had turned out differently, and that he loves me still after all of these years. We laugh and talk just like old friends with a past. I hold no animosity toward Sam, but, I do smile when I think about how Nettie lost at her own game. Having allowed Bryan to remain in school until summer break, I would move him away with me in early June. Having resigned from my job in December, I looked for work immediately. Within one week, I found a job working with adults who were getting their (GED'S) general education diplomas.

Each session was twelve weeks long, and then we had an informal, but nice graduation celebration in their honor. I worked there for eight months, finding it to be quite rewarding. I still had the desire to go back to the public school system, so I applied for a position even though there are seldom any openings midyears; I waited! It was wonderful to see the joy on the faces of the students that received their diplomas. They ranged from ages twenty-two to fifty years old. Some were even older than me, and I made some friends, some of whom I am still in touch with today. Being adults, they had the stresses of caring for families. Sometimes it became a little overwhelming for them.

I have gone to the homes of some of my students after work, to see why they did not come to school. According to the director, our dropout rate was 20 percent, and that needed to change. Charlotte, a student whom I took particular interest in, was just doing the dishes from supper when I knocked on her door. I did not have a phone number in her file to inform her that I wanted to drop by her house. I had gotten her address from the files and decided to give her a visit. One of her six children came to the door. Charlotte was yelling from the kitchen, "Who is that?" The child told her, "It's the lady from your school." I had met her children when we had our company picnic during the summer. They were beautiful children, and so very well mannered.

She was raising them by herself, and I had no doubt, it had been hard. I was still standing in the living room when she peeped around the corner. "Hey, she said, what are you doing here"? "Well, I just stopped by to see why you didn't come to class today." Charlotte finished drying her hands with the towel she brought from the kitchen, and she sat on the sofa. "Have a seat, please," she said nervously. "I just can't do it anymore, Savanah," she said as her eyes watered. "I have too much pressure on me right now." She went on to tell me how the children's father did not help her enough.

She wanted to get her diploma, so she could get a better job. She was barely making ends meet, when the landlord went up on her rent by sixty dollars. "I figure if I quit school, I can at least save money and gas." We talked for about an hour, and she shared so much with me. I had an idea that things were hard for her, but I had no idea the depth. Now I had to convince her that dropping out was not the answer. Quitting school now would prove to be her biggest setback. I helped her to see that she was over half-finished, and to not finish the rest would make her the failure that she was describing to me. I told her she was not a failure because failures don't try to do anything about their situations. She had dropped out of high school after getting pregnant and continued having babies until she had six. She and her ex-husband lived together off and on through pregnancies.

When I was leaving her house, it was almost dark, but she would continue school the next morning. I saw an older man replacing a fence post for the same property, and I wondered if by chance he was the landlord. I got in the car and started it, but something within me kept telling me, "You need to ask." I turned the key back to off, went over to the gentleman, unsure of what I was going to say. He started talking to me before I made it over to him. "You having car trouble?" the man asked. That gave me some confidence that at least he was friendly. I then said, "Looks like you know what you are doing." "Yep," he said, "when you got rent houses you have to learn to do your own work, or you'll go bankrupt mighty quickly! "Oh, so you have several rent houses?" I asked. "Yea, I have about fifteen of them," the gentleman replied. "My goodness, I know that keeps you busy," I said as I walked closer with my hand out to shake his.

He immediately shook my hand saying, "It's been a while since I was close to a young woman as pretty as you." He continued, "I'm seventy years old, and I don't complain because in my day, if a gal wasn't pretty, I paid 'em no mind. Now, I'm so old and wrinkled, they don't pay me any mind." He laughed a big hearty laugh and I laughed along with him. I thanked him for the compliment and said, "You know I really have something I need to talk to you about." He seemed a little shocked, as he leaned the tool against the fence and gave me his undivided attention. "My name is Savanah, and I teach over at the Opportunities Industrialization Center Incorporated (OIC)," I said, still smiling.

He introduced himself as Alvin Hicks. I continued, "Charlotte is enrolled in our program to get her GED. I know that you are aware that she has all those little ones in there. I am here today trying to get her to continue in the program." "Yes, she needs to go on and get that piece of paper," Mr. Hicks agreed. "She is better than half—way finished, with about four weeks to go," I told him, "and we place them on jobs upon completion."

"Man, you can't beat that," he responded. "She was going to quit because you went up on the rent, and she can't afford any more money going out of her household right now," I told him. "I wanted to ask you if you can work with her for at least six months, allowing her to finish school, get a job, and get a few paychecks in her pocket before you actually go up on the rent," I said reluctantly.

I frowned as I asked, not knowing what kind of response I would get to that question. Mr. Hicks looked at me for a few seconds, as if he could not believe what he was hearing. I held my breath, because I had just asked this man for three hundred sixty dollars over a six-month period. He took off his cap, scratched his head and when he began speaking, he said, "Well, I usually don't do things like that, because once you start doing things like that, people take advantage of you. In this case, I am going to delay adding the sixty dollars to her rent, and I am going to deduct an extra forty. This should help her quite a bit, but after six months, I am going to add the forty dollars back, plus the sixty."

That sounded like music to my ear! The man had given up not just three hundred sixty dollars, but six hundred dollars over a six-month period. I could not believe my ears were hearing him correctly. "Mr. Hicks, I thank you so much, I said as I fought back the tears. You have helped Charlotte even more than I could have imagined before I walked up to you. You are a good man with a precious heart, and I thank you so very much!" "Well," he said, "old Charlotte is a good girl, and she is raising all of those little ones by herself. You know, last night when I was thinking about her rent, I kind of felt guilty about raising up the rent. When you asked me to help, it seemed like God was acting through you. Yep, that is the right thing to do," he said as he reached for his tool to finish his work."

I just told her the rent was going up, and here you come and talk me into bringing it down," Mr. Hicks said, "now ain't that something. You hurry up and leave; you must be one of them smooth talkers!" He laughed! "I am gone, and thank you again," I said. Now Charlotte could complete the class with less worry. I asked Mr. Hicks if he would deliver the news to Charlotte before he went home for the night.

He said that he would, and I told him how much I appreciated his helping. We said good night, and I went back to my apartment to prepare for the next school day, feeling a renewed belief in humanity! The next morning, when Charlotte came into class, her smile lit the room. She came straight to me and hugged me and thanked me for talking to the landlord. I didn't want him to tell her I had anything to do with it. Still, it felt good that I was able to help. Charlotte sailed through the following weeks happier than I had seen her during the first few weeks of class. She was five years older than me, but you would have thought I was her big sister. After graduation, I moved to her side of town, and we became really good friends. I got to know her children better and to this day, thirty years later, I am their aunt.

Unfortunately, Charlotte has become quite ill, and we are praying for her recovery. I miss our long talks on the phone and our visits every now and then. She thought that I had all the answers even when I told her I had none. She never believed me when I told her that I was a blind woman, feeling my way through life. Two of Charlotte's children presently live in Houston, Texas, near me, and we are family still. They come to my house every holiday and some weekends. I believe if I were ill, she would be there for my children, just like I try to be there for hers. It was only after I got my third divorce and started to date again that we allowed any distance between us. Yet we could always find each other when either of us had a problem.

In June, I received a call from the city school system telling me to come and interview for a teaching position. I was interviewed and got the job. I held my last graduation celebration for my adult students, and was determined to stay with that last class until they all had their GEDs. They received their GEDs on Friday evening, and I began my new job the following Monday. The first week was teacher preparation days, and I had to get back into the swing of working with children. As much as I enjoyed my adults, I was happy to be back with children again. Of course the pay was better, and I welcomed the new salary. Living in a town where you have no friends can get quite lonely. One of the first people that I met was a guy named Floyd Stegall.

He owned the corner store where I picked up my cigarettes. I was looking for cookies to eat with some ice cream that I had at home. He suggested that I try these new cookies that he had just got in. I am not a stickler for trying new things, so I passed on that suggestion and purchased chocolate chip because they were my all-time favorites. Once I paid for the chocolate chips, I went to the magazine rack to see if there was anything interesting. I did not find anything, so I picked up my bag and went home.

Late on a Saturday night, I decided to eat some ice cream while I watched a movie. Bryan did not come that weekend because he wanted to go with Mama and Daddy to the catfish dinner at the church. I was feeling a little lonely and sorry for myself and my baby. Mama would do anything to entice him to stay there. I missed him being with me! Even next door, I had access to him at all times. I would see him on Sunday, because I did not miss Sunday dinners at Mamas. I went to my bag to get the chocolate chips. What I pulled out were not chocolate chips, they were the macaroon cookies he had suggested I try. Oh my God, I must have put the cookies in my sack by mistake.

I wondered if Floyd had noticed, and thought I was a thief. I did not know what to do. I didn't go back into the store for several days. I could not go in smiling as usual, buy cigarettes and go, because if he knew I took the cookies, what would he think of me, even if he did not press charges? It was about to worry me to death! One night that same week, I went back into the store with the cookies in the same bag, and told him that I accidentally put the cookies in the bag when he was trying to get me to buy them. I told him that I wanted to return them to him.

He laughed really loud and could not stop. There were no customers in the store, and he continued to laugh until tears rolled down his face. Confused, I asked him what was so funny! When he composed himself, he said, he put the cookies in the bag for me to try. I was so relieved, yet mad, because I had spent too much time worrying about these cookies and what he would think of me for taking them. "There is one thing for sure, Savanah, you are an honest woman." Once I tasted the cookies, they were wonderful. I alternated between the macaroon and the chocolate chip from then on.

We needed cookies for a party we were having at work, and I was assigned to bring them. I went by the store to see what kind of deal he would give me if I purchased a whole case. I picked up grocery for myself, as well as the balloons that Jackie ordered because she had to attend a funeral. Since the macaroon and the chocolate chip were the same price, I wanted to buy a case with half macaroon and half chocolate chip. "Not only are you honest but you are thrifty," he said. Once I told him they were for our students' party, he gave us the whole case of cookies free of charge. He carried the case of cookies to my tiny Volkswagen, but the balloons and the grocery were all that would fit.

I told him that I would go empty the car and come back for the cookies. He insisted that he bring the cookies to me in an hour when his employee relieved him. I gave him the address and he delivered the cookies to my apartment. Once inside with the cookies, he looked around and said, "You know, I have been in a couple of the apartments on the other side, but these are much bigger. Is this a one-bedroom?" "No," I said, "the ones on this side are all two and three bedrooms, mine is a two-bedroom." "What do you need with all of this room for little old you? "Floyd said looking surprised. "I have a son who visits me on most weekends, and as soon as school is out, he will be coming here to live with me." "School should be already out shouldn't it?" he asked. "Yes," I replied, "the kids in Arkansas had days to make up from the winter snow.

In fact, I should be picking him up next weekend." "Oh, I didn't know," Floyd said, "you look like you never had a child, I mean look at you, I don't mean to be fresh, but your stomach is as flat as a board." I smiled, a little flattered, "Looks are deceiving you know." It became quite awkward when he could not find anything else to talk about, and neither could I. "Well, you have a nice day. I will see you the next time you come into the store." "OK, Thanks" I said, and he was gone.

The next time I visited the store, Floyd was just getting off of his motorcycle, to relieve his employee whom I found out was his nephew. It was such a beautiful blue bike matching the color of the corvette he drove. "I didn't know you had a bike," I said, as I entered the store. "Yea, in fact, it is brand new. I just picked it up today, he said proudly! Maybe you can go for a ride with me when I go to Greenville, Mississippi, this weekend." "Oh, I don't know, I am kind of scared of those things," I said truthfully.

We talked about the bike while I shopped, and upon paying for my items, he walked out with me to show me certain features about it. "Will you ride with me this weekend?" "Oh, I don't think so, that is too far to ride on a bike," I said. "No," Floyd said, "people do it all the time, so what do you say?" "No, I'll take a rain check on that one until you get use to it and have fully mastered your new toy." He wanted me to know that this was not his first bike, so I was to think about riding with him another time. "I will do just that," I said, "think about it."

Two weeks later, I was parking to go into my apartment, when this motorcycle came cruising through the parking area. I heard it, but did not have my mind on Floyd or his motorcycle, at 5:30p.m, on Thursday evening. I gathered my books and when I lifted my head, he was parked right in front of my car. "I saw you when you turned toward home and decided to follow you." "Where are you going?" I asked as I smiled. "I was looking for a place to get out of the cold," he said smiling back at me. "You want coffee?" I asked. "Sounds like a winner to me," he said. It was at least 85 degrees outside, but the joke was cute!

We went into my apartment, and I put my books away and put on the coffee. We sat there and laughed and talked about everything under the sun it seemed. I really enjoyed his company but it was now 8:30p.m, and I had to go to work the next day. I ended our gathering for the night and escorted him outside. In June when school was out, I went to get Bryan and moved him with me. Mama was giving me the cold shoulder, but I was going to take my baby with me, no matter what. When we were all packed and ready to leave, I kissed Mama on the forehead and told her not to worry; I was going to take good care of Bryan. He was with me four days, when I got a call from Ann. "Savanah, Mama is sick, and it is all because you took Bryan. We took her to the hospital last night."

"Ann you have five kids, give Mama one of them, I want my "one" baby to be with me! What is the doctor saying about Mama?" I asked. They are running test on her now, I guess we will know more tomorrow," she said. I was fit to be tied! Mama and I have fought over this baby all of his life, but I was not going to give this time. Mama was not going to get Daddy to drive ninety miles too many times. Bryan would be going to visit them on weekends, and I would gladly take him on Fridays. He would come back with me on Sundays when I went to Sunday dinners. I stayed up late ironing all of Bryan's clothes and hanging them in the closet. His drawers were organized, and I was so optimistic about our future. I didn't hear anything else that day, but Bryan and I would go to visit mama at the hospital tomorrow.

We got up the next morning getting ready to go visit Mama. Bryan always took his baths at night before bed, so all he had to do was wash his face, brush his teeth, comb his hair, and make his bed. The phone rang and I answered. "Savanah, now listen!" It was Daddy's voice on the other end. "Your Mama has helped raise that boy, and she is attached to him. You need to bring that boy back here now! Are you trying to kill your Mama?" "Daddy," I said, "No! I love you and Mama, you know that, but it started out that she was gonna keep him until I graduated.

I graduated years ago, and we are still fighting over him. He is my baby, and you and Mama has taken him away from me for the last time!" "The boy is used to this place, here with us," Daddy argued. "He is happy here too! Daddy, I am his mother. You didn't give away any of us, but she wants my one! Mama is not going to die Daddy, so no!" I heard the phone click, "Daddy! Daddy!" I repeated! He hung the phone up in my face. I called him right back, and he did not answer. He was not out of the house that quick. I cried and cried! Soon Bryan was standing in front of me. "Mommy what is wrong, Mamo wants me to come back?" "Yea, baby," I said as I continued to cry. "You want me to stay with you don't you, Mommy." I shook my head yes, and eventually spoke, "Yea, more than anything in the world! Mama is in the hospital, and Daddy said she is sick because I took you away.

" His little eyes watered up and he looked so confused. "I don't want her to be sick, Mommy, do you?" he asked. "No, baby, she is my mother, and I love her." "You are my mother and I love you too Mama," he said as I pulled him close and hugged him tight. "I know, baby, and I love you more than anything in this world!" "I know you love me Mommy, but will you get sick if I go back and stay with Mamo until she is better?" "No, baby, is that what you wanna do?" "I guess, because I don't want Mamo to die," he said as his little voice trembled! I was so upset and angry at Mama for putting me through this. I wanted my baby with me so badly and I never expected to have to fight my own mother for my child. I knew she loved him, but I knew, that she knew, there was no right in what she was doing! I packed his things and went to the hospital. In the car, I told Bryan, that I was not going to stay at the hospital, but I was taking him to see Mama there. Mama would see to Daddy taking him home. I had stopped and got food for him, because we did not have breakfast after all of the confusion.

Once we arrived at the hospital, I pulled both luggages to the elevator, and proceeded to the fourth floor. Bryan and I walked over to Mama's room and got his entire luggage situated out of the flow of traffic. I got him set up to eating his food! Since I didn't say anything to Mama, she said nothing to me. I kissed Bryan and told him that I would pick him up every weekend, no exceptions. I then walked over to the bed and said, "You win again, Mama." If she was sick, she sure didn't look like it. She did not part her lips! I turned and walked out of the room, but fell apart in the elevator.

It seemed that the car drove itself all of those miles back to the apartment. I did not remember anything about the drive back. I sat in the car wondering what I did to deserve such treatment. What would have happened had I not had a baby for her to take? I undressed and crawled up under the covers, feeling so alone. First, I lost his dad, and Mama is taking my son. I cried myself to sleep and upon waking, realizing that I had not had a morsel in my mouth all day, I got up to fix a sandwich. I made myself get into the shower, which is always refreshing. After I finished showering, I put on a fresh gown and started to grade papers from Friday's test at school.

There came a knock on my door. "Who's there," I asked. "It's Floyd," the voice from the other side of the door said. As I ran to get my robe, I yelled, "Just a minute." I slipped on my robe, ran by the mirror to check my face, eyes, and hair, and opened the door. "Hi," I said puzzled as to why he was there. Floyd said, "I know I should have called, but I did not have your number. Is everything OK?" "Yea, why do you ask?" I exclaimed. "Well I have been a little disturbed ever since I saw you this evening, and I just had to come to see if you were all right. You know I know you don't have family here." Still puzzled, I said, "You saw me today." "Yes," Floyd said, "you were driving down Chadwick. I was standing next to the street.

I saw you approaching the light and waved my hand almost right in front of your car. I did not get your attention and you looked like you were in a trance or intoxicated or something. When the car almost hit you, I cringed; sure that it was going to be a collision." I am sure I looked dumfounded, because I did not remember any of that. "Maybe I am losing it, I don't know what is wrong with me," I was crying hysterically. Floyd stepped inside and closed the door behind him. He sat me on the sofa, and let me get my cry out. "I don't know what to do, I want to hold you, but I don't want to put you in an even more awkward position." "It's OK," I told him. "I have been upset all day long. I went to get my son, and brought him here, set up his room, ironed his clothes, and today. I had to take him back. He was only here four days and he is gone back!"

"Why?" he asked. "Because my mama wants him to stay with her," and my tears started all over again. I don't know how I ended up in his arms, but I was there. He had sturdiness about his body that made you feel as though you could lean as hard as you needed too. We sat there on the sofa for two hours, but he would not let me talk about me. I wanted to tell him why I was such a wreck. We kissed while the tears were flowing and continued after they stopped. He took me into the bedroom and told me he was going back into the living area while I disrobed and crawled into bed. "Rest assured that I will not bother you in any way, but you don't need to be alone right now."

I trusted him and followed his instructions. When he came back to the room, he turned the lights out and crawled onto the bed beside me fully clothed. "Now, tell me everything you feel comfortable enough to tell me, and I will listen." I poured my heart out in a cup, and he drank it all. Before the night was over, he knew much of my life history. We did not make love, nor did he try in any way. He lay silent, for the most part, just being my sounding board. But he was right there in the bed with me listening the whole time. When I cried, he held me, when I laughed, he laughed with me. When I woke the next morning, he was gone, but a note lay in his spot.

It read:
Thank you for sharing your life with me, and know that there is a light at the end of the tunnel. I listened when you talked, held you when you cried, and while you slept I watched you and listened to you breathe. You are an amazing woman, Savanah, and you will find your way. I had to go, but I want to return again, to share my story with you. You know where to find me!
Floyd

I did not stop by the store for a full week, but when I did, I could see how pleased he was. Through the big glass windows, I could see him smiling. I walked in, and before I could get to the counter, he met me there. He hugged me and I hugged him, and it felt really good. "Who is running this place," I said playfully. "'Tis me, me lady," he said. I told him that I was sorry about the other night, and he insisted that it was his pleasure. He wanted to know if I found his note. I told him "yes"! Then, he wanted to know, how I was now, since he had not seen me in so many days. I told him I was better. I paid for my items and started to leave when he said, "Now, when is it my turn to tell you my story?" "You make the call," I said, "and let me know so that we can arrange it."

"I will do just that," he said. "Ohh!" he said as I was going through the door. "Give me your phone number so that I can call first." I gave him my number and was on my way. I made it a point to talk to Bryan every day so that I could monitor his feelings about everything. He seemed to be fine, but I knew he needed to go to school there with me so I could see that his academics were up to par. His report cards showed that he needed some help. He made Bs and Cs, and that just was not acceptable. Mama was being selfish, and Bryan was paying the cost for it. I was his mama, and I couldn't do anything about it.

Much later in life, I realized that I had been angry for a long time, and it began during my childhood. Once I was much older and had sessions with a psychiatrist she told me almost exactly the same thing. I suppose that is why it took me so long to write this book. I started from the beginning, and each time I tried to verbalize the difficult times in my life, many times I had to stop. I stopped for two weeks, a month, and even up to three months. I knew I needed to finish this book, so when I felt strong enough to tackle it again, I would go right back to my computer until the next difficult point.

Floyd called and wanted his turn on Friday night. I had to say no, because I was going to get my son on Friday. I wanted to give him my undivided attention all weekend. I told Floyd to come on Tuesday instead. I would use Monday night to rest from what I knew was going to be an exhausting weekend. I was taking Bryan to the zoo on Saturday, and we would leave a little early-on Sunday to go to our family church for Friends and Family Day. I came back to my apartment soon after the family dinner and rested. I felt close to my son and much better this Sunday evening than last.

On Tuesday, I allowed Floyd to come over, and I listened to his story. Man, he had a story, one that made mine look like a cake walk. He was sexually abused from age eight until he was fourteen. Since this is my story, I will not divulge details of his story. Yet we became real friends after that day! I don't know why Floyd decided to tell me his story, maybe because he felt that we connected in some way. Both stories were sad, but different.

He became emotional as he told me his story, and it was my turn to hold him when he cried, listen when he talked, and kiss him when he was finished! Floyd made love to me, I made love to him, and we made love to each other. Floyd and I never talked sex, it just happened. We simply became filled with passion. I furnished the condom! He was trying to tell me something, but I stopped him. Nothing was more important to me at the moment, but the heat of that moment. After sex, we just laid there! Our bodies intertwined, as if descending from the highest peak. Once we were on earth again, Floyd said, "That was wonderful!" "Yes, it was wonderful!" I said. I turned my back and his body mimicked my body curves from behind me. We drifted off to sleep, and when I woke, once again, he was gone. Instantly, I felt for the note, and it was there! I smiled as I turned on the lamp beside the bed.

It read:
Savanah, Thank you for listening to my story! I have never shared it with anyone other than my parents and the police at the time of the last occurrence. You have to be special! I will call when I think you are awake. I would be disappointed if you did not have sweet dreams.
Floyd

We saw each other at least twice each week and sometimes three times. He finally got me on the motorcycle and we rode for miles. It was Sunday evening, a beautiful day! I left directly after dinner at Mama's and went back for the ride. After ten minutes of riding behind Floyd, I was comfortable. He had packed sandwiches, and we stopped at one of the state parks. He spread a blanket, and we ate the sandwiches, drank lemonade, and laughed a lot. He was tastefully comical, and I needed that.

Suddenly, Floyd's face turned somber and his eyes saddened a bit. He turned his head in an effort to keep me from seeing, but it was too late. "What is wrong? We are having a great time and you are going to ruin it for yourself!"
"No, I am ruining it for you," he said. "You are not ruining anything for me. What do you mean?" I asked. "Savanah, I have wanted to tell you something since the first time we made love. I tried to tell you before we made love, but you stopped me. I should have taken control and told you before I ever made love to you," he said. "Told me what, Floyd?" He looked at me and said, "I am married!" "My goodness Floyd, huh? You are married? Oh,oh my!" Floyd is crying now saying, "I am so sorry." Remembering what he had been through, now I am crying, knowing what I have been through! I got up off of the blanket, and told Floyd I would be right back.

He looked as if he did not believe me, so I touched his hair and told him, "I will be right back, I promise; I just want to clear my head a bit. He shook his head

OK, and I walked all the way to the other end of the park. I could not see Floyd anymore. I sat down on a bench to think. Floyd was a good person, and he did nothing to me that I did not want! I guess in some small way, I wondered if there was a future in our friendship, but the thought just came to a screeching halt. At that very moment, I smelled his cologne as if some way it had drifted through the air and headed straight to my nostrils. I had been down there so long that the sun was setting. Nobody was in that part of the park. It kind of reminded me of being in my secret place. The bench was right next to the woods, and it was quiet and peaceful. I needed to get back to Floyd, so he would not think I had run away. I jumped up and began the long hike back across the park to join Floyd.

As I lifted my head and looked in that direction, I saw Floyd sitting with his back up against a tree. He was watching me from not very far away. When I saw him, I smiled and walked over to him, as he rose to his feet. I put my arms around his neck and hugged him tight. "We're friends and we can remain friends, just friends," I told him! "We can do this, can't we Floyd?" I asked. His reply was "Yes, we can sure as hell try." We hugged again and walked back to the bike with our arms around each other. He helped me get my helmet on just right, and I planted myself behind him on the motorcycle. The ride back was a little quiet, but we arrived back at my apartment in one piece. I climbed off the back of the cycle, using his shoulder for balance, and thanked him for the ride. As I turned to walk into my first floor apartment, Floyd reached for my hand that still rested on his shoulder.

I turned to him, "Are you OK," he asked. I smiled and said, "As OK as I can be, but it's alright, we can do this." As he drove away, I listened to the sound of his bike until it was no more. I went inside, showered, got ready for bed, and watched television until I fell asleep. We did not see each other the entire week. He did not call, and I did not go by the store. Two weeks passed, and I was better. I did not want to interfere with his marriage, as others had interfered with mine so many times.

On the third week, I decided to bring Fritz home to my apartment. I had left her with Bryan, but he wanted me to take her, so that I would not be lonely. Now that it was definite that Bryan was not coming to live with me, I needed her. I would spend some time with Charlotte, but as much as we liked each other, we were still very different. She had her kids' right there, and although Bryan would be with us most weekends, through the week, I felt lonely for him. Her kids played and squabbled, and Mama would not let mine stay to play and squabble with them. The third week, on a Tuesday, Floyd stopped by. Fritz was all over him, and he was all over Fritz. I had no idea that Floyd was such a dog lover.

It turned out that he owned a dog. We sat and talked briefly, While Fritz sat in his lap. Our conversation was just small talk, and nothing was mentioned about the two of us. As he left, we exchanged a quick hug, and I closed the door. I settled in for the evening knowing that this was a friendship that was doable. We both had problems, and we consoled each other, and that was that.

I stayed completely clear of the store, but Floyd would always find a way to drop in. Now with Fritz there, he would drop by, bring her all kinds of snacks. He even took her for rides in the Corvette from time to time. She quickly got to the point that she recognized both the motorcycle and the Corvette. If he was near, before I would hear his car or motorcycle she would stop whatever she was doing and listen. She then would run all over the house like a crazy dog. She would stop again as if to confirm that he really was coming, then start running again. If he was in the Corvette, she would stop when it pulled into my visitor's parking spot. Once he turned the motor off, she would listen for the lights to fold themselves in and click into place. The race would be on again until he knocked on the door. Once I opened the door, she would already have a running start and jump in the air just in time for him to catch her.

I had never seen such a display of affection between animal and man. I would laugh in amazement, and he would say, "She knows who her daddy is!"
While still holding his daughter, Fritz, he went into his top shirt pocket and handed me a small box. I opened it, and it was a beautiful fashionable ring in the shape of a love knot. "Is this mine?" I asked. "Yeah, it's just a little something I found lying around and thought you might like it." Surprised, I just stood there and looked at it. "Close the door, and while you're at it, close your mouth," he said while laughing. "Is this really mine?" I asked doubtingly. "Yes,

but if you don't want it give it back." he said, as he advanced toward me reaching for it. "No!

Indian-giver," I tucked it behind me as I continued to laugh from the statement he made about my closing my mouth. I thanked him for the ring and thought it extremely nice but totally unexpected. After Floyd left, I rearranged my furniture so that Fritz could have access to the window without getting onto the back of the sofa. Several weeks later, I came in from school, and she did not come to the window. I thought it strange, but it was not particularly alarming. I turned the key and walked in. Fritz was lying on the floor, acting as if she was having a seizure or something. I dropped everything and went to her. She just laid there gagging almost lifeless. I could see where she had gone into the trash in the kitchen, but she was in the living area.

"What is wrong Fritz?" I cried. I tried to pick her up to take her to the veterinarian, but she acted as if I was hurting her. I ran to the phone and called Floyd, he would know what to do. When he answered the phone at the store, I was hysterical. "Fritz is dying," I screamed, "come help me!" His store was just at the corner, so he did not bother driving; he locked the store and ran to my apartment. He examined Fritz, and when he tried to pick her up, she reacted the same as she had with me. He looked around and saw the trash on the floor. "She is choking!" he said. He opened her mouth wide and ran his finger down her throat, and to my astonishment, out popped a chicken bone.

He told me to get the electric fan and turn it on her. Fritz was responding, but still lay there, trying to get enough air to breathe well. "She is going to be all right!" he said. You left chicken bones in the trash, and she wanted them, he scowled at me. "But she was not hungry; I left her food in her bowl!" I cried. He didn't say another word until she was moving her tail. "Get your keys and let's take her to the vet," he said! He called his nephew and told him to hurry down to the store and stay there until he returned. I got my keys and he drove us to the vet. She lay in my lap looking at me through sad eyes! She was still scared, and I could feel her trembling. At the vet's office, they took her back and said that we could come back there after a while.

Floyd told them, he had taken a chicken bone from her throat, and she seemed to be getting better now that she could breathe.

I sat there crying feeling like an unfit mother, the way Floyd had chastised me. "Savanah," he said, "I'm sorry for coming down on you so hard, but it is important that you keep things out of Fritz's reach! Dogs are like children, they don't know what is best for them. She could smell the chicken bones in the trash, and all dogs love bones." "Yeah," I said, "but she has never done that before, and because she has never bothered the trash before, I didn't think she would. She never did it at Mama's house either." "Well," he said, "now you know she will, so think for her, and don't put bones of any kind in the trash." "OK, I won't," I said. We had not waited very long when the doctor came out into the waiting area and got us. "She is going to be fine now, her throat is irritated, but I gave her a shot which will help, and I want you to give her this medicine twice daily until it is all gone.

I just gave her something to calm her, so expect her to sleep. She is a lucky little doggy, because she could have died, you know. Let me see her back here in one week." Dr. Spencer shook both our hands and told us to go through those doors to get our doggy. Floyd thanked the doctor, and we proceeded through the doors to get Fritz. Once she saw us, she was all frisky and wagging her tail as if nothing had happened. "There's your mommy and daddy," the attendant said, as we approached. I thought, how ironic; we are reacting like her mom and dad. Oh, how looks can be deceiving! We took Fritz home, and she positioned herself on the sofa between us and fell fast asleep.

I told Floyd how much I appreciated his coming so quickly, and how I realized that Fritz would have died if it were not for him. He smiled and said he was glad that he could be of help. I had a new awareness of the things I put in the trash. Floyd had no children and neither did his wife. I knew they had a dog, and evidently, it is the center of their lives. He never talked about his wife, but I gathered that they both went their separate ways on a daily basis. He called me to check on Fritz the next day, and I did not hear from him the following day, until 9:30pm.

I had settled into my warm bed when Fritz started running her marathon. When I heard the lights lock in place, I got up and opened the door. There was no doubt that Fritz was back to normal. She was all over him as usual. I told him she was her old self again and we sat on the sofa for a while. "I came down pretty hard on you about Fritz didn't I," he said. I laughed. "No problemo!" I said.

I turned the TV on in the living room and made a bag of popcorn for us to eat. I told him about the movie I was watching in the bedroom, and he happened to have been watching the same movie before he came over. After catching him up on the parts he missed, I sat there and started to fall asleep. "You sleepyhead, wake up, I need some company!" he said. A couple of minutes later I dozed again. I woke up to his lips softly planted on mine. I pulled back and sat erect on the sofa. He touched my face ever so gently and pulled me to him. He breathed deeply and kissed me again more aggressively. I did not pull back, I couldn't!

I longed for more, and more I did receive! He fondled and kissed my breast through my robe until it no longer impeded his view or touch. Knowing I should stop him, I whispered, "We shouldn't, let's stop!" I slide off of the sofa, onto the floor, and he was all over me. He kissed my body until I had no will to stop. Just one more time, I thought, "Just one more time, and I will leave this woman's husband alone God, I promise"! There on the floor of my living room, we fulfilled our lust for each other once again.

When it was over, I lay in his arms feeling sexually fulfilled and emotionally torn. He was another woman's husband, and I loved him as if he were my own. I went into the shower for the second time that night, and returned to find him asleep in my bed under the covers. I called his name, and there was no response! I slide into bed and underneath the cover next to him. He snuggled up to me and went to sleep in my curves once again. When the alarm went off at six, I opened my eyes to find him still lying next to me.

"What are you doing still here?" I asked. "I am still here because I want to be here," he responded. "I know it's wrong, but I am falling in love with you, and I don't know how to stop myself," he said. "I know, I said, I know," as I answered his tug by moving myself into his arms. "We are going to talk this evening Floyd, without forgetting about last night or how wonderful it was," I said. Floyd did not want to talk about it. He wanted to let it ride and allow things to work themselves through. That was too dangerous for me, I cared for him so much, but that made him no less married. I had to stop my heart from breaking before the cracks began to show.

I told Floyd that night that I was not going to see him again! I did not want him to call or drop by to check on me or Fritz. He took it harder than I thought, but I knew he would be fine eventually. I told him to bury himself in his marriage, take her to dinner, on vacation, and try to rediscover what he fell in love with, within her. "Is that what you really want me to do," he asked, looking tired and defeated? "That is the way it has to be, Floyd. You are not ready to leave her, now are you?" He did not answer. "No," I said, "the answer is no, but we can't continue this without somebody getting hurt, and chances are more than not, it would be me." "Do I love you? Yes, but at this point, I can let you go. I don't want a scandal! I have to let you go now while I can. If we go any further, I am going to start putting demands on you, and everything will fall apart; our relationship as well as your marriage, if you stay around, and I start putting demands on you.

If we continue this, you had better be prepared to leave her. When I love, I love hard, and I won't take no for an answer if I should want you to leave her. You will want to back out, and I won't let you, so go!" I paused to calm myself! I walked over to him and said, "Man, I am giving you a break here, walk out that door and don't look back." He turned, and walked out of the door. Fritz and I went to Mama's and spent the entire two-weeks of Christmas break there. January would make a full year since I moved away.

Chapter Six

Upon returning home, I had a box in the mail addressed to me with no return address or name. It was a gold bracelet with diamonds. I could not imagine who sent it. Could it be Floyd? I set it on my dresser and every day I looked at it for a whole week. Then, I put it in a drawer and did not wear it. Maybe the culprit would reveal himself, and I could return it. Maybe Floyd thought I would come by the store to see if he sent it. I was not going to ask, because we were doing good, and it was best to let well enough alone. I was starting the year fresh with no man. I sank myself into church activities, asked God's forgiveness and felt really good about releasing Floyd. I didn't go by his store and used an alternate route leaving home and coming. I reflected back over my life, as if watching a movie I had seen before. I had made a mess of things, but I was still so young. I was not ready to give up on having the things I wanted and certainly was still focused on what I thought I needed to make my life complete. I discovered that if I was going to be happy and content I had to do it myself. My next problem was learning how to do it! It took several more mistakes, to learn how to make myself happy. The pursuit of happiness truly can be a chase of a lifetime.

I must have truly been crazy thinking that a man could define my happiness. In late February, a substitute teacher took a long-term assignment teaching Mathematics and worked directly across the hall from my class. He was kind of cute, his mannerism made him more appealing. He had a shyness about him that made him look down to keep from seeing your reaction to things he would say. That shy way of looking down allowed me to see he had the longest eyelashes. Upon noticing it, I thought, Now what does a man need with such beautiful eyelashes, I need those! We would stand at our doors between class changes, which afforded us a few minutes to small talk. As we became more comfortable speaking and joking between classes, his assignment in that room was over. I wondered if I would ever see him again. He would be too shy to ask for my number. I thought about him a few times the following week, but doubted if I would ever see him again.

One day as I stood at my door between classes, Otis, one of the male teachers who I talked to in the teachers' lounge came scampering down the hall. He said,

"Hey, Savanah, are you going to the lounge today?" I thought it strange that he asked, but I just answered, "Yes." He then said, "OK, I have something to tell you. On my preparation period I went to the lounge.

As soon as I walked in, Otis started smiling. "Hey, you know Mathew, the sub that taught in Armstrong's class a couple weeks ago?" "Oh yes, I remember him," I said. "Well, he wants your number and asked me to get it for him." "Ohhh, he did huh!" I said with a smile that I hoped camouflaged my blushing. "Yes," Otis said, "so can I give it to him?" "You and he are both messy," I said playfully. I was quite pleased that he had taken the initiative, even if he had to do it through Otis. After a couple of big laughs and lots of blushing, I told Otis, "Give it to him." I was tickled to death; I didn't think he could just walk away and not look back. Otis already had my number in the teachers' directory, but he did not want to give him the number without my consent.

Mathew had never been married and had no children. I was pleased at that, because most men I knew, twenty-eight to thirty-four years of age, had at least one child, and most of the time an ex-wife. It took him a couple of days to call. I felt that he was building up his nerve. When he did call, I was kind of glad. He was five or six years younger than me and did not have half the battle scars with relationships as I did. I asked him about any girlfriend he might have, but he assured me that he did not have one at the time. We got off to a good start and spent several nights talking on the phone. Our first date was at church. When he asked if he could see me, I told him yes, if he wanted to go to church with me.

I told him where my church was, and when I drove up, he was patiently waiting on the church steps. When he finally started coming around, it did not take very long for him to become comfortable. One day in April, he took me over to meet his favorite cousins and aunt. Because we had not planned to be in there but for a few minutes, I left my wallet on the floor tucked under the front seat. I had maybe four dollars in the wallet, but my driver's license and credit cards were also in it. Evidently, a woman named Venita, who I was told was his ex-girlfriend, had seen us riding together en route to his cousin's and aunt's house.

While we were inside, Venita went into the car and took my wallet; she wanted to find out anything she could about me. She took the wallet with her and called his cousin and told him she had it. Mathew did not know what on earth to do. He just panicked! I was getting ready to call the police, but his cousin, Nick, told me he would go and get it back.

His name was Nick and my brother's name was Nicholas. We called my brother Nick for short and I thought of my brother each time I called Mathews cousins name. I was appalled. But if he could get it back and nothing was missing, I would accept it and let the whole thing go. I then wanted to know what was really going on with him and Venita. "She is just a girl I used to date; I have not dated her in several months now. It is over between us!" he said, "and she knows it." I wasn't quite convinced that was true! His cousin left and we went to my apartment to wait for the wallet. Within an hour, Nick arrived with the wallet, and nothing was missing, but I could tell she went through it well.

It took me a few days to calm down behind it all, and Mathew stayed pretty close to me for a while. That night was the first night he spent the entire night at my apartment with me. I did not know many people in town; therefore, I looked forward to his company. I told Mathew some of what I had been through, and I moved to Monroe to start my life over again. I told him that if I had to be confronted by women from his past, to please just move on, and we could just be friends. He would not hear of such and promised that nothing of the sort would ever happen again. There was another woman whom he had been seeing, but according to him, she too was a thing of the past. I had this nagging uneasy feeling in the pit of my stomach. I hoped he was telling me the truth.

Mathew and I dated through the summer, and by the next summer, we were engaged to be married. We had a beautiful ceremony in his parents' backyard. Charlotte and a few of the girls from work helped with the planning for the wedding. Charlotte was my maid of honor, and my sisters were my bridesmaids. All of our friends were there, and his parents were thrilled to have a new daughter-in-law. His mother was a delightful woman who appeared much younger than her age. Both parents were gainfully employed and owned their own business. They specialized in home décor, we all did things together and I became as close as a daughter. They had another son, Adam, whom she had when she was thirty-eight. He was twelve years old just like Bryan, and they became really good friends and playmates. Adam spent a lot of time at my and

Mathews' house, especially when Bryan was there. Mathew worked as a bookkeeper for a law firm and made really good money. He was twenty-eight, and I was thirty-two years old. Before we were married, I discovered that he was really more immature than any of the other men in my past life.

He introduced me to very few of his friends, but he kept company with them often. One girl in particular, Bethany, he would visit two or three times each week. He had grown up with her as a next-door neighbor, but when they were teenagers; his parents purchased a new home and used that old property as a rental. After he grew up, it was his duty to care for that rental property! He mowed the yards and cut the hedges once a week, and included that maintenance in the rent. When we married, Bethany had just moved back to town and attended our wedding. After the wedding rehearsal and the dinner, Mathew told me that he and the guys were gonna hang out instead of having a bachelor's party. I was still helping to prepare the backyard and making sure that all of my i's were dotted and t's were crossed for this perfect wedding. Two weeks prior to the wedding, I went shopping to get a few last minute items for the big day.

As I started to leave the bridal shop, I met Floyd coming in. Startled, I said, "Hi Floyd!" "Hello Savanah," he said with a smile, "you haven't been around to the store lately." I shrugged my shoulders, "I know Floyd, how are you"? "I am well," he replied, "I saw your picture in the paper." "Yea," I said while blushing like a school girl. I thought I would give marriage another try." He stood and looked at me for a few seconds, but did not comment. "How did you like your bracelet I sent you?" he asked. "I thought you sent it all along. It is really nice, but I want you to have it back," I said! "Nonsense Savanah, it was my gift to you and I want you to keep it," Floyd said as if he was slightly offended. "Thank you Floyd," I said still blushing. "You have been a great friend, and I will always hold dear, our time together." Floyd looked at me as if he was searching for any reluctance on my part. "Have a great life and if you should ever need me, I have no plans to sell the store," he said playfully. I shook my head "ok" and hurried to my car to carry the decorations to my new mother-in-law to be.

Her club sisters were awesome throughout the planning, implementing, and cleanup after the wedding. Having been married three times already, this was my first real wedding with friends, family, and acquaintances. Although still relatively small, to me, it was the biggest wedding I would ever have, hopefully my last, and I wanted it to be perfect. My new mother-in-law-to-be, Lela, and her club sisters helped to make the wedding one I could only have dreamed about. My parents drove down, and my dad for the very first time, gave me away. Daddy was so handsome in his blue tuxedo. After all the pictures were developed, we were very proud of how they turned out. My mom and his mom were stunning in their dresses, which were exactly alike. The wedding went off without a glitch, and everyone was in awe. On our wedding night, we went back to our little apartment, because we were going to have our honeymoon later in the summer when he was on vacation. I was so disappointed that he went to bed and straight to sleep. I could not believe that he had not stayed awake long enough for us to consummate our vows.

A week after we were married, I teased his friend Calvin about wearing Mathew down the night before the wedding. Calvin said they had planned to wear him down, but Mathew had called and said he wanted to rest. He said, "So don't blame us, blame the wedding rehearsal and dinner." Mathew had told me he was tired because the guys wore him out the night before the wedding, but when I confronted him with the fact that Calvin said he called everything off, his story changed. "I was tired and fell asleep over at Bethany's. I slept on her couch all night." I found that quite strange! Could it be that the reason we did not consummate our wedding vows was because he was with her the night before and couldn't? If he slept on her couch all night, he should have been refreshed and ready to consummate. Thinking it extremely strange, I told Mathew that I wanted his friends to be mine also, and I thought it would be a good idea if we had a small get-together to invite them over so they could get to know me.

He said ok, but it never happened. We were married two months when I went to his mother's house to play bridge with her and her club members. When I got ready to go home, she gave me all of his mail to take to him. There was a statement from a jewelry store among the other mail. We had sat down with our bills before we got married, but there was no mention of a bill from "Action Jewelers." I decided to open that one statement before I went to bed, just to satisfy my curiosity. Mathew worked nights and would not be home until around 2:00a.m. It was a statement showing that he had purchased a lady's dinner ring for $600. I could not believe that he had purchased me another ring when we had elected to save money on my wedding ring and get a $250.00 wedding band for me and a $200 wedding band for him. I called him at work and asked him who he had purchased the ring for. The ring had been purchased about three days before our wedding.

He told me that one of his friends had him to purchase the ring for his girlfriend because his friend's credit was not up to par. I accepted it for the moment, but I would go into more detail when he arrived home. At home, Mathew did not want to tell me which friend he had allowed to use his credit. He said, "What is the problem, he is going to pay the note every month. We will worry if he doesn't, but until then all is well." We argued a little, but I finally dropped the subject. Approximately two months later, Charlotte told me that she had been in the grocery store and overheard Venita telling one of her friends that Mathew had purchased her a ring. She said Venita told the other woman, "Yes, he married her, but I got a ring too." She said she managed to get a good look at it, and it was a beautiful dinner ring, a diamond cluster. If you remember, Venita was the girl who took my wallet out of Mathew's car early in the relationship, while we were visiting his cousin!

I did not mention anything to Charlotte about the statement I had gotten from his mother. I tried to act nonchalant and casually told Charlotte, "Mathew had allowed one of his friends to purchase a ring, because their credit was not good. Maybe the friend was Venita, but I will get to the bottom of it. Either way, the friend is supposed to pay the note every month." When Mathew came home, I decided to put it this way: "Mathew, why did you purchase that ring for Venita?" His feathers fell to the floor! That actually means that he was shocked! He was not a very good liar, so he sat down on the sofa and looked down at the floor. He could not look me in the face. His beautiful eyelashes were still stunning as my anger grew. Of course, any woman who finds that her husband has purchased a ring for his ex-girlfriend would be upset, hurt, and as offended as I was.

He told me that she had taken the news of our wedding so badly that he wanted to do something to make her feel better. "She wanted the ring and said she would pay the notes, so I agreed." The statement showed that one note had been paid, and she didn't pay it. He confirmed the fact that she did not pay the first installment. As far as I was concerned, she lied, or he was lying. I was not going to be the fool either way. I was going to start defending myself by letting people know that I was no pushover. Neither he nor Venita would have the last laugh, I would! She asked for the ring and he gave it to her hoping that would quiet her talking at the office. That is when I found out she also worked at the law firm with Mathew! I told him under no uncertain terms would I accept that kind of nonsense. I told him to leave and do not return until he had that ring in his hands. He left and stayed gone for hours. When he finally returned, he told me that she would not give it to him.

I called her, but nothing could convince her to give up the ring. I was floored and angrier than ever. She had a ring, and would go around flaunting it, telling everyone that my husband purchased it for her. I called the police and told them she had taken my ring from Mathew's car and I wanted it, or I was going to press charges. The police went to her house and came back with the ring. He told my husband that the lady had quite a different story, but because the ring was in my husband's name, the lady had to turn it over. We thanked the officer, and he left. Our ring size was the same, and I wore the ring and got many compliments. The friends of hers that recognized me made it their business to get close enough to see the ring on my finger. Now, if she still wanted to deal with him after that, it was totally up to her. I fussed about it, and we moved on in our marriage. I was somewhat happy but the ring really put a damper on things for a while. I enjoyed my in-laws so much! They were such wonderful people that I just knew I had to stay in the family. I had to make things work with my husband, so making a beautiful marriage was my utmost important goal.

We went several months without any incidences, and I was enjoying my marriage again. The children in my class had gotten to know my husband, and they often told me that my husband's car was on Reddic Street every evening. He was leaving home an hour early every day going to work. He was telling me that he was going in early most days so that he could play catch up on work at the office. After the kids in my class kept talking about seeing his car on Reddic, I finally asked them where on Reddic, did they see his car. They said his car was always parked at the little white house next to the big white house that had the blue trim. That meant that the car was parked at his parents' rent house and the white house with the blue trim was the house his neighbor and childhood playmate, Bethany, lived in. She had come back to town just before our wedding and was in attendance.

The winter came to a close, and spring was in the air. It was time for Mathew to start mowing the lawn again on Saturdays. Every now and then, I would go with him to mow the yard. Whenever I went, I could tell he did not want me to go. Bethany would never come out of the house, but I did see someone peeping out of the curtains when I was there. If he went over alone, she would be out there keeping him company. I drove over one Saturday and carried some lemonade for him to drink. She was out in the yard standing next to him as he sat on the lawn mower. She started walking toward her house when he told her I was coming. I gave him the lemonade and left, but called Charlotte and asked her to drive by the house to see if the woman was outside again.

Charlotte drove by, and within ten minutes after I drove away, she was back out there. Something was terribly wrong with that picture! Again, I suggested that he invite Bethany over to our apartment so that I could get to know her better, but he said his friends thought that I was mean, and probably won't come over. I was deeply offended because his friends did not know me, nor did they know anything about me.

The few guy friends that I knew were more than cordial when they saw us together. The rest and Bethany, I guess I would never know. I could not believe he was cheating, because he knew if I found out, I would be gone. I did not tell him I suspected a thing. I was always told to give a person enough rope and they would hang themselves. As the summer progressed, Mathew left earlier and came home later. About a month later, I spoke with him on the phone just before he left work. He was kind of rushing me off the phone so that he could wrap things up there at the office. He said he needed to run by his parents' house to drop off some papers they needed, and he would be straight home after that. Immediately, I felt that he was going to stop at Bethany's.

I got in my car, drove in Bethany's direction, backed my car in-between two businesses across the street, turned my lights off, and sat there, waiting. I could not believe my eyes! He was no match for me; I have traveled this road far too many times for him to think that I was that naive. She evidently was watching for him, because the light came on the minute he turned into the driveway. I did not wait for him to go into the house; I started my car, turned the lights on, and pulled to the road. He was standing on the steps and she had opened the door and gone back into the house. He paused looking back at the car as he stepped inside. He had nothing in his hands that he could have been dropping off; I looked to be sure, so that when he lied, I would know. I pulled into the street and drove home in disbelief, speechless! He came in about five minutes after I got inside. I wondered what happened to the papers that he needed to take to his parents. They lived another fifteen minutes away! That was "time" he was buying time to spend at Bethany's.

He came into the house once again looking like the cat with the bird in his mouth. I had turned the lights off, and gotten back in bed, but the hall light afforded just enough light for me to see him plainly. It was enough for me that he knew; I knew he had lied to me once again. He was too embarrassed to ask me, and I was to speechless to confront him. After I would not say anything, he did not know what to do. The next morning, as I got ready to walk out to go and get Bryan, I told him, "If I catch you around that fucking Bethany's one more time, I won't be nice at all. Try me! The story will make the newspaper and every television station for miles. I hope you understand me!" I had taken all that I thought I could take of those two. I know he saw her afterward, but it did make them respect me! They began meeting in other places, or it was a total coincidence that they would leave home around the same time and return about the same time as well.

Several months passed with no incidences, and we had gotten much closer. My friends would come over from time to time, and he was getting to know them better. Sometimes we would play cards, cook and have feast. He partook in some of the festivities, but sometimes he would have errands to run. I figured that he seized the moment, because he knew I was preoccupied. I could not prove it, so I let it go. In early December, his phone would ring one time and stop. Within a few minutes, he would need to run to the store or just anywhere to get out of the house. He was sleeping one day and his phone rang one time and stopped. I picked it up and looked at the number that called. It was a number from out of state because the area code was a 312 area code. One day after the phone rang one time; I waited until he left home to go to the store, and called the 312 number.

I identified myself and asked the woman on the other end, what was her name, she told me Jessica and spelled it J E S S I C A, last name McPherson and spelled it M C P H E R S O N. Man, I was blown away. "What is your relationship with my husband?" I asked. Her response almost knocked my socks off. "What do you think? We are fucking, that is what the relationship is!" She then told me to hold on a second. When she returned, she told me that she had another call, and it was important so she had to let me go. Without saying a word, I hung up the phone. I have always been told if you look for something hard enough, you would find it. I looked and I most certainly found it. I knew that the phone call she had just received was from my husband.

When he returned, I flew into him, hitting him with all of my might. He hit me knocking me against the wall. He kept saying stop, but I fought him until he actually hit me with his fist, right on the side of my head. I fell to the floor and began to cry. Mathew was now so mad that he probably would have beaten me to a pulp had I continued. I cried off and on all day. Here we go again, I thought as I wrestled with the idea of asking Mathew to leave. It was my apartment and I had never put his name on the lease. If I insisted, he had no other choice but to go. I was angry that he had anyone in his life that would say those words to me. I felt caught between a rock and a hard place once again and confused was the least of my feelings. Once again, I felt betrayed.

Was there a righteous man in this whole wide world? I understood the Lord's frustrations when he could not find a righteous man through Abraham, Ezekiel, or Jeremiah! Maybe, I was one of the women who should have never tried marriage, but I did not want to be alone. I wanted someone who could love me as much as I loved them. This was the marriage that was supposed to stick! Mathew knew that he had gone too far, and I knew that I should have never hit him, but I was just so fed up with his thinking he was so slick. He apologized for hitting me the same day, but for the next two weeks, the relationship was strained. About two weeks passed and just before Christmas, Mathew went to work as usual, but returned three hours later with his attaché and all the folders from his files.

He had his name plaque that usually sat on his desk, and his pictures that sat on his file cabinet. He came in, sat everything on the dining table and plopped down on the sofa; he had all the characteristics of a desolate man. I wanted to ask him what had happened, why he was home at this hour, but I suppose the devil in me would not let that happen. I was still so very unhappy with all that was going on with our marriage. I was cleaning the house, so I went about my work as if he wasn't there. I hoped nothing was wrong with either his parents or his brother. Those were the people he loved the most. They were the only ones that could make him look so wrestled down. An hour passed and he was still sitting in the same spot. His eyes focused on the television as if it was on.

Because I did not hear anything, I thought the volume was turned down. I walked around just enough to be able to see the black screen. Awe hell, I had better find out what is going on, because whatever it is has his mind warped. Sitting down on the sofa beside him I called his name. He did not respond! I called his name again and put my hand on his leg. "Mathew," I said, "is something wrong?" He looked at me and dropped his head, as only he could do; his lashes reminded me of the things I truly loved about him. "Is there anything I can do to help?" I asked. He answered, "No, there is nothing you can do." One lonely tear rolled from his left eye, and I knew it was maybe more serious than I could imagine.

"Are your parents and Adam doing OK?" I asked. "Yeah, they are fine," he growled. Feeling that he might be getting agitated, I decided to back down until he was ready to talk. "OK," I said, as I placed my hand on his back to try to comfort him a little. "I am going to finish my housework, but I am here if you decide you want to talk about it." I started to get up, and he caught my hand, "No don't go, I might as well tell you now." He took a long deep breath and said, "I got fired!" "Got fired! Got fired! Why?" I squealed! He got up went to the table and got two sheets of paper, one stapled to the other. He handed them to me, and I began to read.

The first one was where he signed to allow two hundred and seventy dollars and thirty six cents to be taken from his last check to pay for telephone calls he made to several different numbers in Chicago, Illinois. One of the numbers was Jessica's number that I called just two weeks ago. Before I said anything, I wanted to read page two. Page two was where they allowed him to resign instead of being fired promising to give him a good recommendation, as he applies for jobs elsewhere. I thought I had been speechless before, but no, I was speechless in a whole different way.

I got up off of the sofa and went to the bedroom, sat on the side of the bed to try to digest what I had just read. I always had a problem digesting bad news! So often I was dumbfounded! The more I tried, the worse things seem to get in this marriage. Now we both looked like zombies, walking around the house like the living dead. I was so glad I had allowed Bryan to go home with his cousin. That night was the first time I asked Mathew to leave. He did not want to go, because he did not want to face his parents with such news. He spent two nights somewhere, but I did not care where. He could have gone anywhere he wanted without the worry of my checking up on him, but I slept very little those nights. He came by the next day, but I did not answer the door. He knew I was home because my car was there. I figured that he decided not to come in after I did not answer his persistent knocking.

Standing there looking through the peephole, I thought, if he has the nerve to use his key and come through that door, I have the nerve to stick this knife straight through him. It's strange, but I did not remember picking up the knife when I heard his car. I didn't remember putting it on the coffee table, but I had to do it, I was home alone. He left, and I was so glad he did. I was probably the unhappiest person in town. My phone rang and rang but I would not answer. I hardly ate anything those two days, but I knew I needed to. I called in a pizza on the second day and when I opened the door to pay for the pizza, Mathew was standing there. He looked as worn as I probably did and the pizza man seemed confused. I paid for the pizza, and Mathew asked to talk to me for a minute. I let him come in, but told him it was only for a minute. He could not even think about going over to his parents without me on Christmas, he said. And what about Bryan, we are supposed to pick him up for Christmas.

We had gotten all of his gifts and some toys. What would he think if Mathew wasn't here? He really liked Mathew a lot. They played basketball and teased each other like crazy. I let Mathew come home, and we went through Christmas as much like a family as we could under the circumstances. He told his parents he got laid off, and I let him tell them whatever lies he wanted. His mother commented about my not eating much. I shrugged my shoulders and told her that I was watching my figure. His favorite cousin "Nick," had moved to Texas and was doing well there; therefore, he talked Mathew into looking for a job in Houston.

Mathew asked me to go with him so we could get a fresh start in a new city. "I am sure things would be much better there," he said. "There are no ex—girlfriends, no buddies, just you and me." It was a hard decision for me, because I had a job that I liked very much. "Why should I drop Everything and start over with you, when you have treated me like shit?" I asked. Mathew then said, "OK, I tell you what, I will go first, get a job, and then you come. I will take care of us, until you find a job.

Come on, Savanah, I know how I have acted, I know how bad things look, but I love you beyond compare. I don't want to try to learn to love nobody else, please, baby!" "Let me think about it, because you are asking a lot of me. I just don't see why I should walk away from my job because you messed up. You have had too many chances and each time you fucked them up." Eventually I said I would give it one more try, but one more was all I was willing to give. Mathew was happy about my decision to move to Houston with him. I had been to Dallas, but never to Houston.

I was a country girl and a little scared of living in the big city. I had heard of so many bad things happening there. Although, I was scared of how Mathew would treat me so far away from my family, scared of living in the city, scared that my marriage was going to fail, scared of being alone, scared that Mama wouldn't let Bryan go with me. Once I resigned myself to the fact that I was moving to Texas, my first priority was my baby boy. He was fourteen years old and I was going to let him make the decision regardless of what Mama said. Matthew left on a Sunday just like Fred did. Was I watching him ride off in the sunset never to feel his touch again? Was this the end of this marriage too? Charlotte came over that night, and we talked about everything in detail.

Many things I told her she had no idea was happening. I had not told any of my sisters, and suffered through the embarrassment alone. My question to her was, would you go if you were me. She said, she thinks that she probably would go, because maybe it would be different in a new city. Maybe the fresh start would be just what the doctor ordered. I told her if all hell broke loose in Houston, she was going to have to drop everything and come help me move back. She promised she would. All of that was said jokingly, but I really meant business.

After we talked, we ordered pizza and I ate half of it. She said I was eating like I hadn't had food for a week. She just did not realize that I had unloaded all of my junk on her, and I felt like eating for the first time the whole month of December. Christmas dinner just would not go down my throat. All I was managing to eat were a few spoonful at a time. I was hungry, and I was going to eat while I could. One never knows what tomorrow may bring to take your appetite away again. In three days, I was going back to work and I had a lot to do. I drove home and told Mama about my plans to move to Texas and that Mathew was already gone. I was surprised to know that he had called her himself and told her about our plans. She knew he was gone, and she said she figured I would be around to discuss Bryan. "Yes, Mama, I am here to discuss Bryan.

I want to take him with me!" I waited for a response but there was not anything said. I continued, "I want him to make the decision, and you and I both have to respect the decision he makes. If he chooses to stay, I won't make him feel guilty. If he chooses to go, I ask that you not make him feel guilty. We have fought over him for twelve years, not counting the two years he stayed with you while I was in school, and we should not fight over him anymore. You must not go to the hospital because that is how you got him back when I moved away to Louisiana. I don't want Daddy calling, telling me that I am going to kill you by taking him. Can we please agree on it for once?" Mama did not speak for a few seconds, and when she did, she told me to go and get her a glass of water. Mama's legs were giving her real problems and she spent most of her time in a wheel chair. I obeyed, but when I returned with the water, I could tell she had a quick cry. My first thought was "she is starting already". She drank her water and passed the glass back to me.

I went to the kitchen and placed the glass in the sink. As I walked back into the room, she yelled, "Bryan, come here, baby." He was watching television in the living room, but came running as soon as she called. She pulled him up to her and said, "Your little skinny Mama is getting ready to move to Houston." His eyes were bigger than usual as he looked up at me as if he had questions. "She wants you to go with her, and I am going to let you do whatever you want to do. If you decide to go, I will be fine, but if you want to stay, she will be fine. You tell us what you want to do, and we will make it happen." He looked at Mama, then at me! I smiled and said, "We are going to let you make your own decision baby. Mama and I are not going to fight over you anymore." He looked at Mama and said, "Mamo, you won't get sick, if I go with my mama?" "No, I won't get sick, she said! To make both he and my mama feel better, I said, "You can come home during the summer whenever you want to, can't he Mama!" She nodded! "Yep, he sure can."

Bryan was leaning against my mama, looking from one to the other. "Well," Bryan said, "I think I am going with you, Mama." I breathed a sigh of relief! Finally I could have my son, and Mama and I could stop fighting over him! "Ok then," I said, "I will be up next weekend to help you pack your things." "When are we leaving, Mama?" Bryan asked. "I can't say exactly, but soon," I told him. He ran out of the room singing, "We're moving to Houston, We' removing to Houston!" "Well I tell you what," Mama said, "you better take care of my baby." "I will Mama, I will!" I left mama's house feeling more optimistic about the move to Houston. I found myself smiling at how God had answered my prayers. As I traveled back to Louisiana, I thanked God!

I drove back up the following weekend and washed and ironed all of his clothes except for a few I left for him to wear to school. Mathew got a job the second week, he was in Houston. He worked for Amerigas but came back with his cousin to drive the Uhaul, and he carried Bryan, Fritz and me to our new home. Bryan was so excited to be moving to the city, and I was praying that we did not have to return in shame. Driving into Houston seeing all of those lanes, I knew my driving days were over. I thought, "I will never in hell be able to drive here." Our apartment was very nice, much like the one we had in Monroe, Louisiana. Bryan could walk to school and he loved it. He had always had to ride the bus about thirty minutes to get to school.

On days when it rained, it took all of five minutes to drop him off. I began looking for a job immediately. I got the phone book, called all of the different school districts and asked them to mail me applications. I filled them out as soon as they were in my mailbox. Several districts called, which resulted in my having five interviews in one week. I prayed for an interview with Pasadena school district and actually received a letter in the mail telling me when to come for the interview. I was learning that area pretty well, since we lived on that side of town. Mathew asked off from work, to take me to three of the interviews, but he later told me that I had to get a map and drive myself, because he could not keep taking off to drive me to every single interview.

I was furious because I knew that I would never make it driving to the other side of town. I was bound to have a wreck, I thought! He got the map one night and showed me exactly where I was going. Not being the best at following a map, I thought I understood, but I still had doubts as to whether I could actually do it. Mathew said, "If all else failed, ask a police officer to help you".

I thought, I was doing just fine at my old job back in Monroe. Because of you, I am out here fumbling my way around in this ocean of iron and metal. If you had kept your shit in your pants, we would be safe and secure back in our old apartment. I would still be sleeping, but no, I had to leave a whole two hours early to be sure not to miss the interview. If I get a job, I am going to have to drive in all of this traffic, just to get to work. I could not see this working out for the life of me. I told Mathew that night, "You got us this apartment on this side of town, but if I get a job on the other side of town, we are moving close to my job. Driving out there is like a punishment, and if anybody takes that punishment it will be you buddy." I was quite overjoyed when I was called for the interview at Pasadena ISD. I went in aiming to impress! When I was called for a second interview, I knew I had my foot in the door.

I signed the contract and began working in February 1982. I loved the job, the kids, the principal, and the drive was only about twelve minutes. We could stay in our apartment, Bryan could stay in the same school, and I went right by his school on my way to work. I was feeling much better about everything. In March, I came down with what I thought was the flu. I was coughing and was as sick as I could be. A new medication had recently hit the store shelves called Comtrex, and I took it as directed until the entire bottle was gone. Still, I had no relief from my illness. Cooking made me extremely nauseous, and there were times when I just had to lie down to get relief.

After about sixteen days of this, I was at my wits' end and decided to go to the doctor. My sister, Nadellie, was visiting us, and she decided to go with me. After being examined, the doctor said he did not find anything that could cause me to feel so bad. He asked if I could be pregnant. "No, Sir," I told him, because at one point I tried to get pregnant and could not. The one and only time I thought I wanted to get pregnant was for Samuel, but God knew better than me and did not allow it. Thank you Jesus! I think I was meant to have one child and one child only. He suggested that we do a pregnancy test just for good measures. I agreed, but I told him there was no way I was pregnant. I urinated in the little cup and gave it to the nurse. They suggested that I take a seat in the waiting area until they were ready to call me back.

I told Nadellie, "Can you imagine they wanted to take a pregnancy test. Girl, I am as far from being pregnant as the Earth is from the Moon." Nadellie started praising God and teasing me about being a new mommy. "Savanah, tell me you wouldn't be happy," she said not giving me time to answer. When the nurse came for me, she asked if Nadellie was my sister. I told her "yes", and Nadellie asked if she could go in with me. The nurse said it had to be up to me to allow her in my session with the doctor.

Nadellie blurted out, "Oh, come on, she doesn't care, she is our baby sister." We followed the nurse and she led us to the doctor's office. He was sitting behind his desk smiling at us coming down the hallway acting silly. He just did not know that we could be much sillier when all five of us girls were together. "Well, I did the test and you are pregnant," said the doctor. I could not believe it. I sat there in total disbelief as Nadellie continued to praise God. I had no idea she would be that happy to see me pregnant. On the way home, she was a little chatterbox. "I can't wait to get to the house to tell Mama," she said, "she is going to be so happy until she will have a fit."

I thought to myself, "Maybe I want to tell Mama", but I dared not to say it. She was so happy; I was willing to let her tell Mama. Once I drove up to the apartment, she jumped out of the car and ran into the house to call Mama. I thought, I would get the chance to tell Mathew, but before I could get to the door, Mathew came out to meet me, smiling. "So is it true?" Mathew said. "Yes, I guess it is, the doctor seems to be sure," I said. "I am thirty-three years old, and will be thirty-four by the time the baby comes in November I'll be in the nursing home before I can get this baby raised."

"No you won't, we are going to do this together," Mathew said as he rubbed his hand over my stomach. Bryan came running outside, "Mama is it true?" Yes, it is true, I told him. He was grinning from ear to ear. "Just one thing, Mama," Bryan said, "it has to be a girl." "I'll try," I said, "but we don't get to choose the baby's sex you know." "Why must it be a girl, baby?" I asked. He responded, "If it's a boy, I will have to go to war if we have one, but if I am the only boy, I might go to service, but they won't send your only son to war." I looked at Bryan, I had never heard that, but it made sense to me. When I finally got inside the house, Nadellie was on the phone with Mama and even she was overjoyed. Nadellie gave me the phone.
I don't know who was worse or best in the praising-God competition, Mama or Nadellie. Mama said she wanted Bryan to have a little brother or sister so that he would not be alone if anything ever happened to me. I told her, "He might wish I had let this baby stay wherever it was, he might have to raise it." Mama laughed, "You will live to raise it, don't worry about that." She told me how happy she was about the whole situation, and we hung up. She said she needed to tell Daddy and the rest of my sisters and brothers.

I was getting ready to call Tisah and Mama was getting ready to call everyone. Who was I going to tell about the pregnancy, everyone else was doing the telling? I knew they were just excited for me so, it was all right. Mathew called his parents on speaker phone, and Adam answered the phone. Mathew told Adam, "Well, dude, are you ready to be an uncle?" "Huh," Adam said waiting for clarity. Mathew repeated, "I said are you ready to be an uncle?" Adam said, "Am I going to be one?" "Yep," Mathew said. Adam started screaming, "Mama, come here, come in here." His mother said, "What's the problem?" "There is no problem, Savanah is going to have a baby," Adam screamed! Amidst all of the screaming, I heard her telling his dad, and then everyone was screaming.

There was one thing for sure; I knew this baby would have loved dripping from its seams. When the smoke cleared and I was able to reflect, I finally realized that I had not my period, so this baby was discovered by pregnancy test extremely early. I was two days away from my period still, and my symptoms started a little over two weeks ago. I had taken so much Comtrex that I hoped it would not affect the baby. I called the doctor, and he said I was not to worry, the baby would be fine.

Mathew's parents made their first trip to see us in early April, and they were still high from the news. His mother kept saying, "I can't believe I am going to be a grandmother. I thought it would never happen," as she smiled happily. We had made friends with a lovely couple, Janice and Marvin Long. She too taught school in Pasadena. He was a businessman who dealt in real estate. I did have the privilege of telling them. They wanted to be the godparents right off the bat. It ended up, that the baby would have two sets of godparents: our friends in Houston, and his parents' best friends in Louisiana.
There were seven teachers on our faculty expecting babies two to three months apart. My principal, such a jovial man, said someone must have put something in the water. His entire faculty was getting pregnant, he said with a hardy laugh. They had one big baby shower for the seven of us, and we all got most of our essentials, thanks to the wonderful teachers at Queens's intermediate school, Pasadena, Texas. Since I became pregnant in February, and my symptoms were so prevalent by March, I gagged, spat, and pushed my way through May. I had June, July, and August to relax and get ready for the new baby. Mathew and I did not want to know the sex, so we asked the doctor not to tell us if he saw any indication of the sex during the ultrasound or any of the other tests.

Since I turned thirty-four years old in June, I was told about the amniocentesis. With this test, I would be told if there was a birth defect of any kind. The test detected the slightest defect, and a woman would have to search her heart of hearts and decide whether she wanted to abort, or risk having the child with a slight defect or a very major birth defect. The test would not tell the severity of the defect. I chose not to have the test, and prayed really hard that I had a healthy baby. Had I had the test and it showed there was a defect; I would not have aborted because I do not believe in abortion. I traveled back to the place of my birth and my friends all had the opportunity to see me pregnant. Most of them reacted the same as my sisters and Mama. Nobody thought I would have another child, especially after Bryan was past ten years old.

I had a lot of fun with my old friends and neighbors. While at Mamas, I looked out and old Nettie's car was parked in my driveway. I had heard that she visited Samuel at my house, but seeing it for myself made me feel quite differently about it. I had asked him once to keep her out of the house we shared together and visit her in her home or he could just move in with her, so that he would not need to entertain her in my house. The other women in his life were not an issue to me, but Nettie portrayed herself as my friend. After about three years and my not being around often, they became bold, comfortable, and careless with their relationship. I decided to put a stop to it once and for all. After not saying one word to them about their carrying on before I left him, nor after I left, this was going a bit too far. I walked out of Mama's house without saying a word to anyone. I knew had I told anyone what I was getting ready to do, they would have stopped me. I could see them through the glass door as I approached, sitting on the sofa together. I went inside without knocking! I didn't care about their relationship, but they both had to get out. It was the principle of the thing, and I felt it disrespectful.

When I walked in, they both looked startled as I spoke softly, but politely, "Now listen, Nettie has a nice home, so my advice is that the both of you get up and go there." He got up, and she remained seated saying, "Sam don't you pay rent here." Just then, because of her sneakiness and smart mouth, I picked up a lamp and threw it across the floor shattering glass everywhere. I then said, "Sam you had better get her out of here and I mean now! Don't let me catch you here again," I said, looking at her coldly, as if she had ice cycles hanging from her shoulders. He slowly walked out through the carport doors, told her to come, and she followed. I walked out behind them, and when Sam turned to lock the door, I said, "Don't worry about locking up, I will do it, I have not forgotten how and My key still fits. I used to live here remember!" I locked the door and turned around to look at the both of them. "Now, let me tell you something that you did not know," I said still looking at Nettie, "You see this man right here," placing my hand on his chest, "this man loves me and he always will.

Don't you ever forget it!" He never opened his mouth to defend that statement, and she stood there looking like a deer caught in headlights. I was remarried, and pregnant with another man's baby, yet that I said was true and they both knew it. She knew that had I wanted him even then, she would have been history! She hoped I would not make that call, for by this time, she loved his dirty underwear.

I turned and went to Mama's to spend my last night before leaving to go to Mathew's parents. I felt justified, I suppose because I had never confronted them, and I knew that I had hit Nettie right where it hurt! Both Nettie's car and Sam's truck finally went up the road toward her house, once their argument subsided a bit. He eventually, about eight years after I left him, married her, for the sake of convenience. Shortly after that, Samuel was injured and had to go on SSI (Supplemental Security Income), which is next to no income at all! All the things he afforded me, Nettie missed out on! His addiction did not end there, it continues. He has broken her heart many times over. Once he dated her best friend's daughter, a much younger, beautiful girl, and I am told, Nettie came very close to a nervous breakdown.

We stopped in Monroe, Louisiana, for a few days, so that Mathew's parents could show me off to their friends. This was going to be their first grandchild, and they were elated to say the least. School started in late August and working a full day, being six months pregnant, going home to prepare dinner was beginning to take its toll. The apartment complex manager had urged us to go ahead and move into the three-bedroom apartment early, and they would allow maintenance to move the furniture while Mathew was at work. She then gave me one of the young men for two days to help with the curtains, hang pictures and emptying boxes. The manager was just awesome! I hired a young lady who was looking for a job to help with the linen, dishes, cabinets, and bathrooms. She and the young man emptied the boxes and put everything in place. In two days, the new apartment was completely in order.

I set up the nursery with furniture, but could not pick colors and nothing else until we knew the baby's sex. On days when I was really active, it moved around a lot, but when I settled down, it seemed to be tired and ready to sleep also. Whatever the sex, it packed a punch out of sight. Bryan moved, but I did not remember him moving this much. Sometimes I worried that something might be wrong, simply because of the punch this baby packed. When I would be sleeping and wanted to reposition myself, if the baby was comfortable in the old position, it would fuss and kick and punch until I returned to the original position. Mathew and I picked boy and girl nursery colors, wall décor, and bedding packages. We wrote everything down along with the article descriptions, and he would pick everything up after we knew the sex.

Everything was ready for the baby's arrival, and so was I. I was getting tired of being pregnant and cried a lot from frustration. I made Fritz, Bryan and Mathews responsibility. I was having enough problems just trying to have a baby. Fritz must have sensed that I was not feeling well, because she stuck right under me. I could not move without her! When I told my mama how clingy Fritz was, she said she could not imagine her being any more clingy than she was before I was pregnant. I assured her that she was much more clinging.

That made mama feel that Fritz would be jealous of the baby once it was born. She suggested that maybe we should consider finding her a good home. I was not about to hear that. She was a part of this family. Every October, a classic rival football game was held between the Texas Southern University and South Louisiana University, but Mathew said he was not going this year. He said, he and three other guys from work had to go to Beaumont, Texas to assist with that branches bookkeeping. He left home that Friday night after he came home from work. It was strange that he took my car, but I didn't question. I guess maybe the pregnancy had taken some of my sharpness away. The next morning, he left early, around 6a.m, and when he finally returned around 7p.m, I had dinner ready. While he ate, I ran his bath. He was so tired and because he had to leave at six the following morning as well, he retired early.

I tried to talk to him about his day but he was very evasive. He answered some of my questions but did not elaborate on too much. I set the alarm to ring the same time as it had the morning before so that Mathew would not be late for work. He woke up earlier saying that he was running late. He jumped in the shower rushing to leave! When the radio alarm turned the radio on, they were discussing Saturday's game. A few minutes later, while he was in the shower, the phone rang. I answered, but the party hung up. I did not have caller ID so I had no idea who it could have been. I thought maybe the guys were calling to rush him along. Then, I got to thinking about the game. It was a game of which many people from Louisiana came to town; Bethany would more than likely be one of them.

Is it possible that he is meeting Bethany? Could he possibly bring all of his trash to Houston after all that this marriage has been through? I jumped out of bed and put the same clothes on that I had worn on Saturday. They were in a pile on the floor for me to take them to the laundry room. I usually would have taken them last night after my bath, but I guess as fate had it, I did not feel like it. After putting on my clothes, I jumped back in bed and pulled the covers all the way to my neck. Mathew submerged from the bathroom fully dressed. Dressed a little too nice to be going to work on a weekend, I pretended to be asleep. He rushed by the bed, and gave me a quick kiss and off he went. I sprang out of bed, grabbed my purse and keys and listened for his car to drive out of our section of the apartment complex. I ran to my car and hoped he would not be out of sight before I could see which direction he took.

Sure enough, his car was in plain sight taking a left out of the parking lot. Upon his exiting, I pulled out after several cars had gone by, to keep out of sight. I followed him straight to the Days Inn Hotel at Hobby airport. My heart skipped several beats I know! No he wasn't still up to his same old tricks! I could not follow him directly to his room; I had to stay out of sight. I parked my car and walked through the hotel to the other side in the direction his car went. By the time I got there, he had gone into a room and I did not know which one. Now what should I do? I could imagine what had taken place yesterday, and what would probably take place again today.

I wasn't having it! Hurt to no end was the least of what I was feeling. Here I am eight months pregnant, and he is staying away all day long, two days in a row, with some bimbo. I went back to my car and just sat there, in total disbelief once again. How could he? Feeling helpless, I called my girlfriend Janice, and told her what was happening. "What!" she said. "Where are you now?" "I am sitting in the parking lot," I said. "Oh, baby, I am so sorry, but you stay right there, I am on my way!" she said. It took all of ten minutes and she and her husband, Marvin, drove up. I did not know she was going to bring him, but what the hell! They both got out and came over to my car and got in.

"Girl, I bailed out of the bed and tried my best to leave him, but I couldn't," she said. "No, Savanah, I was asking her where she was going and all she would say is, 'I'll be back in a few minutes.' I knew something was happening and I jumped in the car too," he said. "I could not get her to say what was going on, and then on the way she started telling me how she was going to whip somebody's ass for you." "No, I don't want her to fight for me, but if I were able to fight for myself, I would hurt both of them. Now that I had followed him to the hotel, I knew it was a woman, and I would bet it was Bethany. My baby is too important to me, for me to lose it over its screwed-up daddy and some bitch," I replied.

"Marvin, you and Janice didn't have to come, I just wanted to talk to her on the phone," I told them. "No, we need to be here with you, Savanah. Girl, I am so sorry!" Janice said. "Don't feel bad for me. It has been this way, my whole marriage. We came here to get a new start and here we are again! He has done this before, I should not be surprised or hurt, but it does hurt me so much!" I said, as I started to cry. "I thought the baby would help build and complete our marriage, not pull it apart."

"Marvin, he is coming out of that room, and now!" I said, as I opened the car door. I went into the lobby, picked up one of their brochures from the counter. I went into the phone booth and dialed the phone number to the hotel. I asked for Bethany's room and to my total surprise, the phone started ringing. Marvin had come into the lobby behind me and was standing as if waiting for me to finish my call. "Hello!" Bethany said. I took a deep breath, because I needed to sound in control. "Hi Bethany, how are you?" I said. "I am fine thank you," she replied. "Listen, this is Savanah, and I am standing out here at the Days Inn waiting for my husband to finish his business in your room, so would you tell him I said hurry!" She gasped, shocked as hell! "That's right bitch, I gotcha ass!" I told her.

She threw the phone down, hanging it up, and I in return hung up as well. I walked out of the booth, past Marvin and back to the car, where Janice waited anxiously. I was sure the hotel staff was not aware that anything out of the ordinary was taking place. I was as quiet and as poised as I could fictitiously be, under the circumstances. I knew. I had messed up any chance Mathew had of keeping a hard-on with that move! I felt somewhat empowered because knowing Mathew, they were, under no uncertain terms, running around like caged birds when the cat was watching. Marvin came running behind me asking, "What did you do?" When I told him, he had to laugh, and Janice thought that was the coolest move ever. I too, thought it was a swift move, but it hurt nonetheless! I was angry and I told them, "Today marks the end of this marriage." I knew myself better than anyone else, especially in situations of the heart.

Marvin then decided that he would go in alone, and actually duplicated my idea, to help defuse the situation. He told Janice to keep me in the car, he would be back shortly. As he walked away, he told her again, "If you let her get out of this car, I am not going to be very unhappy with you, Janice." "OK! OK!," she said, "I get it!" As he walked away, she said, "Girl, don't get out of this car, because he means it. Did you see that look he gave me?" I nodded, "Yes." We watched him disappear into the hotel. He went toward the counter, and then came back toward the phone booth. After a minute or two, he walked through the hotel and out of the doors on the other side toward the back section. He was back there maybe fifteen to twenty minutes, and then came back to the car.

Once he was back at the car, he started telling us he had spoken with Mathew and the lady; as he explained, I saw Mathew's car go out of the drive and onto the street. He was driving very fast and seemed to be traveling alone. Marvin said Bethany was scared shitless, and Mathew was in almost the same condition. We sat in the parking lot and talked for a few minutes, but I knew Marvin helped Mathew, Bethany, and me by keeping me in place while Mathew got away. In some ways, I wanted to be angry with him, but I knew Marvin handled it the right way for a more desirable outcome. During the entire ordeal, I felt pressure and cramping in the bottom of my stomach.

Janice drove my car home, and they took me to the hospital just to be checked out. Because I was pregnant, they saw me immediately in the emergency room. My doctor was called, but I was examined by another physician. They felt I might have been trying to go into early labor and gave me a shot of some kind. I was to go home, get in bed and rest the entire evening. If the pain got worse, I was told to return to the hospital, and I would possibly be admitted for observation.

The shot made me really tired and sleepy, but I was not yet ready to retire for the day. If I could just stay awake long enough to say what I wanted to Mathew,

I would gladly go to sleep. I did not tell the doctor what had happened. How could I tell anyone such a horrible story? The only reason I told Janice was to vent and keep myself from busting wide open with anger and frustration. Here I am at the hospital, and only God knows where my so called husband was. When a woman is pregnant, a man can destroy her, the marriage, any affection she has for him by doing what Mathew has done to me. I never felt the same toward Mathew after that day. I did as much as the doctor informed me to do. I went home, took a shower, and after I was safely tucked into bed, Janice and Marvin went home to prepare for their work week. They had an adventurous Sunday at my expense, but I was thankful for them.

I slept maybe three hours and was awakened about 6p.m when I heard the phone ringing. It was Mathew's cousin, Nick calling to test the waters for him. I knew Mathew had to be there because he had nowhere else to go. Our best friends were with me, and he only had dealings with Marvin and his cousin Nick. He tried to pretend he knew nothing and it was a casual call. I told him not to play games with me; I had all the games I could take. Because he knew I had been through plenty with his cousin, he could not lie, even with Mathew looking down his throat. Now you tell Mathew that I said, "Come home and get his shit, and get as far away from me as he can." He finally admitted that Mathew was there and wanted to come home so that we could talk. "Talk! Talk! Talk about what?" I asked.

You tell him I said, "Talk to this," and I hung up the phone. Remembering that I did not need to be upset further, I took the phone off of the hook and laid it back down. I had to control myself; I did not want to lose my baby! In reality I had always wanted Bryan to have a sibling, just in case something happened to me, so that he would not be alone. That was the idea when I almost let Samuel talk me into trying to get pregnant. I had wanted this baby for too long to let him and Bethany make me lose it. I prayed, but I could not concentrate on it. My mind would wander way off into left field somewhere, then back to Mathew and Bethany. I suddenly remembered that I had let Fritz out doors to use the bathroom, and had planned to let her back in, but I fell asleep.

I immediately jumped up and ran to the door, but she was not there. I asked our neighbors' son if he had seen her, but he had only been outside for about fifteen minutes. Fritz had been locked out for about three hours when I woke up. The medication had caused me fall asleep. I send the neighbor to look for her. He returned about thirty minutes later saying that he did not find her anywhere. My God, I had lost my dog! I know she did not know what to think after she returned to the door and I did not let her in. I was sad!

Bryan had gone out of town with his best friend and his parents, and he arrived home at 6:30p.m. He always would come in, come straight to my bed, and sit and talk. He was excited that the baby was coming real soon, and he stayed close to me most of the time. He liked his stepfather, so I did not want him to know what had happened today. I told Bryan about Fritz and he rushed out of the house to find her. He came back without her and we were both sad. I only hoped that whoever took her would be good to her. She was freshly groomed, pretty and white with pink bows. It would be easy for someone to want her. Mathew came home while Bryan and I were talking, so I sent him to the store so that I could tell "Mr. Asshole" a piece of my mind.

Mathew always had a way of trying to make me feel that he was concerned by not addressing the real problem. It was as though he thought, if he did not bring things up, a supernatural miracle would take place and I would overlook whatever dirt he had done. He walked into the bedroom, and seeing me lying down, he asked, "You OK?" I stared at him long and hard, and told him, "Yes, I am just fine," as calmly as I could.
I truly wanted to say, "What the fuck do you think, bastard?" He started to go into his pleading, pitiful act, as he sat down on the bed, but I stopped him in his tracks. "It doesn't matter, Mathew, please don't start.

Spare me your fake, pointless apology! Yet know this, I am going to have this baby, and it will be over, but if you want to spare us both the discomfort, you can go now. Frankly, I don't care what you do." Bryan and I continued to grieve over Fritz, and looked to see her in someone's possession, but never saw her again! She had lots of good years left, but mama said it may have been God's will and she probably had a good home! She said that she was so spoiled that she would never have understood the baby taking so much of our time.

We prepared for the birth together, and the excitement of a new baby was in the atmosphere of the little apartment we called home. We actually made bets about the sex of the baby. Mathew tricked me by letting me go first. If it was a girl like I wanted, Mathew was to buy me anything I asked for. I chose a new television set. If it were a boy like he wanted, I would buy him anything he wanted. He chose a new Chevrolet van. There was no way in hell I could afford a new Chevy van, and he knew it. I felt in my heart that our marriage was going to remain in trouble after the birth of our baby, but whatever was going to happen was going to happen. I could not worry about it anymore. I had a baby to deliver and I did not want to do it alone. I made up my mind that I was not going to fuss anymore. Once the baby was safely delivered, issues would get better or worsen. I would deal with it when the time comes.

I went through the labor and delivery, happy he was there for me. I was happy I did not have to try to squirm out of the purchase of a van, not that I would have anyway. We had a little girl, but he did not show disappointment in any way. We named her Mathew Lynn after her father and grandfather, thus their world was complete. It was Mathew's first and only child, if I had anything to do with it, so he was ecstatic just to be a father.

His mother came and stayed, helping me for almost two weeks after her birth. I was so appreciative, because twenty-one hours of labor wore me to a frazzle. We all enjoyed her together, Mathew, Bryan, Mathew's mom, and I. Mathew's mother always said, we all sat and watched her just like we were watching TV. That was extra funny, because it was so true. I had my near-perfect family, with my handsome son and now a beautiful daughter. If only I had the wonderful husband, that would put the icing on the cake. From a tiny baby, she drank her milk so fast you could actually hear it when it made it to her small stomach.

Bryan got the biggest kick out of watching her drink, taking long sucks until she was so full it seemed that she would just pass out. He loved to feed her just so he could watch that part. I could always tell when she drifted off to sleep, because he would fill the house with laughter. As 5p.m was on her evening feeding schedule, Bryan would arrive home around the same time after showering at the school from football practice. He asked me, "Mom, don't feed her before I get home, because I want to do it. I have to see her pass out." I always waited so he could have that time with his little sister. He enjoyed her and was so happy she actually did turn out to be a girl, just like he had hoped. Mathew Lynn was growing like a weed. It seemed that she changed daily, and before I knew it she was one year old.

Matlynn as we called her for short dominated her surroundings. She was cheerful, talkative, and smart. She talked in full sentences at fourteen months. If you wanted something kept quiet, you had better not say it around her, because she repeated it with accuracy. With Mathew, there was still something missing, for I was never enough. We always got our gas at the same service station, and Mathew suddenly had to go to the store or the service station every day or so in the evening around the same time.

Matlynn was two years old and always wanted to go with him. For a while, he would take her, but finally after she told me "Mommy, Daddy talked to that boy too much! He let me stay in the car too long!" I responded, "He did? Daddy had better not have left you in the car too long." I did not think anything of it, because Matlynn said Daddy was always talking to a guy. So what? Guys talk about football, basketball, and just plain guy stuff. Knowing how Mathew loved sports, I could see that happening. When he stopped taking her, I would be working on the laundry or doing something else around the house, and he would leave her crying, and pleading to go. I thought, "How can he be so cruel to her?"

One evening, Matlynn and I were coming from the store and stopped by the service station to get her favorite lollipops. The community store did not carry that brand. As we drove up she said, "Mommy, that's the boy Daddy talks to, too much!" "No, sweetheart, that is a woman," I said. I got out and walked to the window. The woman wore her hair slick back in a small ball style, causing Matlynn to think she was a boy. Oh! I see, I thought. He would take Matlynn everywhere with him usually. I watched Mathew's pattern very closely, and a pattern it truly turned out to be. He was talking to this woman during the day when I was at work and visiting with her a few minutes in the evening, as many evenings as he could find excuses.

I decided to record the calls during the day for a few days, just to see if my suspicions were true. Surely enough that is exactly what was happening. Some days she worked twelve hours, which allowed them time to talk when I was at work. It was hilarious! He would call and talk, but sometimes the owner would be there and answer. He would start speaking in a Spanish accent. I was amazed at the lengths this man would go for a woman. By this time, it was funny, and I let it go on for several weeks without saying a word.

We went through the motion of living from day to day, growing colder and colder toward one another. Just before Matlynn's third birthday, I met a young lady named Lisa. She, her two sons and a husband had moved upstairs just two months prior to my meeting her. They both taught school as well, and had move to Houston from Tennessee. She already had friends in town, so she went to quite a few social events. We usually arrived home from school about the same time, and many times, we chatted outside on my porch. She happened to mention that she danced at least two nights each week. One night, she invited me to go along, and I took her up on the offer. I had always loved dancing since childhood.

With Daddy owning a teen café, I was quite a dancer at one time. Maybe I could actually learn some of the modern stuff. I enjoyed myself so much that I started going with her once each week but finally worked my way into going twice a week also. I had found an outlet, something that I really liked to do. On nights when I went out, I saw to it that Bryan had his homework done before I left.

Our going out was slowed a bit when both families purchased homes. As we looked, I told Mathew I wanted to purchase something that I could afford alone because I did not know how long we would be together. Mathew realized beyond a shadow of doubt, I did not care about him like before. Once our homes were in order, Lisa and I picked up where we left off. We would meet at different clubs to dance and sometimes have a drink or two.

I more often than not, had one drink as soon as I got to the club. I had a twofold reason for that. It relaxed me enough for me to attempt any dance they were doing, and after three hours of dancing, it would not affect my driving ability. If it was Lisa's night to drive, I sometimes had two drinks. Whenever I tried to feel guilty about going out, I would get hell in me and say, "Why should I feel guilty about leaving her with him, hell, I carried her nine months, labored twenty-one hours, and took all of his shit this whole marriage." I went out when I wanted and stayed as long as I wanted. It was my turn to let him think whatever he wanted to think.

Just prior to Matlynn turning three years old, Mathew lost his job again. This time, I did not know why! I wondered if he was stupid enough to get caught up in the same old stuff at work again. He was stupid enough to screw off over and over again. I did not care, and did not let it weigh upon my mind! Mathew began job-hunting immediately. He looked for work for several months to no avail. He was offered a job in Virginia, and the company would pay for our relocating. Mathew wanted that job, and I wanted him to have it, but I was not going to move, not even three steps. I had my fill of following him, making new starts that would only prove to be disastrous. He was not getting me any farther from home than Houston.

I had gotten used to Houston and really liked living there. Mathew had always gone to church, but seemed to have lost interest since he was away from his home church. Our life together became more somber than I would ever have imagined. Like the other husbands, he too felt he had enough to share the wealth. It is a fact that most men think they are "all that" in the bedroom, but it was my experience that most of them barely had enough sexual stamina for me. The thought of their trying to share that little bit was almost comical.

I was tough, hardened by my many experiences with men. As he prepared to move to Virginia, I helped him as much as I could. His car was old, had many miles on it, and could not be trusted to make a long trip like that. Since I was the only one employed, I had to purchase an automobile for him to make the long drive and have transportation to and from work in Virginia. I did it, because he was still my husband and he had to have reliable transportation. I also thought about the fact that he needed a job to be able to help us sustain back in

Houston. Several times I wanted to say, "Now look who is having to, once again, stand behind your sorry ass." We talked intensely the night before he left, and I told him to search his heart, find whatever the hell he was looking for, because I was not it. He continued to proclaim his undying love for me, but why could I not feel it?

Mathew was inexperienced in the area of marriage, and I was hardened by past experiences in love and marriage. As he prepared to leave, I told him, "Away from me, you do everything you think you are big enough to do! I won't be there to meddle." Then I quoted something I had heard and contemplated many times. It was supposed to have been a quoted by someone named "Britt". It read something like this: If you love something, let them go. If it returns, it is yours to keep, if it doesn't, then it was never yours! Mathew left for Virginia in May, and I was alone, but this time it was different.

I did not cry or miss him as much as I thought I might. I carried on with my life as if I were a single parent. Things I heard about Mathew when friends from Monroe called, did not hurt so badly. Another phase of my life was ending, and I was totally OK with it. I hated the idea of having another child fatherless; but for what I had endured, it seemed a small price to pay.

Out of the seven kids born to my parents, all seven had been divorced at least one time. "Daddy attributed it to the changes in society and the generations in which we were raised. We were sitting around talking and the subject came up. We had all been raised by parents who were loving toward each other and who stayed together through the raising of their seven children. Only two children of the seven divorced and never remarried, and four married a second time.

I was the only one who had multiple marriages. We all laughed thinking how ironic that we all had been divorced at some point. Daddy thought that since George and I were the babies of the family, I too was a product of the generation of which I was raised, resulting in multiple marriages. Daddy then said, "Savanah is a good catch dog, but she just can't hold!" Everybody laughed, and so did I, but it was not particularly funny. The joke was on me! I must admit, it felt awkward to hear him refer to my marriages so comically.

I was great at preparing men to be better husbands to their second or third marriages, because by the time I released them to the wild, they were more careful the next time around. Strangely enough, they all loved me and wanted me to remain their wife, but not enough to be devoted. I had vowed not to accept infidelity, and I still held fast to that vow, even if it did take some time for me to get to the point of divorce. The only time I wavered was when I thought Fred had fathered Linda's baby. By the time Mathew came into my life, AIDS was running rapid throughout the US, and I wanted no parts of that stuff. I would take the chance of raising my children alone.

My dream of a happy marriage and family life was over. I went about my business, making my children the center of my life. I had my happy family without marriage being a part of the act. I guessed I must have been equipped with an emotional and biological mechanism that made me overly susceptible and vulnerably attracted to men who cheated. I had always been the type that showered my man with love, and although I required love in return and got it, I dared not turn my back. After Mathew had gone away, I began to look back over at my life. It was the first time I came to the realization that, I had wondered through my adult life, without thinking through my direction.

I was twenty-years old, when I discovered Fred's infidelity and left him at age twenty-three. I was thirty-eight, when I watched Mathew drive away into the sunset, just as I had watched Fred drive away sixteen years before. To my amazement, I had married all of my boyfriends! There were a few dates here and there with other guys, but they were only dates that never made it to second base. I don't know whether marrying four times, if we are going to count the few weeks I lived with Jimmy as a marriage, was a good thing or a bad thing. I guess I could probably find advantages and disadvantages either way. I had watched girlfriends change men almost as fast as they changed their shoes.

They left relationship after relationship with nothing but a wet butt, without getting the cost of the soap they used to wash with. At least I came through each failed relationship with stuff: diamonds, gold, furniture, eventually three homes, and the children that I always wanted! Still, when all was said and done, I was disappointed in the end, just as my friends were.

Finding a husband was always easy for me. Each one wanted me for their wife, and was eager and excited placing a ring on my finger. Still, those men did not have good examples to follow in knowing how to treat a woman. They did what they saw their fathers do, thinking I would accept the treatment their mothers took. When we don't, they do not understand! The cycle repeats itself in the children born into the situation for generations to come. Many years ago, few men and women left town after graduation from high school. This practice tied them to living as they were accustomed to living. It is only when they change environments, and see how things are done differently, that some discover exactly how easy it is to love a woman. A woman truly loved, can build a family and her husband is adored.

There was some satisfaction in knowing that they thought enough of me to marry me. I knew, I did not want to try it again, not now, not ever, unless God himself told me. I remembered when Bryan was small and would look at me so strangely when I was hurting as a result of that failed marriage to Fred. He never knew why I was hurting, but he often said, "Mommy, don't be sad." He was only three when he said that to me the first time, but, that was not the last, by far. I would always try so hard to be cheerful for him, even if I felt rotten. I didn't give him enough of myself! Some of the reason was because Mama stood in the way. I should have stood up for my son, instead of letting him be crippled academically by my parents.

I should have been stronger, but I didn't know how to be stronger. Instead, I found other things to fill the void—men, friends and dancing! With Bryan, I tried to play catch up academically and personally after we moved to Texas. I would say we accomplished as much as we could under the circumstances. I stopped going out when Matlynn was four, because she was such a demanding child.
When she said to me one night, "Mommy, please don't go out, stay with me, please!" The look on her face was as serious as I had ever noticed in any child. I put down my purse and keys, called and told my friends that I would not be going out anymore. I had been thinking that maybe I should put my going out on the back-burner. That was my confirmation! What happened with Bryan was not going to be repeated. I was her mom, and it was my responsibility to see that she developed physically, mentally, socially, emotionally, academically, and spiritually.

It was my job to protect her, love her, be there for her, play with her, support her, and assist her in becoming a healthy, well rounded, and productive member of a society that was becoming more challenging with each new generation. Bryan graduated from high school, and we had a big party. Mama and the rest of our family from Arkansas came to his graduation and to party with us. Mathew and his family were there to join in the celebration. Mama enjoyed being there with all of us, although rheumatoid arthritis had resulted in her being confined to a wheelchair.

Daddy did not come, but sent Bryan a crisp $100 bill. He seldom closed his café, because it was the weekends when he made the most money. He was in the process of buying a van with a handicap lift, to accommodate mama and her wheelchair. Regular automobiles had proven to be so difficult, but my brothers had to be sure she was at Bryan's graduation. She would have it no other way!

Bryan went off to college, but decided after a year that he did not want to be there. He was capable academically, but he had to study. He lost focus after this little girl decided he had to be the father of her daughters, each born a year apart. I was hurt but I did everything I could for the young lady and the babies. I even kept her at my house for her six-week recovery periods, and paid nursery for the babies and for Matlynn, at the same time. He was a boy that drove an automobile; therefore his insurance cost was eating my lunch. When she named him as the father of her second child, I thought I would die. He became discouraged, left school, and got a job, after my pleading for him to return to school fell upon deaf ears.

He continued to live at home until he was twenty-two years of age. He then moved out, leaving Matlynn and me alone. I really wanted him to stay, but he insisted that he needed his own space. I still visited him often, trying to make sure he stayed grounded and away from all the evil the world had to offer. He was living his own life, paying his own way, and I was still trying to make up for lost time.

When Bryan's babies mother became unhappy with the amount of money he was giving her monthly for the two kids, she filed for child support. Since they were not married, his attorney asked for a paternity test. When the test results returned, neither of the children was his. It affected his whole existence! He loved these two baby girls more than he loved himself. I felt so sorry for my son that I cried uncontrollably. I loved them so much, and now what were we to do? She was only tenth grade when she conceived the first child and eleventh grade when she conceived the second.

I did not think that a tenth grader would be so promiscuous. Mathew never believed Bryan was the father but it never crossed my mind that she could be lying to me. One thought that I could never get past was, Where in the hell was her mother? That is until I met the mother! Bryan became distant and went through many changes as a result of such a devastating disappointment. When I would try to talk to him about it, he was not comfortable with it. I wanted him to see a psychiatrist to help him work through it, but he would not hear of it. Eventually, he started dating again and I prayed he was all right.

After two years in Virginia, Mathew was transferred to Fort Worth, Texas, and continued to be his usual self. Matlynn was recuperating from a severe asthma attack. I had taken her to the emergency room and she was given a shot, prednisone, and a breathing treatment. I called off from work the next day because we did not get home until 5:00 a.m. I put Matlynn in the bed with me, so I could be close to her as she slept. She seemed to be doing much better at first, but when I woke up, her breathing was so shallow that I decided to wake her up. She looked at me and said, "Mommy, what are you going to do if I die?" I jumped up from the bed, wrapped her in a blanket, and told her, "You are not going to die, baby," and headed back to the hospital.

Matlynn was so different from any child I had ever been around. She used to tell me at least thirty minutes before she became sick with her asthma that she was getting ready to be sick. Her prediction never failed. Within thirty minutes or so, she would be as sick as she could be. Once we arrived at the hospital, they immediately placed an IV in her arm and admitted her.

When I told Mathew about her being in the hospital, he told me that he would come if I needed him, but his job there in Fort Worth was relatively new, and he really needed to be there. I told him to go on and stay at work and I would keep him informed about her progress. Once we were given a room, a nurse stayed right there next to her. While checking the IV, she stuck little probes onto Matlynn's chest that ran to another machine that was recording those reading too. When they came in with the oxygen tent, I thought that I should call Mathew and let him know he should prepare to come to Houston. The nurse was being evasive when I asked her questions and I began to get really scared. I wondered if it was just her personality or if she was withholding information about my baby's condition. I did not get an answer on his cell phone, so I called the office. The secretary told me that he was not in, his daughter was ill in Houston, and he was on his way there. I waited for him to walk in the door at any time. His parents were waiting by the phone to be kept abreast of her progress.

After several hours and he did not show up, I called his parents to inquire about him. They were under the impression that he was at work also. Della, Mathew's friend's wife, called my cell to check on Matlynn's condition. I asked her how she found out about the baby being ill. She said that Kenneth, her husband, said Mathew was in Monroe and told him Matlynn was ill.

"Monroe! I questioned? I called his office and the secretary told me he was on his way to Houston!" I replied. "No," she said, "he is here in Monroe." "Did Kenneth say why he was in Monroe?" I asked, "the secretary said he was on his way here to see about Matlynn!" "Savanah, if I tell you this, you had better never let Mathew know because he will tell Kenneth and it will be my ass," she replied. "OK, I won't, you know that," I said. "He is moving that girlfriend of his up there with him," she said softly. "You are lying, Della, tell me you are lying!" I said. "No, Savanah, it's true," she said even softer.

I sat there for a few seconds before I could speak. "Della, call me tomorrow and I will update you on Matlynn's condition, and oh, thanks," and I hung up the phone. No, he didn't use our sick baby as an excuse to leave work, just to move his girlfriend to Fort Worth! I thought. That was the straw that broke the camel's back. Matlynn was in the hospital for five days, and I was there the entire five days all alone. I left only to pack a bag with changing clothes. He called to check on her frequently, but he never came to the hospital.

After Matlynn was doing well again, I filed for divorce. I never confronted him because what good would it has done? The only thing I hated now was losing his family as my in-laws. I loved them dearly, but not enough to stay Mathew's wife. It was super clear that not even Matlynn was very high on his list of priorities.

Somebody Should Have Told ME!

Chapter Seven

From the age of thirty eight, I would spend eight years alone, dating every now and then, but focusing on Matlynn as my number one priority. Living fast causes mistakes that sometimes are not repairable. My mind drifted back to my upbringing. My life was somewhat sheltered. My mother was not able to tell me a lot about relationships, because she had only one. My mother was safe within her marriage. She never lived in the world of divorce and confusion. She could not tell me how to function when turmoil struck my life, or how to handle heartbreak. She could only imagine and feel sorry for me when I suffered. We as her children were her number one priority, but the world was changing from the way it was when she was a girl. People were separating divorcing, partying, living together instead of marrying and she thought all hell had broken loose. All parents should let their children be their number one priority in all that they do.

Take them to church, get them in Sunday school, so they will know what thus says the Lord. Never fail to discipline, but do it with love! Sometimes, depending on the child, you may have to demand, but do it gently. They learn and pattern themselves after those of us who raise them. My mother did all of this for us. We knew what thus said the Lord. We went to Sunday school, and was in church every time the door opened. Yet, even these days no parent has all of the answers. Your children will treat your grandchildren the way you have taught them via modeling.

Our children are the future, don't you show up negatively through them in the future. When I married the first time and it ended so painfully, it affected me so much, that I allowed it to filter over into each relationship thereafter. After Fred, when I saw my marriages going in the wrong direction and it seemed I could not get them back on track, I walked away. That was my shield of protection! Over the eight years that I was alone, I learned much about myself, and I set out to be the better for it. Being married does not give you ownership of anyone.

Marriage is a contract that can be and often is broken. It is that feeling of ownership that causes us so much pain when the marriage or relationship comes to an end. That is why it is so important to concentrate on page number

6 of this book. If nobody tells you, what somebody should tell you, "ask," "observe," and take your time. Allow yourself to be human, it is OK to hurt, but know, it always gets better! When it does, you will emerge victorious, but above all, never fail to listen! Men and women alike are just sometimes attracted to the opposite sex. In the case that there is a marriage, and one or the other is found to be less than faithful, feelings of betrayal and deceit, puts the marriage in a very bad place. It is sometimes saved, and quite often it ends in divorce.

Hillary Clinton made the choice to give her marriage a chance, and so far, so good. She did this with the world watching, and I admired her bravery. John Edwards's wife was dying and he strayed, Sandra bullock ditched Jessie James and did not look back. Tiger Woods lost half of his fortune, you might as well say. However, cheating husbands have always been something expected, but frowned upon when the exact same thing is done by a woman. Some believe in the old idiom, "live and let live" or "What is good for the goose is good for the gander." Until the aids virus, I might have been inclined to agree, but now the decision is made and stands! I chose to live! Arnold Schwarzenegger's long time romance even got in on the act just last year!

Everyday folks like us go through this all of the time, and how lucky we are that our dirty laundry only get to be known by a few. Here again, children are caught in the middle, while grown folk suffer through the healing process. We have to know when it is time to roll and when to fold. You feel it and you know it's over, even if you can't let go, yet, you will let go! It is your choice whether you want to do it with dignity! Men don't always love the women they frolic around with. Still ignorance has never been an excuse for carefree living on the part of neither male nor female. Those that get a second chance after infidelity had better grab and hold with all of their might. Chances are it is your last!

I dedicated those years of my life to raising Matlynn different from the way I was raised, and from the way I had allowed Bryan to be raised. I did not have all of the answers just like my mother, but I gave her my all. All through elementary, middle school, and high school, I watched over my daughter. I did not allow her to spend the night away from home but a precious few nights. My niece, Katie, moved to Houston when Matlynn was six years old. She had a daughter three years older than Matlynn. Katelyn was a very studious child who was raised by a loving mother as well. If Matlynn did not spend the night with Katelyn, she was home. One other time, I allowed her to spend the night with her friend, Jennifer, when she had a pajama party. Jennifer's mother was quite particular with her daughter as well. Jennifer had spent the night with Matlynn several times, and I felt terrible saying no every time Matlynn was asked to stay over there.

Because Matlynn was and still is an only grandchild, on the paternal side of the family, she would always spend several weeks in the summer with her grandparents in Monroe, Louisiana. On the maternal side of her family she third to the last grandchild out of a total twenty six grandchildren. Although she was loves, my parent had to spread their love around. of If Mathew saw her, it had to be in Houston or at her granny's house. It was never because I distrusted him, but the girlfriend who eventually became his wife, had three sons and a daughter.

All of Mathew's stepchildren were older than our child. I was taking no chances on my daughter going to spend any time there. They were not her "true" brothers, and Matlynn's father had to work. Most children are mischievous and curious by nature, and boys and girls alike at a certain age, experiment. There would be no experimenting with my daughter.

Had Mathew pushed the issue, I would have reluctantly complied with the law, but thank God he did not. You know what you have been through, but you never know what is waiting up ahead. As a result of my not allowing Matlynn to visit, Mathew would only see her when she visited is parents home. He had one child in this world, and he placed himself in the situation to be step-father to four children. This affected Mathew and Matlynn's relationship for several years. He kept in contact with her through regular phone calls, and never missed sending birthday and Christmas gifts. He always supported her financially of which I was most appreciative.

Think of the possible consequence before you allow your child to do certain things. I am by far no authority and I cannot tell young women how to live their lives, nor how to raise their children, but when a person has lived and been through the school of hard knocks themselves, their stories should be told in order that young women and young men alike will be able to look at the big picture. Parents need to share certain experiences with their daughters and keep an open line of communication for daughters to feel comfortable enough to sit down and discuss almost anything. I certainly did that with Matlynn. It is dangerous to allow children to feel their way through life. It is the same as asking a blind man to find a single baseball in a baseball field.

When Matlynn was twelve years old, I met Douglas through a mutual friend. I had just purchased a new Toyota Camry, and wanted to have the windows tinted. Summer in Houston is hot and the tint would help keep the car cooler on the inside. My friend, Carla went with me to "Auto Shield", a business where Douglas was part owner. As I waited for my car, we became engaged in a conversation with him. He was a handsome man, but did not have the pretty-boy attitude that some men can have. When they finished and pulled my car out front, I was proud that I had decided to have the windows done. It was already a pretty car, but the tint really set it off. They told me when I left I needed to let my windows stay up for seven days, before rolling them down. I complained that I sure hope I did not forget. Douglas decided to place tape over the windows' lock buttons which would remind me not to let them down. As soon as Carla and I drove away, she started going on and on about how Douglas was falling all over himself watching me. I really had not noticed, and told her that he was talking to both of us. She went on and on, but I finally told her to shut up. I was not looking for a boyfriend, or a friend boy. She laughed and laughed.

On the seventh day, Douglas called to remind me that I could use my windows again starting immediately. I thanked him because I truly had forgotten. We talked briefly and said goodbye. A few days after I started rolling my windows up and down again, I noticed the rubber that lies against the window was loose. Each time I rolled the window up, that rubber would lift. It had never done that before, so I decided to take it to the dealership. They told me whoever tinted my windows, cut the rubber, causing it to rise up when I roll the windows down. I looked back on my caller ID and found the number where Douglas had called me. Thank God, I thought as the number rolled up on the screen. I called to give Douglas a piece of my mind. When he answered, I identified myself, and it was apparent that he was pleased that I had called. I told him that the guys he had install the tint cut my rubber around the window on the driver's side front. Prepared to get an argument, I told him that I wanted it fixed immediately. To my surprise, he offered no resistance but asked me to meet with him so that he could look at the damage. I met him and after looking at it, he told me to get an estimate for the repair, and he would take care of it.

After getting the estimate, I met him again to pick up the two hundred forty-three dollars needed for the repairs. When he paid me, he filled my car with gas and bought me breakfast. As I sat across the table from him, he was funny and I laughed louder and harder than I had in years. Even after the meal, I was in no hurry. Although it was a nice outing, there was something that I could not quite put my finger on with him. He leaned in closer to me from across the table. Now I am sure that Carla was right about his liking what he had seen that day. I had dedicated so much of my time to Matlynn and closed the door to ever getting serious about a man again. I didn't even know if I was still cute. I was feeling old at age forty-five. It was summer, and Matlynn was with her grandparents in Louisiana. By this time, Matlyn's physicians had found the correct medications that prevented her Asthma from appearing so severe. She seldom had any kind of attacks anymore.

The Rodeo was one thing that caused flare ups in her condition. All I was going to do that day was go back home and clean. I learned that Douglas worked a full-time job as well as being part owner in the business. He found out at breakfast I did not have a boyfriend, so he asked if he could call me sometimes. I agreed for him to do so, knowing it was going nowhere. He would call from work and ask what I was doing. If I was busy, he would ask if it was OK for him to call later. He wanted to know how late was too late for him to call. It was summer and I was not teaching summer school, so I gave him a green light to call me at his leisure. I sat up late watching movies anyway. He got used to calling, and some mornings, I would meet him for breakfast and another funny laughing session. He occupied my time during the whole summer, a welcome change from the usual boredom.

When Matlynn returned home, Mommy had a new friend. He had not been to my home as of yet, but the following weekend, he came by with his nephew driving him. He met Matlynn, and she liked him right away. That was a little different for her because she usually took a while to warm up to strangers. I watched Douglas make friends with my daughter that day. Inside, both Douglas and his nephew, Cedric, commented on how nice my house was. It was nice, a home for me to raise Matlynn, and where I was to spend the rest of my life. It was a small three-bedroom house with two baths and two-car garage in suburban Houston. It was in a relatively upscale side of town in an area called Friendswood. Douglas and I talked on the phone but the visits were seldom. In September, I was back in the classroom, and Matlynn was enrolled at the same school where I was teaching. Just as school was over, one Wednesday, Matlynn and I went to my car, to find Douglas and his sister parked next to us. He had been to the doctor and she was driving him. The doctor had told him not to drive, and he wanted to spend some time with me.

I picked up food for Matlynn, Douglas, and myself, and then proceeded to drive the three of us to my house. Once Matlynn had eaten, she knew to begin on her homework right away so that she would have time to play. I checked her work and drilled her on the spelling test for the next day. Douglas sat and patiently waited and watched TV as we worked. Matlynn went out to play in the backyard, with her dog, Chili. Now Douglas and I had time to talk! He told me that he was losing his sight to an eye disease called "Retinitus Pigmentosa". He had known for several months that he was losing his sight, but he did not want to tell me because he thought that I would not want to continue our friendship. I was sad for Douglas who had the most beautiful, light brown eyes. How can those eyes not see? I wondered. That was the little thing I could not put my finger on.

When he leaned over the table when we would have breakfast, he was trying to get a better look at me. I remembered his telling me that I was beautiful, and I thanked him, but how did he come to that conclusion if he could not see me well. "So am I to disregard the comment you made about me being beautiful?" I asked, jokingly. "No," he said, "you are beautiful, Savanah." It must have been scary knowing that one day he would be in total darkness. I had never heard of Retinitus Pigmentosa, but he educated me within a few minutes. He said it was a degenerative disease of the retina of both of his eyes. The disease was inherited from his mother, and only he and one sister contracted the disease. The disease caused little freckles to grow on the retina, eventually covering up the entire retina, leaving him in darkness. I had never had the pleasure of meeting any of his family other than his nephew, Cedric, and the one sister that I met briefly that same day at my job. There were six other girls and two boys, making his mother have a total of eight children.

I hugged him and assured him that everything would work out if he trusted and believed in God. He had driven for the last time and that was probably the next hardest thing he had been told, second to his losing his sight. The doctor had checked him the week before and gave him the results of the test today also. Douglas had diabetes! When he told me that, my heart literally melted in sadness for him! "Oh Douglas, I am so sorry, sweetie," I said! Now I knew why he wanted to come over today, he needed to be with someone, and maybe family was not what he needed at that moment. With Douglas not working anymore, the company gave him long-term disability, and he filed for social security. He had three children by two previous marriages, and they two would receive benefits from social security. Douglas's job paid really well, and he had prepared for the rainy days. He would be able to take care of his children and still have a decent living for himself.

Douglas lived about forty-three miles from my home in an area called Cypress. Matlynn's bedtime was 9p.m, so I had my niece to come over and stay with her while I dropped Douglas off at home. It was the first time I had gone to his area, and with it being dark, I could not see the house. I could tell from the homes that were well lit that he too, lived in a somewhat upscale area. As time passed, I learned that it could be years before he became totally blind. He visited more often since he lived a leisurely lifestyle, but he did not impose during the week days. We mostly talked on the phone once I was in the bed, until I was ready to go to sleep. We talked a lot about his health, and he was getting a lot of information from the commission for the blind. Every night he told me more and more about what the commission offered and how it all applied to him. I could spare one hour after I got in bed talking to him.

Matlynn was sad, when she found out that Douglas was losing his sight. I don't know whether she remember that or not, and neither did I until I started to write this part of my story. I have to wonder if she developed her desire to work in the healthcare field because of that. She told me once as we talked about her going into healthcare, that she just might find a cure for Douglas's disease. Granny and Papa came up from Monroe for Christmas. Douglas spent a lot of time over during the Christmas holidays and made a mash hit with both Granny and Papa. He really liked them a lot too. We all got along so well together that others could not believe they were Mathew's parents. In February, Douglas was faced with making another decision. The commission for the blind had offered

Douglas a mobility training-life skills class that would last three months, but he would have to go to Austin, Texas, to Cris Cole Center for the Blind to take advantage of that opportunity. Douglas was very reluctant to leave Houston and everyone he knew in his comfortable surroundings.

I knew that the training was something that would benefit him so much, and I encouraged him to go. I promised him that Matlynn and I would visit on every other weekend, and we did. I drove and we used it as a tool to help Matlynn learn to read maps better. She navigated me into Austin and straight to Cris Cole Center's door every other weekend. The class began on March first, and Matlynn and I went down and helped him get unpacked and set up in his room. It was a lovely facility for learning, and learning he did. Upon returning home, I rushed and got everything done to prepare for the work week and Matlynn's school. We did homework while we were in Austin, and made sure that Matlynn was in bed before 9p.m. I, on the other hand, still had ironing to do. I made it a habit of getting all clothing for both Matlynn and me ready for the whole week. I finished everything by 11p.m and crawled into bed. I was dozing off to sleep when the phone rang. It was Douglas, trying to see if we made it home safely. I apologized for not calling as I said, but I was behind schedule and had a lot to do. We spoke for a very short time and I went to sleep.

I woke up a little tired, but told Matlynn we would turn in an hour earlier tonight. For several days, I did not feel the greatest, and neither did Matlynn. Things kind of leveled out and we had the next weekend free. I talked to Douglas every night as usual, and he was glad to see us when two weeks rolled around. In Austin again, I became ill, so ill that I could hardly drive. Matlynn had already told me she was getting sick. It was Saturday, and because we did not know what was going on with the both of us, we both checked into the emergency room. I was too sick to attend and comfort her, but Douglas was there and she was OK with it. The doctor said that the cedar gets to many people who come to Austin between the months of November and March. After treatment, Matlynn and I went back to our room and Douglas took care of us. Matlynn and I had one bed and Douglas had the other.

He checked on us all through the night, and I was glad he was there. We had our prescriptions filled, and by Sunday morning, we felt much better. It was time to go back to Houston, directly after lunch. That was not a productive weekend, but we were all together. We met so many blind individuals that were functioning quite well. It is amazing that what the eyes cannot see, the ears supplement for. After frequenting the center several times, those who were familiar with me, recognized me when I approached without my speaking a word.

They listened to my footsteps and would often say to another, "Go to the desk, call Douglas and tell him that Savanah and Matlynn are here." Some of it could have been because I had Matlynn with me and she was a chatterbox. I was blown away at the intelligence and all that these people with no sight could do. They cooked very well and went wherever they wanted to go in the city. They knew how to use their canes and listen to the traffic to determine when to walk and when to stay curbside. Although I had much experience with special needs children, my kids would never be mobile enough to do the things these blind individuals could; seldom did I have one to walk.

These people were normal in every way, other than being blind. Every other weekend, Douglas began having dinner ready when Matlynn and I arrived. I was seeing this man in a whole different light. In May, he completed his three months of training; he graduated with a certificate and Matlynn and I were proud. School was out for the summer on Friday and Douglas graduated on Saturday, so we celebrated! We walked up the trail on the side of the mountain that over looked Lake Travis and looked down on the homes all equipped with boats, jet skis, and everything for leisurely living. That was the highlight of Matlynn's day. As we stood looking down on the breathtaking view, it occurred to me that Douglas could not see why we were so astonished.

I began telling him in detail all that we saw. He stood there smiling and those light brown eyes looked so perfect. We sat down to eat the burgers we had stopped and purchased, and enjoyed the view that we probably would not see for some time. On the ride back home, Douglas told us many funny stories of things that happened to the different residents during his stay. We laughed and had a fun ride back home. As we entered Houston city limits, I told Douglas that I did not know how to get to his house since we were coming from a totally different direction. He asked me to tell him where we were exactly. We were on Highway 290, at the Mason Road exit. OK, he said, that will be easy.

He told me exactly where to go and we ended up at his home. On Sunday, Matlynn was excited that her grandparents were coming down the following weekend, and she would be off to Monroe, Louisiana to spend the summer. It was a joyous week, as it was every time my ex-in-laws visited. Matlynn functioned in first gear any time her grandparents were around, knowing she is the center of their world. When we got home we found that Chili, Matlynns dog was missing. We looked everywhere for him to no avail. Our neighbor told us that she had seen a man walking down the street with a dog that she thought was "Chili" in his arms. There was no way that Chili had gotten out of the yard by himself. Every board was tight and there were no holes for him to slip underneath. Chili was a Chinese pug and as cute as could be. She pointed to the house where she had seen the man go in with Chili.

Matlynn cried and cried about her dog, so I decided that we would walk down there and just ask if maybe they had seen him. We rang the doorbell and a nice looking woman came to the door. We asked about Chili and described him to the lady. She seemed surprised that we were asking about the dog and stepped outside closing the door behind her as if she did not want usa to look inside. She was quite evasive and wanted to rush us along. As she turned to go back inside, I took my time about turning to leave so that I could get a glimpse of inside of her house.

There was a man standing back inside kind of peeping around her to see us. Just as the door closed I was sure that I heard the whining of a dog. The whining sounded much like Chili! "They have a dog too Matlynn," I said. "That dog sound like Chili mommy," Matlynn stated.
"Well, probably not sweetie," I said, because I did not want to encourage her curiosity. "Mommy" Matlynn said, "let's ask them to let us see their dog, because that was Chili crying to come home." "Oh sweetheart, we can't just accuse them of taking Chili without proof, I suggested! Matlynn cried but we did not turn back. I hoped they would not just go and get her out of our back yard. We left her plenty of food and water, and when I looked, most of the food was gone. That meant that she was home most of the weekend. It was Saturday evening when Denise saw him with the dog that looked like Chili.

On late Sunday evening we rushed to have the flyers with his picture placed all over the community. Surely someone would recognize him and bring him home. All night I thought about Chili and Matlynn was so restless I allowed her to sleep in my bed with me. My poor baby loved her dog, they were playmates. She called for him in her sleep, and I knew that she was dreaming about her Chili. We had prayed that Chili would return to us before going to sleep, but when we left for school on Monday morning, there was no word of her. On Monday evening after school, I called for Matlynn to come and eat. She was doing homework while I prepared dinner, but she did not answer. I went into her room and she was not there. I called her louder, and looked in every room, but she was gone. Panick set in after I did not find her outside in either the back or front yard. I called the police and told them that my daughter was missing. They told me that someone would be there shortly.

When I started back into the front yard, I met Matlynn running into the garage out of breath. "Mommy, Mommy, I told you that was Chili down there in those peoples house". "Matlynn, don't you ever leave here without telling me, you know you know better," I said as I hugged her tight! You made me call the police, I said! You should have asked me if you could go, I said thinking more of my baby than Chili at the moment! She dropped her head and with sad eyes, she looked directly into my eyes and said, "you wouldn't have let me go." "Did you see Chilli," I asked.

Yes, "mommy but the man saw me and I ran home," she said. Just then, the police pulled into the driveway. I made them aware that Matlynn was fine, but she slipped off and went to find our dog that was taken out of our yard this past weekend. We described Chilli as a medium tan Chinese Pug with one white foot on the front right paw. Matlynn took over, "I peeped through their fence in the back yard and Chili was in the back yard playing with their dog". She described their dog as being a white poodle. She said she tried to pull the board back so that Chili could get out, but it was too tight. The man who lived there came out and heard her talking to Chili. That was when she thought she had better run back to tell me. The two police officers went to speak with the owners of the house, Matlynn and I went right behind them. The wife said that the husband was not home.

The little white poodle was standing at the door with her this time. She said she did not know where her husband, was and he had been gone for quite a while. This child saw him a few minutes ago here at home, they told her! She paused, and then said, she must have been mistaken.
The police officer questioned Matlynn again, and she told him the same story. She showed him where she was standing when she saw Chilli, and where the husband was standing in the yard when she decided to run back home. He asked Matlynn again, are you sure you saw your dog? Matlynn was adamant about what she knew! The officer let the wife know that he did not think Matlynn was lying. And that she was old enough to know her pawn dog. He told her to have her husband contact the police department as soon as he arrived back home. He was instructed to ask for detective "Forsythe". Before the officers left they told me that I could file a claim in small claims court, if I so choose to.

On Tuesday we got a call from the police saying that the man did indeed come to the station to meet with the detective, but he did not admit to having the dog. "I had spoken with Matlynn about the matter and she insisted that the man left home in his truck when she was running back toward home. If that was true, he probably left with the dog after Matlynn recognized him. Matlynn had high hopes of getting her dog back on Tuesday evening, and was so disappointed when she did not. She cried and cried and each night she was more restless. On Wednesday morning when we were driving to school she said "mommy the police is no good at all about solving crimes are they"? "Well, yes they are good at solving crimes but they can not do anything about Chilli because you are a child telling on an older man.

They just don't know who to believe", I said. "They should believe me because I am telling the truth, she said; it is not fair for them not to believe me because I am a child. Children know how to tell the truth"! Well, the only thing a grown up would do is to take him to court, and sometimes the Judge will listen to each side. Depending upon who he believes he will make a ruling in favor of one or the other, I told my daughter! Let's go talk to a judge mommy, responded Matlynn. I was blown away that she was willing to keep pushing the man even into court, something she knew nothing about.

Well Matlynn, let's have a good day at school and I will think about what we should do. We will decide what our next step is tonight, ok I requested. She seemed a little satisfied with that, and she went to her classroom. Matlynn was going to school where I worked and I was glad so that I could keep an eye on her especially at times like this.

As soon as she got in the car that evening, she wanted to know if I had thought about what we should do about Chilli. I told her that I would let her take the man to court. I knew his neighbor, so we obtained his name and address from them. After school on Wednesday, she and I stopped by the Judges office and filed a claim in small claims court on Matlynn's behalf, asking for her dog back, or the cost of a new one. I thought it to be the perfect opportunity to show Matlynn how our laws work. She could tell her story to the Judge and he would make a ruling on the matter. I tried to prepare her for the fact that the judge could rule against us and we would not get Chilli back, nor get a new puppy.
I asked her if she still wanted to go through with it. She was very sure that she wanted to do so, but I did let her know that I would be right by her side through the entire ordeal. There was only one problem and that was her grandparents were supposed to be picking her up on Friday. Court had been set three weeks away, so she called her grandparents and told them of her dilemma. They told her that they would pick her up as planned, bring her back for court in three weeks and then go back to Louisiana so that she could finish her summer with them. I would pick her up so that they would not have to drive that distance a third time.

Three weeks passed and Matlynn was back to go to court. We went in and the man was sitting there waiting. It was about ten minutes before time for court to start. We walked in and Matlynn pointed at him, "Mommy that is the man that stole my dog". I was so embarrassed that she said it out loud and everyone in the courtroom started to laugh. I shushed her up right away and told her that courtrooms demand silence. "The Judge will get us if we talk too loud", I said. "Oh, ok mommy," she said just as innocent as she boldly pointed the man out. Matlynn had a way of being out spoken all of her life.

She did and said things that could only leave me shaking my head. The man was so embarrassed that Matlynn had pointed him out that it made him very nervous. I could imagine that he was thinking, "I am in big trouble with this little girl"! Court began and we were the first case. When we were called first, I was happy that we would not have to sit through all of the other cases.

Matlynn walked up there beside me and I stated my case on her behalf. When the Judge started talking to Matlynn, she did not hesitate to answer. Anyone listening would have believed her. She was very matter of fact about everything she said.

The man was nervous and it was so apparent. When he said he did not have the dog, Matlynn said, yes he did your honor. I was watching my dog through the fence, and he came out in the back yard and heard me talking to Chili.
When I saw him I ran home to mommy! When I looked back, he was in his truck leaving. I thought he was coming for me. So I ran faster. He must have put Chili in his truck and taken him somewhere else. He never admitted to having Chili, but, when it was all over, the Judge gave the man three days to get us $500.00 to replace our dog. He reprimanded him about taking a child's dog. Matlynn and I talked about replacing Chili, but she could never decide what kind of dog she wanted. After six months she had still not decided on a dog. We put the money in her college fund, and never have gotten another dog. It hurts too much to get them and lose them, especially since I had lost Fritz a few years before hand.

No other dog could have taken either dogs place; therefore, to get another was setting us up for heartbreak. Sometimes Matlynn and I reminisce about Chili to this very day. She never knew Fritz, but I have told her about her. Mathew had Terra, but I was ready to get rid of her when she started smelling Matlynn when she was a baby. I never got too attached to Terra, because I was still getting over the loss of Fritz. Once Friday came, I had said goodbye to them, and immediately began cleaning the house. I had finished, taken my bath and was just getting ready to check on Douglas as I did each night before I retired, if he did not beat me to the punch. That night as in most nights, he beat me to the punch again.

We talked for over an hour and he thanked me as he had done so many other times, for being his friend and supporting him while he was going through a difficult period. I assured him that it was fun for Matlynn and me. It gave us something out of the ordinary to do, and the money he gave us for food and travel helped enable us to do it. I was going to Miller outdoor theater on Saturday evening to see the yearly production of "Motown Live". I asked him if he wanted to tag along and he immediately took me up on the offer. I think that it was the best production I had seen so far, and he enjoyed the music, as well.

After the show, I was getting ready to take him home when he told me that he hated to see me drive him all the way home and have to take the long drive back alone. He said if I was not doing anything important the next day, he would sleep in one of the spare bedroom, and I could take him home the next day. That sounded fine to me, because I really was dreading the drive. At home, I fixed us sandwiches before bedtime and we watched a movie. He could still see the TV if he sat very close, but he did not want to sit close, so I told him some of what was going on. That helped fill in the missed parts for him, and we both enjoyed the movie. It was one o'clock in the morning and we were laughing and being silly as though it were 6p.m. He told me many things about himself, his life as a child and as an adult, before his disease was revealed to him.

He had a somewhat hard life growing up with both parents with his father having a mistress on the side. Every time his mother had a baby, his mistress had one soon afterward. His mother was the breadwinner of the family, even though his father worked as a neighborhood dry-cleaner. He gave his mother little money to help support the family, so she quite often worked two jobs. He remembered how they took turns going to the bus stop to meet his mother to help carry any bags she might bring home from the grocery store or the lady she worked for would give her things to bring home to help with the children. She would bring clothes including coats, shoes, toys, and groceries from work. At Christmas, his mom was always given a bonuses, and turkeys, hams, Christmas toys, and clothes. That was a great time for the children of the family because food was always an issue at their house. He talked of how four of them slept in one bed, with two at the head and two at the foot.

They only had two bedrooms; his mother and father had one to themselves, and the children had one room with two beds. Some of the older sisters had married and left home, and for privacy, a sheet was hung on a line in the middle of the room. The line was attached to opposite sides of the wall.

One chicken had to be eaten by ten people, and they utilized every part of it. A long piece of Baby Ruth candy bar was cut into twelve pieces and a hamburger was cut in half as two people shared a bag of potato chips; that was a meal. He had gone to bed hungry many times, but they knew how to make a meal. They become very resourceful when it came to making their own meals and attire when their mom was away. One slice of bacon was broken into three pieces and laid on a piece of bread to make a sandwich if there was enough bread. When he mentioned a sugar sandwich, I could not identify. How do you make a sugar sandwich? Their popsicles were homemade in ice trays with Kool Aid, and we both laughed when I told him that they were eating pop cubes. Mayonnaise sandwiches, mustard sandwiches, ketchup sandwiches filled their starvation for the time being. If their shoes were too big, they stuffed toilet paper in the toes to make them fit.

Sometimes if the shoes were too small, they had to wear them anyway, even if they had to cut the shoe in some areas. He said that the one thing his mom did not play about was the fact that they had to bathe every night. His mother would take one bar of Ivory soap and cut it in half, one for the girls to use and one for the boys. Sometimes if their toothbrushes were worn out, they would place toothpaste on their fingers and scrub their teeth. Both his mom and dad were from Louisiana, so they traveled packed in a car like sardines in a can. He said they always had a car to ride in, because his dad would buy a new car, but would never pay a note on it. He would get tickets in the car and sign his name as Bill Long, with Bill Long's address on it. Bill Long lived on the next street over, but could not drive a car and had never owned one.

Bill Long would always get arrested for his father's crime. Once the car dealership began looking for the car that his dad never paid a note on, he would hide the car in the alley. Once the dealership finally repossessed the car, his dad would go to the next dealership and come driving up in another new car again. The entire process would begin all over. His dad never owned a driver's license his whole life. By the time he finished telling his stories, which I have verified through his other family members were true, I laughed so hard my side hurt and tears rolled from my eyes.

He said finally his mother got tired of his dad and she put him out of the house, but not before she and his girlfriend had one hell of a fight. Douglas went to the bus stop to meet his mother one evening and she did not get off of the bus. He didn't know what to think of that, since it had never happened before. He went back home and the children waited for their mother, but she never came. Just before bedtime one of their aunts came to the house to tell the children that their mother would not be coming home tonight because she had to work late. The older sisters came over to care for their younger siblings. What had actually happened was that his mother went to the mistress's job and called her out.
She confronted her about the husband she was growing tired of. It could have been her last effort to save her farce of a marriage, who knows? A confrontation took place and Douglas mother was arrested and spent one night in jail. That is when she finally put him out of the house. His father married his girlfriend and lived with her until his death. Douglas says that his father's case was that of one man loving two women at the same time.

His story was an amazing one, and although it has some humor, it was filled with what I knew had to be painful experiences, like my own. His father died early in life, but his mother lived many years after she divorced him. She met a man, who married her with all her excess baggage. Her life was not so hard anymore and she became saved, sanctified, and filled with the Holy Spirit. When she took her children down to the social security office to draw benefits from their father, she went to the mistress, now the wife's house and carried her children to sign them up for their benefits as well. All I can say about that is "some kind of special woman she was!" She took her children to church, and they all are in the church today! Throughout Douglas's life, she talked to him about what kind of man she wanted him to be.

He remembered his father, and she asked him not to reflect such negative actions. On her deathbed, his mother reiterated what she had always preached to him, one last time. "Be good to your wife; promise me you won't be anything like your father." Although things happen and he has been married a couple of times already, he is a good man who only needed love, just like myself! Mrs. Caldwell was some lady who, I wish I would have had the pleasure of knowing.

Douglas second divorce was not final as of yet, but it was in the process. He said his ex-wife was placing blame and pointing fingers in an attempt to turn the children against him. He loved his children, and I reassured him that it would get better with time. Prayer changes things, sometimes far down the road, but it does! Douglas was too good for any force to work in his life that was not of God. We became extremely close that summer, and with Matlynn gone, I welcomed his company. I knew that Douglas was a fine, decent person who was losing his sight and although he tried not to show it, he was scared to death about what his future held. One night, we were sitting out on the patio in the dark and I had put music on. I was drinking multiple glasses of wine, whereas he had only one glass due to his diabetes.

I think I had three glasses and was just a little tipsy, but still with all my faculties functioning well. He told me that I was pretty, and I stopped and gave him one long stare. "Now how do you know that?" I asked, "I might look like Sack Billy!" "You are very pretty, and I know that. With all of the time I have been around you, I have gotten a much better look at you than you think," Douglas said.
I leaned over to him in the dark and said playfully, "How do I look right now?" He seized the moment and pulled me into his lap and kissed me. "Douglas Tyler, what has gotten into you," I said, giggly from the wine. He laughed, and in the dark, his teeth seemed to illuminate.

He and I kissed again and again, and it felt perfect, it felt right! We got to know each other and became friends first, before kissing or even talking about the two of us being together. Before the summer was over, Douglas had shown himself to be the ideal handyman. Things broken, he fixed, and I was amazed at this man, who was going blind. He was smart, intelligent, thoughtful, kind, and gentle, and I really liked him a lot, and he liked me! I thought about him when he was not there and missed him when he did not come over. He never failed to call and let me know whatever was going on with him. I developed a beautiful relationship with his oldest daughter, Tiffany, and her daughter, Amber.

Tiffany was born to his first marriage. His son, Douglas Jr., and his middle child, Kimberly, are both products of his second marriage, gradually joined the fold after they matured enough to have a little independence. This family is now becoming what Douglas and I have prayed for so very long. My life was good, I was happy, and everything that had happened in my past did not matter anymore.

That summer, we made love so much that we both lost weight! I mean, real weight like ten pounds was a lot for me, at five feet six inches tall. My normal weight was only one hundred forty pounds. Douglas was five-ten with a stocky frame, kind of like a boxer. He was all man, all of that and a bag of chips. He made everything better; he made me smile.

I am an improved woman because of him. When there were ups and downs with my children, he gave me the space and support I needed to deal with situations and welcomed me with open arms when I returned to him. He kissed away the tears when I cried, rubbed my back when it hurt, loved me in spite of my flaws. He became an excellent father to my daughter, while encouraging continuous love between her and her biological father. He is a friend to my son and has filled a void the best he could in his father's absence. After three years of consistency, I had found my husband, the man I had been looking for all of my life. When my crosses became too heavy for me to bear, he helped me hold them up through prayer and the lending of his shoulder. I will forever try to measure up to the outstanding qualities this man possesses. I married this special man on June 2, 1995.

My mother's health was failing, but she told me, "Don't let that one be the one that got away." I listened! Because my parents could not travel, Mathew's parents assumed the role of my parents at my and Douglas's wedding, and we are all still just as close today as we were in 1995.

Our wedding was held in one of the ball rooms at the Holiday Inn. It was a spectacular occasion! The room was filled with guest from both sides of the family. The children from each marriage were given a gold anchor on a gold chain to wear around their necks; symbolizing that our combined family would hold together strongly. My son gave me away to Douglas proudly. He said that he knew that this marriage was a good one and it would last. He also served as our disc jockey for the reception. After my first dance with Douglas, my son and I danced. He was so handsome in his white tuxedo with tails.

He looks so much like Fred every day, but that day especially. Matlynn was one of the bridesmaids, and could not wait to get out of high heels that she was not use to wearing. She was only thirteen, but wanted her shoes as high as the rest. We toasted and partied the night away. Our gifts exceeded our expectations and we were glad to lay our bodies down to sleep!

My mama passed away in June 1997 at the age of 79, leaving daddy alone at the age of 83. Daddy did not run the old café anymore, but he continued to drive and visit with the friends he had left. He looked forward to our visits home, because he and Douglas really hit it off. He was close to Tisah's husband Raymond, who visited him most Sunday evenings. Raymond was an outdoorsman who hunted, fished and gardened. Daddy enjoyed hearing about the big fish that got away, or in many cases that Raymond caught. He loved Raymond's stories about deer hunting too. Daddy was past the stage of planting, although he pushed my brothers to do his planting for several years after he physically could not do it.

My Sister Tisah and Raymond had two children. The girl, "Angel", married, divorced, and remarried the same man. After it did not work the second time, she never tried marriage again. Their son was in the same class with Bryan and Nadelle's son Westley. In grade school, and part of intermediate, the three boys were inseparable. After we moved to Houston and boys were all graduated from high school they all had chosen their life's skills and were employed. NiJul was killed in a motor cycle accident, and this had a tremendous devastating effect on the family.

Mama had lost her second grandchild and she was very sad. I dare to say that Douglas was the first son-in-law daddy had that became his buddy. They would ride around town acting like teenagers, laughing and talking about everything under the sun. When daddy knew that we were coming home, he would be sitting on the porch when we arrived. I would call letting him know our location every hour or two as we traveled. As soon as Douglas had rested from the ride for no more than an hour, daddy would say "well, let's get out of here." Douglas would jump up saying, "I wondered what we were waiting for old man." Daddy would then stop in his tracks "did you say old man, he'd ask?" "Did I say something wrong, Douglas would reply?" Daddy would laugh, and say, "Just call me Casey boy, forget all of that old man stuff!" They would then have a big laugh, and off they would go!

We teased Douglas that daddy was going to spill both of them up the road somewhere. Daddy still drove fairly well, but he could make some mistakes because of his age. Douglas said he and daddy would be riding around town and come to a stop sign. Daddy would look one way for approaching traffic and ask Douglas, how does it look over there boy, and pull right out into the road. He was sure daddy must have looked already, because dad knew that he could not see. As Douglas told me that night, he said, I sure as hell hope he is looking and is just teasing me."

At the age of 87, daddy remarried and we all decided that if it made him happy, we would not show concern. The marriage became rocky after a while, because she did not want any of us to be close to daddy anymore. Only Ann was close to her, and we suspected that Ann encouraged the marriage. We seldom frequented the house we had been raised in anymore, but we sometimes visited daddy on the front porch during the summer. We missed the daddy we had loved so much, but to keep her from fussing at him, we stayed away. He would visit with my sisters and brothers and it was only then that we could enjoy our daddy. Douglas and I started staying with my other siblings when we would travel back home because we were not welcome. Only Ann attended the little ceremony in the nearby state of Mississippi. None of us knew about it until the day of the wedding.

When I heard that daddy was getting married, I was shocked. Then, when I found out who he was marrying, I was even more shocked. He was marrying his friend who died a couple of years before, wife! I was on my way to homecoming ceremonies for the University of Arkansas. I always stayed with my cousins as did some of our other friends. We all attended the same University of which we were proud. It was customary that their mother was always there. We were guaranteed to eat well every year. Their dad, my dad's brother had died of a heart attack two years before. I was so caught up in greeting everyone that I forgot to tell Aunt Lucy about daddy getting married. When I told her, she sat there and looked at me in disbelief. She took a swig off beer and finally asked "who the hell is William marrying" I said "Mrs. Daisy Fields"! Her mouth fell open and she could not close it.

She never said a word, so I went on talking with everybody. Suddenly she said "Shit, William just shit and fell back in it! That woman is a fool! Why you think her dead husband walked with his head down and barely spoke? He was afraid to speak for fear that she would act a fool." That news changed homecoming for Aunt Lucy.
Yes, she enjoyed the festivities, but every so often she would belt out something about how daddy would see what he had real soon. "I don't know why he thinks she's going to treat him any better than she did Clark. Mark my word, "he is going to hate the day he ever met that fool." At that time, I believed Aunt Lucy, but I had no idea the magnitude in which she spoke. He certainly found out, and so did we. He could not speak to anyone without being accused of going with them. She accused him of going with his own granddaughter and that was pretty bad. Daddy was way past the stage of having any sexual

activity, and money was limited since he was living on one income. She never paid a bill, purchased grocery or any of the sorts unless it was done with daddy's money.

Her money was to be saved. We did not like that, but it was daddy's wife and only he could deal with it. Later, other people started telling us that she was a fool and, that she carried a gun and did not hesitate to pull it. They told a story of her son in law turning into her driveway, and because she was mad at him, she pulled her gun and told him to get out of her yard right now. This happened when the woman was 86 years old. She listened to all of daddy's phone calls, even when it was his children. We never really got to enjoy our daddy to much after the marriage.

By the age of ninety four years old, daddy was having much pain in his hip. I had gone home and stopped by because I had decided that she was not going to keep me away from my daddy. I purchased Muscle rub in Houston to see if it would help his hip. Upon arriving, massaged his hip, visited for a minute and left to go to my brothers where I was staying while there. Daddy called me about two hours after I left and said that his hip felt better with that massage than it had in such a long time. The only other time he got massaged was when my Niece Sarah would arrive into town. She was a certified massage therapist that knew her stuff. She once massaged me and I came out feeling like I was sixteen again. I told daddy that I would come back early in the morning and massage him before he got out of bed. I asked Mrs. Daisy if she would call me before daddy got out of bed and she answered "sure" sarcastically! The next morning just like she said, she called. "Your dad is awake". I thanked her and told her that I would be their shortly. Upon arriving, I heard some yelling, and stopped on the front porch to listen. They were having a drastic argument.

I heard my father say, "I want you to get everything you got here and go back where you come from"! It was time for me to get inside to see what was really going on. When I walked in, daddy was out of bed sitting in the recliner. "What on earth is going on, I asked. She was standing in the dining room with a dish cloth in her hand. I could not believe that two old folks were having such a humongous argument.

My daddy answered my question, "I am going to tell you what is going on, I will tell you what God loves and that is the truth. She does not want my children to come here! Her children can come here and stay as long as they like, with nothing said, but she gets and attitude when my children come! Mama and I worked hard to have what we got. It ain't the best, but it is ours. This house belongs to my children whenever I close my eyes. I am sick of it, and I want her to get anything that looks like it might belong to her and get out of here!" Wow, I said, Mrs. Daisy is it true that you don't want us here?" She replied, "Your daddy has Alzheimer's. I love to see his children come to see him. I am going back into the kitchen to finish his breakfast. Daddy chimed in, "don't you fix me anything, and you just get out of here"!

I could not believe daddy was standing up to her like that. She was always known as the boss hog. I commented, "Well, you both stop right now! First daddy has not been diagnosed with Alzheimer's, and his mind functions well. As far as you not wanting us here, I don't know how the rest of them feel, but I am coming to see my daddy. I was born in this house"! Daddy was so mad he was shaking and he meant that he wanted her to go!

"Go to town and buy me some breakfast Savanah. I don't want a thing she cooks"! "Ok, I am going, but I want you both to stop this arguing, I pleaded, and daddy don't accuse her of things you may not be sure of ok. You both are too old to be getting upset. You are supposed to be enjoying your last days, and here you are arguing over what should be considered as natural for one family as the other. I am going to get him some breakfast, so why don't you just stop cooking whatever and I will bring breakfast for the both of you." "No," she said, " I am almost finished so I will eat it" Ok, now while I am gone, there will be no more arguing. It is over!" "Ok daddy", I asked! Daddy nodded! "Ok Mrs. Daisy," I asked! She replied, "if he don't say nothing to me, I won't say nothing to him. "Ok fine", I responded, and turned and walked out of the door.

Upon returning with daddy's breakfast", she sat on the sofa reading the Bible! That is what she did when she and daddy got into it. I helped him up so that he could go to the bathroom to wash his hands and face. He had no teeth, so I got his toothbrush, put toothpaste on it and said, "Now here brush those old gums". He chuckled. I hoped that was a sign that he was calming down. He had stopped shaking. Although his false teeth were soaking in a cleaning solution, I brushed the as well. As I handed them to him, he looked me in my eyes and said, "Savanah, she is a mean woman." All I could say was "I know daddy! It was as though he wanted me to help in some way. "You married her, so try to make it work if you can", I stated! We returned and he sat down to the dining table and ate his breakfast.

My Nephew Woodrow was getting married and I had to be at the wedding for four o clock PM. It was 10:30a.m already. Now Mrs. Daisy, daddy, and I sat in the living room and I initiated conversation that we all could be involved in. I asked her about her children, asked how to cook Taco Soup, asked daddy if it was good, hoping that he would not say anything negative about it. "It taste fine, but I don't like as much corn in mine. She has always put less corn ever since I told her, he responded." I like Taco soup any way I can get it! I left them alone, but before I left I told them that I would buy their lunches so they would not have to cook.

I asked daddy what he wanted, and he said "you know I am easy pleased, and you know just about what I like, so just pick me something from the menu." "Ok now, Mrs. Daisy what do you have a taste for, I asked." Don't bother to bring me nothing; I'll be fine, she said, not so sarcastically this time.

I went back to George's house ate myself and showered for the wedding. At 2:30p.m, I went to get daddy's lunch and picked up some bananas, peanut butter
cheese crackers and grapes so that he could get some potassium to help with muscle spasms, and he would have something to hold him over until nine or ten o clock. It is three PM now, I am going to the wedding and reception, and I will bring you more food when I come home. I probably won't get back until around ten o clock tonight, so you snack on the bananas, grapes and peanut butter cheese crackers until I come back. Mrs. Daisy, I bought enough of everything for you too. I will call you and see what the two of you want to eat later, but it has to be something light.

You should not go to bed with full stomachs". She nodded, as if to say "ok" and I left! I hoped things would smooth over and they would be alright. One thing about it, I was proud of my daddy because he stood up for himself and for his children, that day! When passing daddy's house on the way to the wedding, I noticed that he was sitting on the front porch. She was not out there with him, so I kind of hoped that she would be joining him soon.

My brother Nick was now a pastor, therefore he performed the wedding. It was a beautiful wedding and Woodrow had his bride a new carriage parked in front of the church when they exited to go to the reception hall. It was a real nice SUV, and she was so surprised! I stayed at the reception for a couple of hours, but I knew I needed to take daddy some food, so I called to see what they wanted. She answered the phone, but said she did not want anything to eat, but she would go outside to see what he wanted. When she returned she told me that he said that I should surprise him because he did not know what he wanted.

I asked her why was daddy outside at that hour of the night. He usually would never be outside past dark! Her reply was, "well I guess he is waiting for me to leave before he comes inside. He called my daughter and told her to come and get me, and said that he was through with me"! Oh my, I said, "well I am going back inside and tell Nick so that he can come down there!" "OK she said, maybe he can talk some sense into your daddy!" There was a sound of urgency in her voice that said she did not want to leave.

I wondered if she was realizing that daddy truly was tired of her shit. Maybe if she stayed, she would change her ways. She must have been ashamed for her family to know that daddy wanted her to leave bad enough to call her daughter. I responded, "Tell your daughter to hold off until Nick gets there!" "Oh, it is too late for that; she has been here and gone with all of my things. I just would not leave until some of you all got here, she said"! I ran back inside and told Nick what Mrs. Daisy had told me, and we both left there on two wheels. Nick arrived first because I had to stop for food.

When I walked in the door, Nick was speaking "Now you both called yourselves in love when you got married, and you took the vow, until death do you part, right"? They both agreed that they were in love, and they took the vow seriously. My brother handled it quite well even though they both kept trying to tell on the other. My daddy said, "but she is a mean woman, and I did not know that she was going to be so mean." She chimed in, "I am not mean, I just say what I mean and mean what I say"! "Nick," daddy replied, she does not want my children to come here and I have let it go on too long. Her children come almost every weekend, and we have a big time, but when my children come, she won't half talk, and if she does, it's short and unconcerned.

He finally got them to acknowledge that they needed to try to make the marriage work. I could tell that daddy did not really want it, but I guess he just went along with Nick. We really worried about his being there alone, so we encouraged him to let her stay. I spoke up and told them that I wanted to take daddy to Hot Springs, Arkansas to have a professional bath and massage. I told them I wanted them both to go and have the experience together. I have always gone to Hot Springs at least two time each year, and knew first hand that the baths were therapeutic and the massages were healing. They agreed that we could all get up in the morning, get in the car and take the two hour ride the next morning. I thought that was a great way to get them to relax!

The next morning when I arrived, daddy was dressed and ready to go. She sat there in an old robe of daddy's. "Why aren't you ready Mrs. Daisy," I asked? She replied, "I don't have any clothes down here, so you all just go ahead. "No, we can wait until they bring you some clothes," I declared, but she would not hear of our waiting for her. She still acted quite angry and cold, as if something had changed since last night.

Reluctantly, Faye, Matlynn, daddy, David "Nadelle baby son," and I, hopped into my brothers Ford SUV and we were off to Hot Springs, bath house row. The Buckstaff bathhouse was the only active house up and running on bath house row, because the rest were under reconstruction. I hated to leave Mrs. Daisy because although she said she could not go and we should go ahead without her, she had a tendency to become offended later. I knew if she went along, she would not find a reason to fuss at my daddy later. It was the month of December therefore it was cold, but once we arrived in Hot Springs, the temperature dropped lower than we could have ever imagined. We arrived to find out that only one person was scheduled for their bath and massage, when I clearly told the woman that it was four of us looking to have service.

We had driven all of the way there and I was highly upset. They had allowed two of their massage therapist to leave early because clientele was low. I argued with the massage desk about the other three massages and she became extremely rude. "I specifically stated when I made the arrangements that there would be four people getting messages, I told her! Well lady, I don't have you down for but one so you may as well decide which one will receive the service, she stated. I told her "we did not drive all of this way for one to be serviced, so can you make an acceptation and call someone in.
"No I cannot, she exclaimed. "Well, I need to speak with an administrator, I told her. She replied, "You and your whole gang can administrate right out of here, I refuse service to all of you, how about that! That is my right"! Oh, so you do huh, thank you very much, I said. I told everyone in my party to come with me and I turned and went to the front desk. I told the desk clerk that the attendant was rude and I did not appreciate it! She got the manager on the line, who offered us a full one night stay in a luxurious hotel suit for the night.

All of our food was free of charge, and we could all be serviced the next morning. That satisfied us just fine, so we spent the night in a gorgeous suit with patios doors and windows that faced the mountains. We called Mrs. Daisy to let her know that we would be spending the night in order for daddy to get his massage, and she said suspiciously "that is fine, but I figured something would come up!" We ended up having a wonderful time. We got up the next morning, had breakfast, then our massages and went home feeling great!

Upon arriving home we went in telling Mrs. Daisy about how the manager of the hotel gave us our free suite, and why. She acted nonchalant, and totally disinterested. I became distracted when I received a call from Bryan. He was calling to tell me that he was in Kansas visiting with his father and his family. Bryan was traveling, doing work all over the United States for the Post Office systems. He had another opportunity to get close to Kansas and dropped in for a few days. Daddy informed me later that Mrs. Daisy accused us of taking him off to meet with another woman age ninety four! She said, that we had it planned to spend the night, before we left. I thought "my poor daddy"! It was six months from that day that he died.

He had not been ill, accept for the pain in his hip and thigh, but he had become dependent on oxygen to breath. The evening before his death, he kept asking everyone not to leave him, but nobody knew why. Ann told me that daddy was getting pretty sick and I decided to come go home to see him. He was getting old and I needed to visit with him one more time. I called Mrs. Daisy and asked if daddy was asleep. She informed me about 8:30 pm that he was indeed asleep. George stayed with him all evening and into the night and he finally fell asleep after midnight. I am told; he acted as if he was afraid to go to sleep. After he fell asleep, George decided to go home, but was to return early before daddy woke up.

At five o'clock in the morning approximately four hours after George left, Mrs. Daisy called him and told him that she could not wake daddy up! George bailed out of bed and went down there. Daddy was sitting half way up with his back leaning against the headboard of the bed. His body tilted slightly toward the right side of the bed. His eyes were open but he was dead. His oxygen was way across the room, and George wondered why. His nostrils were flared as if he was trying to catch his breath. Our daddy died that night and we will never know the circumstances surrounding his death! He died June 1st, 2009, at the ripe old age of 94, but had he lived to be 95, his insurance policy would have only paid what was paid into it, instead of the $50,000 it was worth.

His funeral was truly a home going celebration much like our mama's. My brother officiated our dad's funeral at the church where he pastored. It was the church we all grew up in, and he was buried next to our mother as he had requested. They share a beautiful headstone with both their identifying information.

Of the five children that Ann had, there were three girls and two boys, the five that Faye had; there were also three girls and two boys. Of the six children plus the adopted son that Nadellie had, there were six boys and one girl. Nick had two daughters prior to marriage, but soon married and divorced. He later married Gladys and had two more children, a girl and a boy, giving him a total of four. George married and divorced, then remarried his wife again and divorced again after a few years. They had two children one girl and one boy. I remained close to all of the children, after I graduated from college.

After the one girl Tina became pregnant, and died in the car accident in 1973, years later in 2008, Ann lost another daughter, "Brenda" to cancer. The elder child Sarah and I had been extremely close all of her life, but she moved away to Oklahoma City, Oklahoma after she was married. After living away for ten years, she, her son and daughter moved back to Arkansas, when her marriage ended in divorce.

My sisters and I grew distant from Ann after daddy remarried. It was partly because we felt that she encouraged the marriage between our father and his wife. Because of that, Ann was the only sister welcome to visit our dad! Ann's remaining daughter Sarah became distant with us as well, mostly because we were distant from her mother. She practiced working against any accomplishment I made. After a few years of one disappointment after another, I gave up on ever being friends or having an Aunt and Niece relationship. We speak when in one another's company, but that is about the size of it. I think we love one another, but differences just seem to keep coming up.

Sometimes to agree to disagree is the best way to maintain a cordial relationship! I truly believe that seldom visits make longer lasting friendships! I believe that if we all practice doing unto others as we want others to do unto us, life would run much smoother! I feel that if we all consider the fact that there will one day be a day of reckoning, we would be more careful how we live our lives. I believe that prayer and supplication is the answer to all of our problems. I believe in the age old adage "live and let live"! Criticizing others is easy to do, when we forget what we have done in our past. Gone are the days when mothers and fathers smack kids in the mouth or into the middle of next week for talking about sex, boyfriends, and girlfriends.

Listen and talk to your children intelligently about whatever they wish to discuss. Do not discourage or scold them so that they will not come to you. Anything that you cannot discuss with them, find someone who can, maybe your pastor, or if sex is the subject and you don't feel comfortable with your pastor, maybe a friend who in the medical field could be helpful.

Douglas and I have been married for eighteen years now, the couple of rough spots have smoothened, and we are progressing toward old age ourselves. Douglas still maintains a small degree of his sight. When people who are not familiar with his blindness visit our home, they are surprised when they finally realize that he is legally blind. Douglas is more man blind, than any I have ever known, with sight! He moves around with ease, because our home is organized with him in mind. He cooks most of the meals and does many other things one would not believe a blind person could do. This fish did not get away, and if he tries, I am going with him! We both are active within our church, and we praise God together as one.

Douglas son now has his master's degree and his younger daughter is a registered nurse. His elder daughter Tiffany has her associates' degree and is presently back in school to complete her bachelor's degree in communications. Amber is in the third grade. My granddaughter Britany is 16 and looking forward to going to college in a couple years and Bryan Jr. is ninth grade, and as smart as a whip. He plays basketball, and thinks he is the next Lebron James.

Whenever Bryan Sr. can comes to visit, every which is available get together and we have big family fun. Quite often, Douglas, Bryan Jr, and I take off to visit with Bryan Sr. for a week. In the summer, we stay sometimes two or three weeks. Through space, time, and distance, he led Douglas and me to one another, finally! Whenever we get together as a family is a joyous occasion. "Mrs. R M C, you would be very proud!" Because no child will tell you everything, you have to use your own common sense in making decisions for them. I was not going to take the chance of Matlynn's life being stagnated by an unwanted pregnancy. I carried her to the doctor at age sixteen and asked him to give her a contraceptive. It ended up being birth control pills. I administered that medication every day, until she was responsible enough to take them without failure. By age seventeen, I had instilled in her the values it was going to take for her to walk through life with her eyes wide open. I called her dad and told him that he could come and take her to Fort Worth any time he wanted.

He and his wife came for her and she spent Thanksgiving with them for the very first time when she was in twelfth grade. She has alternated holidays between us ever since, and now, we all are happy. Matlynn went away to college in Ohio, because she got a full scholarship. Half of the scholarship was for running track and the other half for academics. By her junior year, she was given a full academic Scholarship. Burned out with track, after running in high school for four years and in college two years, she graduated from college Magna Cum Laude, with a Bachelor of Science degree in Chemistry. Now she managed her own asthma and did so well that she never has attacks anymore. It has been years and she told me that she takes maybe two breathing treatments each year. She feels that she has outgrown the condition for the most part. Matlyn, Mathew, Douglas and I had completed our first task, and were on to the next financial adventure. She was off to medical school to pursue a degree in Physician's Assistant Studies. Mathew and I sat and had a drink together at her graduation party.

We were both proud parents because it was our joint effort, and her persistence and determination that got her to that point. We joked that we both could spend a little money on ourselves for a change! She graduated with honors, and is now an instructor at Baylor College Of Medicine, and works in the trauma center at a local hospital, in Houston, Texas. She continues to alternate holidays between her father and me, when she is not working. I have taught her all that I could teach; and the rest of her life belongs to her. Through it all, I listened to her problems, in all areas of her life. I have offered my opinions; some advice she took and some she rejected, but I was there whether she succeeded or not. When she fell on her face, I supported her and wiped her tears; when she succeeded, I applauded her. My open-door policy is always in effect for both of my children. They know how much I like Mohammed Ali's quote, "He who is not courageous enough to take risks will accomplish nothing in life."

Bryan married and divorced, but not before giving me two of the most beautiful grandchildren ever. I still stick a little close to him, probably, because I harbor a little guilt for his not getting the best of me, early in life. In 2009, we lost our first sibling to cancer. It was Nadelle, our sweetest most compassionate sister. She was 69 years old! There will be problems with all children, I had problems with mine, but I stood firm. I disciplined when necessary, but never failed to talk to them and explain why. Often they pretended that they did not understand, but they did! What I learned in those eight years was to be a strong and positive role model for my daughter and at the same time learn to motivate and appreciate the woman that I became in the mist of my life's journey.

I discovered through self-experience, and trials and tribulations, my recipe for living the rest of my life, as it applied to me and the raising of my children. I was into motivational readings that were emotionally and mentally stimulating. I gave a lot of careful thought as to how I was going to correct the mistakes in my past, and in the raising of my children and set out to make the difference in Matlynn's life, and in the life of my grandchildren. I applied as much as I could to Bryan's life as well, but had little time to do it. It did not help that he did not have a positive role model as a father after he left my parents. He and Mathew were friends, and Mathew was extremely good to my son, but he needed more than a friend.

Not having a strong father figure causes some to turn to their peers. Peers cannot raise peers, they can only lead one another astray It is difficult for a woman to teach a boy how to be a man. It should make every young man who grows up without a father; want to be there for their sons and daughters. Quite often, fatherless children, become less of a father to their own children. When divorce and trial and tribulations of the living comes into the lives of fatherless children, it can make bad matters worse. I see the difference in my children every day. I love them both and they know it beyond a shadow of doubt. Yet, I shall always regret not overriding my loyalty as a daughter, with my duty as a mother.

THE END

Somebody Should Have Told ME!

Below you will find 18 thoughts that I try to apply to my daily life.
They are found on the Poetic expressions website at
www.poeticexpressions.co.uk

Mike and his team gave me exclusive permission to print these thoughts
Please visit their website and make a Contribution no matter how small!
Cancer does not discriminate.

"Poetic Expressions is a proud supporter of Marie Curie whose Nurses provide free nursing care to cancer patients and those with other terminal illnesses in their own homes".

Poetic Expressions

18 Thoughts

Be kinder than necessary because everyone you meet is fighting some kind of battle.

A sharp tongue can cut your own throat.

If you want your dreams to come true, you mustn't oversleep.

Of all the things you wear, your expression is the most important.

The best vitamin for making friends is Vitamin B1.

The happiness of your life depends on the quality of your thoughts.

The heaviest thing you can carry is a grudge..

One thing you can give and still keep is your word.

You lie the loudest when you lie to yourself.

If you lack the courage to start, you have already finished.

One thing you can't recycle is wasted time.

Ideas won't work unless 'You' do.

Your mind is like a parachute . . . it functions only when open.

The 10 commandments are not a multiple choice.
The pursuit of happiness is the chase of a lifetime!

It is never too late to become what you might have been.

Life is too short to wake up with regrets.

If you get a second chance, grab it with both hands.

"**Poetic Expressions** is a proud supporter of **Marie Curie Cancer Care** whose Nurses provide free nursing care to cancer patients and those with terminal illness in their own homes"
"Please take the time and donate what you can by visiting any of the website address below
www.poeticexpressions.co.uk or www.justgiving.com/poeticexpressions"
Thank you
The Poetic Expressions Team
"Words of comfort and joy"

'Words of Comfort and Joy'
    While you live, LOVE
        While you breathe, SING
            While you walk, DANCE
                While you work, SHINE
                    While you see, DREAM
                        While you can, Forgive

When you forgive, you set a prisoner free. You are that prisoner!
Forgive and live!

Somebody Should Have Told ME!

Printed in the USA

Paula Mann Publishing

www.ingramcontent.com/pod-product-compliance
Lightning Source LLC
LaVergne TN
LVHW051550070426
835507LV00021B/2496